Cost Accounting and Accounting Systems

Cost Accounting and Accounting Systems

K.K. Sharma

Cost Accounting and Accounting Systems

ISBN 978-93-5111-641-7

Published in 2015 in India by

RANDOM PUBLICATIONS

4376-A/4B, Gali Murari Lal, Ansari Road
New Delhi-110 002
Phone : +9111-43580356, 011-23289044, 011-43142548
e-mail: sales@randompublications.com,
info@randompublications.com, randomexports@gmail.com

Reprinted 2022

Type Setting by : Friends Media, Delhi-110089
Printed at : Replika Press Pvt. Ltd.

Preface

The importance of cost accounting has risen due to this competitive environment. It is a significant aspect in the field of Commerce, Management and other important functional areas.

In accounting, historical cost is the original monetary value of an economic item. Historical cost is based on the stable measuring unit assumption. In some circumstances, assets and liabilities may be shown at their historical cost, as if there had been no change in value since the date of acquisition. The balance sheet value of the item may therefore differ from the "true" value. While historical cost is criticised for its inaccuracy (deviation from "true" value), it remains in use in most accounting systems. Various corrections to historical cost are used, many of which require the use of management judgment and may be difficult to implement or verify. he trend in most accounting standards is a move to more accurate reflection of the fair or market value, although the historical cost principle remains in use, particularly for assets of little importance. Depreciation affects the carrying value of an asset on the balance sheet. The historical cost will equal the carrying value if there has been no change recorded in the value of the asset since acquisition.

All manufacturing companies sell their products to make profit. The profit on each product sold can be defined as the difference between the selling price of the product and the total cost of making the product. Cost therefore plays a very important role in the product design process. To be successful, a product must not only satisfy a set of functions defined in the product design specification, but it must also be possible to build the product within the cost criteria set out at the start of the project. Before the development of any product begins, it is essential to perform some form of economic analysis on the product to determine if it is worth making. This may involve some form of market analysis to determine what the customer is willing to pay for a product.

Accounting systems are comprised of manual or computerized records of financial transactions for the purpose of recording, categorizing, analyzing and reporting timely financial management information. When selecting an accounting system, understand your needs and the categories of accounting systems.

The knowledge and understanding of cost accounting is an integral part of learning the overall nature of accounting and is one of the varied aspects of accounting available for careers in this field. I would like to thank my team for standing beside me throughout my career and writing this book. My special thanks go to "Random Publications" who have published the book.

– *K.K. Sharma*

Contents

1

The Changing Role of Accounting

Accounting is shaped by the environment in which it operates. As a result, accounting systems vary from country to country. The most obvious differences concern financial reporting, as this is the area where there are most likely to be rules and regulations in place.

One of the most important issues affecting the development of accounting today is the need for internationally comparable financial information and the drive for harmonisation of accounting practices. Many businesses operate globally and face costs of having to prepare financial reports in different ways to satisfy different regulators.

Also, investors from one country may wish to buy shares in or make loans to businesses in another country. These investors need to be able to compare all businesses fairly in order to decide where to invest their funds. In order for businesses all over the world to be treated similarly and reduce their reporting costs, different accounting regimes need to agree a common set of rules.

As you can imagine, this is a difficult process, and one that is dominated by a handful of the most influential bodies.

The management uses of accounting information are also developing. Businesses face increasingly complex decisions in an increasingly complex world. Advances in technology create both new markets, and new tools and capacities for recording and analysing data.

For instance, the increasing importance of social and environmental reporting means that accountants need to develop new ways of collecting, classifying and measuring non-financial data. This information may include the levels of pollutants emitted by a factory, or whether the factory meets health and safety standards. Some businesses are choosing to report this kind of information in order to avoid negative publicity or to gain business from 'green' consumers (or finance from 'ethical' investors).

There is also an increasing demand for government and public sector bodies to be held accountable to tax-payers and citizens for their actions. For example, schools publish their examination results, and hospitals their waiting lists. Although social and environmental reporting are outside the scope of this unit, thinking about these issues helps us to understand the changing nature of accounting throughout time.

TOWARDS A DEFINITION OF ACCOUNTING

Perhaps the best way of thinking about the role and development of accounting is to consider the functions that accounting information performs. Not all of these functions have been expected or required of accounting at all times in the past, and it is likely that additional functions will be demanded in the future. Therefore, if accounting is defined by the functions it performs, you can see that this definition changes through time. The earliest roles of accounting information were to measure and record financial transactions and provide information for stewardship purposes.

At present, accounting is generally viewed as serving the following functions:

- *Recording*: accounting systems supply a means of recording data so as to enable the production of reports or for use in calculations. For example, for the preparation of financial statements, the calculation of performance indicators on which managerial bonuses are based, or for costing inventory.
- *Classification*: accounting systems assist in categorising data so as to enable the production of reports or for use in calculations. For example, identifying whether an item is an asset or an expense, or which costs should be included in inventory.
- *Measurement*: accounting systems quantify data so as to enable the production of reports or for use in calculations. For example, determining how much profit a business has earned in a year, or the value of a piece of machinery.
- *Stewardship*: accounting systems provide information which enables owners to determine how funds entrusted to managers have been used by them, and to what ends.
- *Information for decisions*: accounting systems provide information which enables users to make decisions about the future. For example, to assist investors or managers in deciding how to allocate their limited resources.
- *Monitoring and control*: accounting systems provide information which enables management to monitor performance, and take corrective action if necessary.
- *Performance evaluation and compensation*: accounting systems provide information on the performance of different individuals and parts of the business in order to determine how much managers and employees should be rewarded, just as to the terms of their contracts.

- *Communication*: accounting systems provide a means by which information is transmitted to users. For example, to external users via the financial statements, or to internal users via the budget-setting process.

These functions can be divided into two types. The first three functions concern the production of accounting information. The last five functions concern the uses of the information produced.

WHAT IS ACCOUNTING?

This is not an easy question. What do you think accounting is? The scope and definition of accounting changes throughout time. In general, it is argued that accounting is concerned with the provision of information about the position and performance of an enterprise that is useful to a wide range of potential users in making decisions. Historically, this information has been financial, but accounting is increasingly being used to address the 'triple-bottom-line' of social and environmental, as well as economic, concerns. In this part, we focus on financial uses of accounting but you can study social and environmental reporting, Auditing. Similarly, in this course the types of enterprises that as suggested, focus on are businesses whose aim is to make profit or otherwise to increase their owners' wealth.

However, it is important to remember that other types of enterprises such as charities, other non-government organisations, and public sector bodies such as schools, universities, hospitals, and local and national government, also use accounting. You can also find out more about accounting for these types of enterprises, Auditing.

The decisions that users of accounting information make may be economic or legal in nature. Economic decisions are concerned with the allocation of resources, for example, whether to sell or invest in a business, or invest in the equipment to manufacture a new product. 'Legal' decisions are concerned with determining whether managers have made a good job of running a business on the owners' behalf (stewardship), and how much managers should be paid, or they concern matters such as how much tax a business should pay, or whether a business has broken the terms of its borrowing agreements. Users of accounting information are usually thought of as individuals, but there is also a social role for accounting, and it can be regarded as a 'public good' which aims to improve the allocation of scarce resources for the welfare of society in general.

A BRIEF HISTORY

Accounting originally served a stewardship function, as a result of the separation of ownership and control of resources. First wealthy landowners, and later company shareholders, hired managers or 'stewards' to run their properties and businesses. The landowners and shareholders owned the resources, but the stewards and managers controlled them. As the business owners could not always be on hand to watch their stewards or managers perform their duties, they required the stewards to make regular reports on their activities, using accounting to prepare the figures. This is what we call financial reporting. The separation of ownership and control has grown wider and wider throughout the last century, as companies increased in number, and became larger and more complicated.

Their owners became an increasingly distant and diverse body, often buying and selling shares on stock exchanges with no direct dealings with the company at all. As the opportunities to hide or manipulate information have therefore also increased, financial reporting by businesses to their owners has required more and more regulation.

Step by step with the increased demand for financial reporting, demand has arisen for independent audits to check the reported information. Recent accounting and auditing scandals such as that involving Enron and Arthur Andersen have thrown the problems with financial reporting into the spotlight. Alongside the growth in financial reporting, has been the development of the use of accounting for the benefit of the business managers themselves.

The practice of using accounting information as a direct aid to management arose later than financial reporting, but is no less important. Increasing business complexity and changes to the economic environment have meant that more and more sophisticated systems of collecting and recording information are required. In contrast to financial accounting, this information is used to help make decisions about the future, not just report on past events.

Different types of information, and different tools with which to analyse it, are required. Finally, as accounting has been recognised as a social science, the impact of the use of accounting information (whether as and aid to management, or for financial reporting purposes) on the employees of the business has been widely explored. Managers or employees who are paid salary bonuses based on figures provided by accounting systems may change their actions as a result of the incentives (or disincentives!) this provides.

NATURE OF ACCOUNTING SYSTEMS

An accounting system is a process whereby a specific output is produced by a given input. In an information accounting system, data is processed to provide information. Data is a collection of unprocessed facts, while information is data or facts that have been processed into a meaningful form.

In the normal course of events, a business undertaking will enter into a large variety of transactions. The details of a particular transaction are referred to as transaction data. The term transaction data therefore refers to the facts that completely describe a specific transaction.

The aim of an accounting system is to record the transaction data and then to process this data to provide information that is ultimately collected in the financial and management reports of the enterprise. There are two stages in the development of an accounting system, namely systems analysis and system design.

A good accounting system must comply with at least the following fundamental requirements. The system must provide decision–makers with timely and accurate information relevant to the responsibilities and requirements; the internal control measures must be adequate to ensure the protection of assets and the provision of reliable information and the system must be sufficiently flexible to accommodate changes in the volume of activities and in the operating procedures without requiring drastic modifications.

A thorough knowledge of the activities of the undertaking and its information and control requirements is an essential prerequisite for the development of an effective accounting system that meets the necessary criteria. The procedure of surveying the undertaking's activities and information and control requirements is known as system analysis.

In the system's design process the system is designed to comply with the specifications determined by systems analysis. Initial transactions are recorded in source documents and the in journals and finally they are classified and stored in ledger accounts. The processed information is extracted from the ledger accounts for drawing up the financial reports. The design of any accounting system within this framework comprises of, planning the procedures just as to which the system will function, the design of the source documents, journals, ledger accounts and final reports and finally the design of the necessary internal control measures.

From a management information point of view it is important that the information needs of a user are determined and that the accounting report meets these needs. Rapid development in the field of computer accounting has led to the effectiveness of the accounting process, enabling more usable, more accurate and more timely output of accounting data.

Efficiency increases as the value of the system increases in relation to the cost thereof. Computerised systems have made the accountants job in designing the accounting process that much easier than the manual systems of days gone by.

TYPES OF ACCOUNTING

Accounting is believed to be one of the most important elements in the business world where money is almost everything. It is termed as a process in which finances of an organization are recorded for further assessment. By employing the purpose of accounting and this process of financial management, businesses are able to determine if they are earning profits or going in losses.

In contrary to a common misconception, the practice of accountancy was carried out even in the early ages. It is only with new types of accounting and Information Technology (IT) that it has advanced to a greater level. The principles of accounting are the basis of carrying out the accounting process. Let us get to know about the general types of accounting in the industry.

COMMON TYPES OF ACCOUNTING

Financial Accounting

For carrying out this type of accounting, professionals use guidelines laid down by certain financial institutions such as the Securities and Exchange Commission (SEC) and the International Accounting Standards Committee (IASC). A financial accountant is handed over the responsibility to assess financial conditions which would help companies determine further steps in investments.

Management Accounting

Management accounting is one of the most important types of accounting careers. It deals with studying, analyzing, and recording the financial aspects of business firms. Few of the sub sections of this field of accounting are asset management, internal auditing, financial planning and budgeting, etc. Professionals working in management accounting really need to be adept in using related computer accounting software for data management.

Governmental Accounting

As the name suggests, governmental accounting is a field that relates to financial management of the federal, state or regional government. It is concentrated more on providing data management services instead of earning profits. An accountant employed in this sector usually looks after the audits, budgeting, and financial management of government facilities.

Fiduciary Accounting

The task of fiduciary accounting is normally handed over to a trustee or an administrator in a non- profit organization or a specific community. This accounting is likely to be administrated or initiated by the court. A fiduciary accountant performs traditional accounting duties like record maintenance, financial assessment, and even asset management.

National Income Accounting

National income accounting is associated with the social and economic factors of a nation, unlike just the financial management in a company. It covers a much broader scope which eventually gives out results such as the purchasing capacity of a country per year. The use of national income accounting also enables a country to find out the market value of goods and services manufactured in the country for a specific time period.

Project Accounting

Project accounting is very much similar to management accounting. However, both types of accounting are conducted in business; it is only that project accounting is concerned with the financial advancements on a particular project. It is believed to be a very effective tool in project management. This helps organizations to schedule the deliverables in accordance with the project progress reports.

OTHER TYPES OF ACCOUNTING

Private or Industrial Accounting

This type of accounting refers to accounting activity that is limited only to a single firm. A private accountant provides his skills and services to a single employer and receives salary on an employer-employee basis.

The term private is applied to the accountant and the accounting service he renders. The term is used when an employer-employee type of relationship exists even though the employer is some case is a public corporation.

Public Accounting

Public accounting refers to the accounting service offered by a public accountant to the general public. When a practitioner-client relationship exists, the accountant is referred to as a public accountant. Public accounting is considered to be more professional than private accounting.

Both certified and non- certified public accountants can provide public accounting services. Certified accountants can be single practitioners or by partnership ranging in size from two to hundreds of members. The scope of these accounting firms can include local, national and international clientele.

Governmental Accounting

Governmental accounting refers to accounting for a branch or unit of government at any level, may it be federal, state, or local. Governmental accounting is very similar to conventional accounting methods. Both the governmental and conventional accounting methods use the double-entry system of accounting and journals and ledgers.

The object of government accounting units is to give service rather than make profits. Since profit motive cannot be used as a measure of efficiency in government units, other control measures must be developed.

To enhance control, special funds accounting is used. Governmental units can use the services of both private and public accountant just as any business entity.

Fiduciary Accounting

Fiduciary accounting lies in the notion of trust. This type of accounting is done by a trustee, administrator, executor, or anyone in a position of trust. His work is to keep the records and prepares the reports. This may be authorized by or under the jurisdiction of a court of law. The fiduciary accountant should seek out and control all property subject to the estate or trust. The concept of proprietorship that is common in the usual types of accounting is non-existent or greatly modified in fiduciary accounting.

National Income Accounting

National income accounting uses the economic or social concept in establishing accounting rather than the usual business entity concept. The national income accounting is responsible in providing the public an estimate of the nation's annual purchasing power. The GNP or the gross national product is a related term, which refers to the total market value of all the goods and services produced by a country within a given period of time, usually a calendar year.

ACCOUNTING CONVENTIONS

The most commonly encountered convention is the "historical cost convention". This requires transactions to be recorded at the price ruling at the time, and for assets to be valued at their original cost. Under the "historical cost convention", therefore, no account is taken of changing prices in the economy.

MONETARY MEASUREMENT

Accountants do not account for items unless they can be quantified in monetary terms. Items that are not accounted for (unless someone is prepared to pay something for them) include things like workforce skill, morale, market leadership, brand recognition, quality of management etc.

SEPARATE ENTITY

This convention seeks to ensure that private transactions and matters relating to the owners of a business are segregated from transactions that relate to the business.

REALISATION

With this convention, accounts recognise transactions (and any profits arising from them) at the point of sale or transfer of legal ownership—rather than just when cash actually changes hands. For example, a company that makes a sale to a customer can recognise that sale when the transaction is legal—at the point of contract. The actual payment due from the customer may not arise until several weeks (or months) later—if the customer has been granted some credit terms.

MATERIALITY

An important convention. As we can see from the application of accounting standards and accounting policies, the preparation of accounts involves a high degree of judgement.

Where decisions are required about the appropriateness of a particular accounting judgement, the "materiality" convention suggests that this should only be an issue if the judgement is "significant" or "material" to a user of the accounts. The concept of "materiality" is an important issue for auditors of financial accounts.

DOUBLE ENTRY SYSTEM

The double entry system of bookkeeping owes its origin to an Italian merchant named Lucas Pacioli who wrote the first book on *double entry bookkeeping* entitled "Decomputis et Scripturis". It was published in Venice in 1544. All modern methods of accounting are simply adaptation of the system invented by that ancient pioneer.

DEFINITION AND EXPLANATION

The double entry theory of bookkeeping can be defined as the system of recording transactions having two fundamental aspects—one involving the receiving of a benefit and the other to giving the benefit—in the same set of books. In this theory, as the two fold aspects of each transaction are recorded, the name "double entry" has been given to this system.

Every transaction involves two fold aspects *e.g.,* an aspect of receiving and an aspect of giving. One who receives is a debtor (Dr) and one who gives is a creditor (Cr). Under the double entry system, both the aspects of giving and receiving are recorded in terms of accounts.

The account which receives the benefit is debited and the account which gives the benefit is credited. It is the ultimate result of this system that every debit must have corresponding credit and vice versa and on any particular day the total of the debit entries and the credit entries on the various accounts must be equal.

ADVANTAGES OF DOUBLE ENTRY SYSTEM

The main advantages of double entry theory of book–keeping are as follows:

- Trial balance can be drawn up on any day to prove the arithmetical accuracy of record.
- The nominal sides of transactions being recorded: it is possible to prepare Trading and Profit and Loss Account from which the Gross

Profit and Net Profit made by the business during a particular period can be easily ascertained.
- As all personal accounts of debtors and creditors as well as real accounts are kept, it is possible to prepare Balance Sheet.
- The transactions being recorded in the most scientific and systematic way gives the most reliable information of business.
- It prevents fraud by rendering any alteration in any account more difficult.
- It enables the trader to compare the different items, such as sales, purchases, opening stock and closing stock of one period with similar items of preceding period and the trader may thus know whether his business is progressing or not.

DISADVANTAGES OF DOUBLE ENTRY SYSTEM

The following are the main disadvantages of this system:
- This system requires the maintenance of a number of books of accounts which is not practical in small concerns.
- The system is costly because a number of records are to be maintained.
- There is no guarantee of absolute accuracy of the books of accounts inspite of agreement of the trial balance.

ACCOUNTING THEORY AND PRACTICE

The nature of any theory is to provide a logical basis for the practice or procedure to which the theory is applied. Accounting theory has evolved over a long passage of time during which substantial changes in human behaviour and market structures have taken place.

There are two main types of accounting theory that impact the practice of accounting. Normative theory concerns how things should be done. For example, ideas about the meaning of economic income can influence the way in which regulators decide that accounting systems should measure profit.

In contrast, positive accounting theory tries to explain why things are the way they are. For example, why managers choose a particular accounting method over another, or choose not to invest in research and development activities.

For policy-makers to make changes to accounting systems, they not only need to know what they are trying to achieve (*i.e.* they need to form an opinion as to the desired outcome), they also need to understand why people are currently behaving differently and how any changes will affect them. They will refer to normative theory for the former, and positive theory for the latter.

Positive accounting theory is tested by gathering and analysing data. Usually, researchers either study a single organisation in great depth over a long period of time, or they collect a smaller amount of data about a much larger number of organisations. Analysing a single organisation may mean that the research findings are not generalisable to other organisations. However, analysing a large number of organisations to reach conclusions about the 'average' organisation, does not tell you very much about individual cases.

ACCOUNTING INFORMATION AND ITS USES

We have seen that financial reporting provides information to users who are not normally involved in actually running the organisation. These users are external to the business. They include actual and potential shareholders, lenders and other investors.

They may also include customers, suppliers, the government, and the general public. We have also seen that management use accounting information themselves. Directors, other managers, and employees are internal to the business, and use information to make economic decisions (for example, which new product to manufacture, or what price to charge to a new customer).

External users may wish to make both economic decisions (for example, whether or not to invest their money in the business by buying shares) and legal/stewardship decisions (for example, the government needs to calculate how much tax to charge, and shareholders need to determine how well the managers have performed in managing their funds). These different types of decisions require different types of information.

There is usually a trade-off between:

- Relevant information (that can influence decisions about the future or confirm the outcome of a past transaction); and
- Reliable information.

Economic decisions need forward-looking information. This information is unlikely to be reliable as no one has a crystal ball that can predict the future with total accuracy! Legal and stewardship decisions need information about the past. It is usually important that this information is very reliable, as getting it wrong may result in fines and penalties.

ACCOUNTING EQUATION

The accounting equation represents the basic equation associated with double-entry accounting.

Essentially, the accounting equation establishes the formula for representing the relationship that exists between assets, liabilities, and net worth. As the most common of all balance sheet equations, the accounting equation is also fundamental to learning how to properly read and utilize a balance sheet.

For the purposes of understanding how the accounting equation works, it is important to have some grasp of what is meant by each of the three basic components in the equation. Assets refer to the worth of goods or products in the possession of the owner. Liabilities represent the amount of cash or resources that were borrowed in order to acquire the assets. Net worth is the financial worth of the individual, less any outstanding debts to outside entities. Essentially, the point of the accounting equation is to arrive at this final component of net worth, or as it is sometimes referred to, the equity.

To show the way that the accounting equation works to determine net worth, assume that an investor currently has a net worth of two thousand dollars, with no current liabilities.

The owner chooses to acquire a new asset for the amount of one thousand dollars. In order to acquire the asset, the owner chose to use five hundred dollars of assets that were already in his or her possession, and then borrow five hundred dollars to complete the purchase. Assuming there is no depreciation associated with the acquired asset, the owner now has control of assets worth a total of three thousand Rupees (₹).

However, he or she now has liabilities in the amount of five hundred Rupees (₹). This will result in a net worth of two thousand, five hundred Rupees (₹). As long as the sum of the net worth and the liabilities equal the assets, all is well in the accounting process.

Simply speaking, the accounting equation shows that net worth is determined by taking the value of current assets in hand and subtracting the value of any current liabilities. When it comes to use of the accounting equation as the foundational balance sheet equation, this means that the bottom line on the balance sheet will always show the net worth of the individual or entity. As long as the final net worth figure and the amount of liabilities balance with the assets, all is well. However, if the combination of liabilities and net worth does not equal the total of the assets, there is something wrong in the accounting process, and an investigation to uncover the origin of the imbalance should take place immediately.

GENERALLY ACCEPTED ACCOUNTING PRINCIPLES

Generally Accepted Accounting Principles (GAAP) is a term used to refer to the standard framework of guidelines for financial accounting used in any given jurisdiction which are generally known as Accounting Standards. GAAP includes the standards, conventions, and rules accountants follow in recording and summarizing transactions, and in the preparation of financial statements.

The term "GAAP" is an abbreviation for Generally Accepted Accounting Principles (GAAP). GAAP is a codification of how CPA firms and corporations prepare and present their business income and expense, assets and liabilities on their financial statements. GAAP is not a single accounting rule, but rather the aggregate of many rules on how to account for various transactions.

When preparing financial statements prepared using GAAP, most American corporations and other business entities use the many rules of how to report business transactions based upon the various GAAP rules. This provides for consistency in the reporting of companies and businesses so that financial analysis, Banks, Shareholders and the SEC can have all reporting companies preparing their financial statements using the same rules and reporting procedures. This allows for an "Apple to Apple" comparison of any corporation or business entity with another. Thus, if Company A reports ₹1,000,000 of net income, using GAAP, than the public and other users of financial statements can compare that net income to another company that is reporting ₹500,000 of net income, using GAAP.

The rules and procedures for reporting under GAAP are complex and have developed over a long period of time. Currently there are more than 150 "pronouncements" as to how to account for different types of transactions, ranging from how to report regular income from the sale of goods, and its related inventory values, to accounting for incentive stock option distributions. By using consistent principles, all companies reporting under GAAP report these transactions on their financial statements in a consistent manner.

The various rules and pronouncements come from the Financial Accounting Standards Board (FASB) which is a non-profit organization that the accounting profession has created to promulgate the rules of GAAP reporting and to amend the rules of GAAP reporting as occasion requires. The more recent pronouncements come as Statements of the Financial Accounting Board.

Changes in the GAAP rules can carry tremendous impact upon American business. For example, when FASB stopped requiring banks to mark their assets (loans) to the lower of cost or market (*i.e.* value of a foreclosed home loan). the effect on a bank's "net worth" as defined by GAAP can change dramatically. While generally neutral, there is some pressure on the FASB to yield to industry or political pressure when it makes its rules. Nonetheless, since all companies report using the same set of rules, know the rules of GAAP reporting can tell the user of financial statements a great deal. The study of accounting, in large part, entails learning the many rules and promulgations set forth by FASB and how to apply those rules to actual business events.

GAAP is slowly being phased out in favour of the International Accounting Standards as the global business becomes more pervasive. GAAP applies only to United States financial reporting and thus an American company reporting under GAAP might show different results if it was compared to a British company, that uses the International Standards.

While there is tremendous similarity in between GAAP and the International Rules. the differences can lead a financial statement user to incorrectly believe that company A made more money than company B simply because they report using different rules. The move towards International Standards seeks to eliminate this kind of disparity.

Financial Accounting is information that must be assembled and reported objectively. Third-parties who must rely on such information have a right to be assured that the data are free from bias and inconsistency, whether deliberate or not. For this reason, financial accounting relies on certain standards or guides that are called "Generally Accepted Accounting Principles" (GAAP).

Principles derive from tradition, such as the concept of matching. In any report of financial statements (audit, compilation, review, etc.), the preparer/ auditor must indicate to the reader whether or not the information contained within the statements complies with GAAP.

- *Principle of regularity*: Regularity can be defined as conformity to enforced rules and laws.
- *Principle of consistency*: This principle states that when a business has once fixed a method for the accounting treatment of an item, it will enter all similar items that follow in exactly the same way.
- *Principle of sincerity*: This principle, the accounting unit should reflect in good faith the reality of the company's financial status.
- *Principle of the permanence of methods*: This principle aims at allowing the coherence and comparison of the financial information published by the company.
- *Principle of non-compensation*: One should show the full details of the financial information and not seek to compensate a debt with an asset, a revenue with an expense, etc.
- *Principle of prudence*: This principle aims at showing the reality "as is": one should not try to make things look prettier than they are. Typically, a revenue should be recorded only when it is *certain* and a provision should be entered for an expense which is *probable*.
- *Principle of continuity*: When stating financial information, one should assume that the business will not be interrupted. This principle mitigates the principle of prudence: assets do not have to be accounted at their disposable value, but it is accepted that they are at their historical value.
- *Principle of periodicity*: Each accounting entry should be allocated to a given period, and split accordingly if it covers several periods. If a client pre-pays a subscription (or lease, etc.), the given revenue should be split to the entire time-span and not counted for entirely on the date of the transaction.
- *Principle of Full Disclosure/Materiality*: All information and values pertaining to the financial position of a business must be disclosed in the records.

- *Principle of Utmost Good Faith*: All the information regarding to the firm should be disclosed to the insurer before the insurance policy is taken.

INTERNATIONAL ACCOUNTING STANDARDS AND RULES

Many countries use or are converging on the International Financial Reporting Standards (IFRS), established and maintained by the International Accounting Standards Board. In some countries, local accounting principles are applied for regular companies but listed or large companies must conforms to IFRS, so statutory reporting is comparable internationally, across jurisdictions.

INDEPENDENCE AND PUBLIC ACCOUNTING

Independence is a more fundamental and pervasive concept in accounting than in the other professions. Indeed, former Chief Justice Burger stated that independence is a critical concept that sets CPAs apart from other professions. This is true because the core mission of the CPA is as auditor, one who certifies the public reports that describe a corporation's financial status. This is the only exclusive function that the CPA performs for society.

In rendering an opinion the independent auditor assumes a public duty. Moreover, this public duty must transcend any employment relationship or other duty towards the client. The CPA has what Burger calls a "public watchdog" function that demands that the auditor subordinate responsibility towards the client in order to maintain complete fidelity to the public trust.

So important and ingrained is independence in the public accounting profession that it may be regarded as a cornerstone upon which much of the ethics peculiar to the profession is built. Note the radical change in focus when the accounting profession speaks of independence. The perceived peril in lack of independence is not to the client but to an outside third party. This third party may be any person who reads and relies upon the financial statements upon which the auditor has rendered an opinion.

We find that to serve the third party the auditor must take an unbiased viewpoint when he performs audit tests, evaluates the results of those tests, and then issues an audit report and opinion with respect to the financial statements. Traditionally accountants have viewed independence on three ethical planes. First, in order to take an unbiased viewpoint, an auditor must possess the virtues of honesty, objectivity, and responsibility. In other words, on this plane we are concerned with the character of the auditor. We may regard this as the highest form of independence.

At the second level independence refers to the relationship of the CPA and the client. Here independence means avoiding any relationship that would likely, even subconsciously, tend to impair the CPA's ability to take the unbiased viewpoint. The public accountant must avoid personal and business relationships with clients that could cause even the most well-meaning person to slip or compromise in professional judgement.

On the final level, independence means the CPA should avoid any relationship that might suggest to a reasonable observer that a conflict of interest exists. Even when the professional is completely satisfied that no relationship impairs her judgement as a professional, she has not gone far enough. She must concern herself with the jaundiced eye of the beholder. So, even is she is completely satisfied that she can render an impartial judgement or opinion for a client with whom she has a particular business relationship, the standards of the profession still might prohibit her from acting as independent auditor. In this respect we can compare the accounting profession with the legal profession, which demands of the judiciary that no appearance of impropriety exists.

We thus see that on two levels independence is a condition of the mind and character of the professional. On the third level the issue is not about the professional herself but the way others view her. The common expressions used in professional circles to describe these phenomena are independence in fact and independence in appearance.

INDEPENDENCE IN FACT

Independence in fact is one of the most elusive aspects of ethics in the accounting profession. Most public accountants are ready to assert that for the most part independence in fact is the norm in daily professional life. Yet they are at a loss to provide evidence for this assertion or even to explain why they believe it is true.

After all, it is difficult to discern the virtues necessary for independence in fact. Moreover, we have little basis to doubt the existence of independence in fact in a particular circumstance until the most dramatic of events, the audit failure, comes to light. An audit failure is said to occur when a CPA opines to third parties that a client's financial statements are fairly presented in accordance with generally accepted accounting principles when in fact they are not. Often the root of the audit failure is found to be a lack of independence in fact.

Some frequently cited examples of a lack of independence in fact include lacking objectivity and skepticism, accepting the work of management for something that normally requires independent verification, agreeing to a significant client-imposed restriction on the scope of the audit, or knowingly neglecting the critical evaluation of a significant client transaction. Failure to test the accounts receivable by independent confirmation would be a concrete example. Some people also believe incompetence is a manifestation of a lack of independence in fact. In each of these cases, the virtues required to render an unbiased opinion are missing. Independence is thus violated on its highest plane.

Another dimension of independence in fact originates in relationships with clients. The Securities and Exchange Commission, in Accounting Series Release 234, has tightened the restrictions here. "The application of an independent viewpoint is particularly important with respect to judgements exercised in the determination of appropriate principles and methods applied to the recording, classification and presentation of financial data. By their nature such judgements cannot subsequently be evaluated on an impartial and objective basis by the same accountant who made them." In other words, the CPA cannot serve two masters: he cannot hold himself out to the public in a traditional auditor-client mode while at the same time serving that client as a controller, treasurer, or internal auditor. Neither can the CPA hold a direct financial or a material indirect financial interest in a client about whom he is rendering an opinion.

INDEPENDENCE IN APPEARANCE

Independence in fact exists when an auditor is actually able to maintain an unbiased attitude in the conduct of the audit. By contrast, independence in appearance refers to the interpretation or perception of others about the auditor's independence. Most of the value of the audit report stems from the independent status of the auditor. Therefore, if auditors are independent in fact, but readers of the financial statements or members of the public at large believe them to be advocates for the client, most of the value of the audit function would be lost. These users of financial information can have faith in an auditor's representations only when they are confident that the auditor has acted as an impartial judge.

The entire reason for a profession of public accounting rests upon the foundation of independence in appearance. Otherwise the audit function could be performed by internal auditors who work for the company. These men and women are honorable people who possess requisite virtue for performing audits. Moreover, organizational systems could be devised to protect them from management retaliation. It is therefore at least possible that they could be independent in fact.

Nevertheless, users would almost always have a lingering doubt about the statements' impartiality and freedom from bias. Readers might suspect that the auditors were really serving the best interests of the company for which they worked. In other words, the internal auditor would not appear independent.

Hence her representations would not have value to the user. An analogous phenomenon may be found in our government, where an independent prosecutor is appointed when a federal official, especially one in the Justice Department, is accused of a crime.

Concern about lack of independence in fact not only lowers the value of a particular audit report but also can have an adverse effect on the profession. Certified public accounts are given special status in society—the status of "professional"—because of the perceived role that they play in that society.

The role of the auditor is to give an unbiased opinion on reported financial information based upon professional judgement. If CPAs on the whole are not viewed as independent, the validity of the auditors' role in society is threatened.

The very credibility of the profession, public accounting, depends ultimately upon society's perception about independence rather than the fact of independence.

AREAS OF CONCERN

Four areas in particular are significant with respect to independence in appearance:

- The competition that now exists among audit firms;
- The increasing role of management advisory services offered by auditors;
- The large and growing size of audit firms; and
- The length of time an audit firm has been filling the audit needs of a given client. Each of these areas has the potential of weakening public perception about certified public accountants' independence.

The competition we observe today among auditors was brought about because of action of the Federal Trade Commission and a Supreme Court decision. Before these events CPAs kept themselves above the fray, so to speak. They seemed content with their existing client base and were constrained by the then existing code of ethics from doing much to change that base. This way of doing business, despite being declared illegal, at least gave the illusion of being "professional."

Today auditors conduct business in a more capitalistic fashion utilizing advertising, personal selling, and other advanced marketing techniques to capture as much of the audit market as they can. It is all perfectly legal and legitimate business activity, but somehow it does not seem as "professional." The lingering question in the mind of the outside observer is whether a professional might not be willing to sacrifice independence in order to gain business advantage in an unrestrained competitive environment. Notice that the primary problem here is the appearance rather than the fact of independence.

The role of CPAs as business consultants through their management advisory services creates a similar problem. This role of the auditor is admittedly an old one. Yet today it is increasingly important to the practice of public accounting because competition for audit clients has made audit service less profitable. Moreover, the profitability of these services has been followed by increased publicity concerning the activities of CPAs in the consulting area.

This is compounded by the fact that CPA firms have expanded into more and more diverse areas of consulting. The problem once again is how the public perceives all of this. Can a person play this increasingly important role as an advisor to clients on how to conduct their businesses and at the same time give an unbiased opinion about the reported financial information? The profession strongly defends the position that by keeping auditing and consulting activities separate, independence is in fact maintained. Perhaps this is true. Yet the very fact that the question is raised means that independence in appearance is threatened.

A third problem with respect to independence in appearance arises due to the sheer size of the firms in which many certified public accountants practice. Increasingly the profession is being dominated by huge, multinational firms known as the Big Six. Ethically, there is nothing wrong here. But to the public these large firms are beginning to look more and more like big business. Therefore, these firms must be especially careful to guard against perceptions of a lack of independence.

A final factor that can erode independence in appearance is the length of time a particular client is served by a single auditor. In many cases an auditor-client relationship has stretched across decades. As time passes the client and the firm are increasingly identified with one another in the public eye. Again, the danger here is in appearance. The organizations may seem to be too close in the eye of the beholder even if the strictest measure of independence in fact is maintained.

Problems of credibility in each of the above cases almost always arise outside the profession. Therefore accountants must be constantly aware of the perception issue, which can have an adverse impact upon auditing firms and the direct and indirect users of their services. The issue is rarely concerned with the validity of negative perceptions, but rather the *belief* that users and society hold with respect to objectivity and freedom from bias.

2

Cost: Concept and Principles

COST CONCEPTS

COST UNIT

A cost unit refers to a unit of product, service or time in relation to which costs may be ascertained or expressed. In other words, cost unit is the unit of output for which cost is ascertained. For examples, the cost of air–conditioner is ascertained per unit. The selection of cost unit is important in cost accounting. It should be carefully selected to suit the nature of business operation. The selected unit should be neither too small nor too big, but ideal for cost ascertainment. Cost unit may be expressed in terms of number, weight, area, length etc. The following are the cost units in various industries.

Industry	Cost Unit
Refrigerators, Cars, Scooters	Per unit
Television sets, Motor Cycles	Per unit
Watches, Radios	Per unit
Sugar	Per quintal
Cement, Steel, Coal	Per tonne
Paper	Per tonne
Textiles	Per metre
Chemicals	Per kg/tonne/litre
Electricity	Per kilowatt hour
Passenger transport	Per passenger k.m.
Goods transport	Per tonne k.m.
Ceramic tiles	Per square foot or per unit
Bricks	Per 1,000 Nos.
Road contract	Per. k.m.3

Thus, cost units may vary from industry to industry. An enterprise which produces more than one type of product may have more than one cost unit.

COST CENTRE

A large business is divided into a number of functional departments for administrative convenience. These departments are further divided into smaller divisions for cost ascertainment and control. These smaller divisions are called cost centers. A cost centre is a location, person or item of equipment in relation to which cost can be ascertained and controlled. In simple words, it is a subdivision of the organization to which cost can be charged. A cost centre can be:

- A location *i.e.* an area such as works department, store yard
- A person such as supervisor, sales man
- An item of equipment *e.g.* delivery van, or a particular machine.

The determination of suitable cost centre is very important for the purpose of cost ascertainment and control. The manager of a cost centre is held responsible for control of cost of his cost centre. The number and size of cost centers vary from organization to organization.

The selection of a suitable cost centre depends on the following factors:

- Nature and size of the business.
- Layout and organization of the factory.
- Availability of various cost data and information.
- Management policy regarding cost ascertainment and control.
- *Types of cost centres*: Cost centres may be of the following types.
- *Production cost centre*: A cost centre is which production is carried on is known as production cost centre. *e.g.*, machine shop, welding shop, assembly shop, etc.
- *Service cost centre*: A cost centre which renders service to production cost centre is known as service centre *e.g.* power house, stores department, maintenance department etc.
- *Personal cost centre*: It consists of a person or a group of persons *e.g.* Sales manager, Works manager etc.
- *Impersonal cost centre*: It consists of a location or a machine or a group of machines. *e.g.* canteen.
- *Operation cost centre*: It consists of machines and/ or persons carrying out similar operations. *e.g.* machines and operators engaged in welding or turning.

PROFIT CENTRE

A profit centre is a responsibility centre which accumulates revenues as well as costs. In other words, it is a department or segment of the organization which has been assigned control over both revenues and cost. For instance, if there are two divisions in a textile company, say readymade and clothing, each one may be regarded as a profit centre.

DISTINGUISH BETWEEN COST CENTRE AND PROFIT CENTRE

Important differences between cost centre and profit centre are:

- Cost centre is created by the cost accountant. On the other hand, a profit centre is created by the top management.

- Cost centre is created for the purpose of cot ascertainment and control. But the profit centre is created for the purpose of evaluation of performance.
- Cost centre is a small segment, whereas profit centre is a large segment.
- Cost centres do not enjoy autonomy. But, profit centres enjoy autonomy.
- Cost centre does not have a target of costs. But a profit centre has a target of profit for performance evaluation.

COST CONTROL

Cost control can be defined as the comparative analysis of actual costs with appropriate standards of budgets to facilitate performance evaluation and formulation of corrective measures. It aims at accomplishing conformity between actual result and standards or budgets. Cost control is keeping expenditures within prescribed limits.

Cost control has the following features:

- Creation of responsibility centres with defined authority and responsibility for cost incurrence.
- Formulation of standards and budgets that incorporate objectives and goals to be achieved.
- Timely cost control reports describing the variances between budgets and standards and actual performance.
- Formulation of corrective measures to eliminate and reduce unfavourable variances.
- A systematic and fair plan or motivation to encourage workers to accomplish budgetary goals.
- Follow–up to ensure that corrective measures are being effectively applied.

Cost control does not necessarily mean reducing the cost but its aim is to have the maximum utility of the cost incurred. In other words, the objective of cost control is the performance of the same job at a lower cost or a better performance for the same cost.

COST REDUCTION

Cost reduction may be defined as an attempt to bring costs down. Cost reduction implies real and permanent reduction in the unit cost of goods manufactured or services rendered without impairing their suitability for the use intended.

The goal of cost reduction is achieved in two says:

- By reducing the cost per unit and
- By increasing productivity.

The steps for cost reduction include elimination of waste, improving operations, increasing productivity, search for cheaper materials, improved standards of quality, finding other means to reduce unit costs. Cost reduction has to be achieved using internal factors within the organisation. Reduction of costs due to external factors such as reduction in taxes, government subsidies, grants etc. do not come under the concept of cost reduction.

COSTING

All manufacturing companies sell their products to make profit. The profit on each product sold can be defined as the difference between the selling price of the product and the total cost of making the product. Cost therefore plays a very important role in the product design process.

To be successful, a product must not only satisfy a set of functions defined in the product design specification, but it must also be possible to build the product within the cost criteria set out at the start of the project. Before the development of any product begins, it is essential to perform some form of economic analysis on the product to determine if it is worth making. This may involve some form of market analysis to determine what the customer is willing to pay for a product.

The costs involved in any product can be spilt into development costs and the product cost. Interestingly, some companies do not actually know what their costs are which leaves them open to the possibility that their actual costs may be more than the selling price of their product!

An example of this was the Mini when it was first produced in the early 60's. Market research suggested that the car should be sold for less than £500 so the company priced the car at £499. Later when they analysed the cost of producing the car they found that the car cost around £530 to build, resulting in large losses for the manufacturer.

ELEMENTS OF COST

DEFINITION

Presented here are typical cost elements that must be considered when arriving at a total project cost estimate. These examples must be considered generic in nature. They are not definitive examples since the accounting practices of different firms and organizations may vary greatly. The definition of these cost parameters is usually not the responsibility of the engineering organization.

Rather, a financial or estimating organization is responsible for determining the cost data, which is combined with engineering (and fabrication, manufacturing, test and integration, purchasing, etc., as appropriate) estimates of the work to be performed. The point here is to give you some sense of the various components that may enter into the total project cost.

Direct Labour

Direct labour is the cost of all the time (hours) that people spend on a particular activity that is directly related to the contract objectives. This direct labour cost is the estimated number of hours spent by an individual on the job, times the dollars per hour that person is paid. These individual costs for all the people working on a job are then added up to get a total direct labour cost. Various techniques are used to determine the dollars per hour that are used to calculate the direct labour cost. A common approach is to use labour cost pool rates, where the average of the actual pay rates for all employees with the same job classification is used. These pool rates could be broken into categories such as Engineer, Senior Engineer, Foreman, Machinist I, Machinist II, etc. If your technical proposal names specific people to accomplish all or part of the proposed work, the actual pay of these individuals must be included in your cost estimates.

Another technique that is sometimes employed is to use the actual pay rate of all the individual(s) who will be working on the proposed job. The total direct labour cost is then determined by adding together the individual labour costs of all the people to be assigned to the project.

If the proposed project will last for a significant length of time, escalation factors must be applied to the current labour rates to account for future changes in these rates. This escalation will be due to items such as pay raises, attrition, and increases in starting pay for new hires. These escalation factors are often based on historical data.

Labour Overhead

The cost of an individual to a contract is more than just the pay that that person receives. There are expenses associated with employing that person that are referred to as labour overhead, or indirect, costs. Click here to see a number of these cost elements that may be included in the labour overhead. The estimated expense of these various items is usually based on historical data or expected future costs, or these expenses may be based on a combination of historical data and actual cost data.

These expenses are lumped together into a labour overhead factor that is multiplied by the direct labour cost to determine the overhead labour cost. This overhead represents costs related to people or labour working on the contract, and therefore this overhead cost follows the base or direct labour costs.

Facilities

This type of cost can be considered either direct or indirect, depending on the nature of the company. If a company's facility exists to serve only one contract, then the cost of facilities should be a direct cost to the contract. If space is used to house employees that work on several contracts, however, this type of cost should be an indirect that follows the direct labour of people working on the contract.

Materials

Included in this cost category are the expenses incurred in purchasing raw materials for use during the fabrication and assembly of hardware for testing and/or for delivery to the customer. For a test programme these material costs would be associated with the test hardware. For a test and hardware delivery project, the material costs would include materials required for both the test and for delivered hardware. These costs can include the purchase of metal stocks, bulk wire, screws and fasteners, and all parts that are used in the delivered product.

Other Costs

There are often other miscellaneous direct costs that will be charged to the contract, such as travel, postage, rentals, and insurance.

Subcontracts

Often another firm, under a subcontractor to your firm, will accomplish a portion of the work required by your contract, for example when a second organization has a special capability or product line that you require to accomplish the job. In this case you would have the potential subcontractor(s) respond to an RFP for the required services or hardware. If there are a number of potential sources, this would be a competitive situation and you would select the subcontractor whose participation would place your company in the most advantageous position for the overall project.

General and Administrative (G&A) Expenses

G&A expenses are other costs associated with doing business. These G&A expenses are expressed in terms of a factor that is applied to the total cost, less material and subcontracts. Click here to view the several elements that contribute to the total G&A expense. These expenses are associated with overall company management and the pursuit of new business opportunities. Historical data is often used to project these expenses into the future.

Fee

The fee is the amount you add to your bid that is the profit you hope your firm will make on the contract. A number of factors enter into determining the proposed fee for a specific contract. These include considerations such as:

- Required schedule performance and associated risk.
- Cost performance constraints and associated risk
- Personnel expertise required to accomplish the work.

In general, the higher the risk associated with the proposed work, the higher the fee that will be proposed.

Determining what fee to propose is a decision made collectively by the proposal management and by company management. Many considerations enter into determining this fee.

If the project has a high risk associated with successful completion, you may choose to bid a higher fee than you would for a simpler project. Also, if winning the project is very important to your long-range business position, you may choose to propose a lower fee.

Unallowable Costs

As defined in the FAR, there are a number of costs that are deemed to be unallowable for federal government contracts. These costs should not be included in your proposal cost estimates, as they will not be reimbursable. Some of the major unallowable costs include:

- Airfare costs in excess of the lowest customary standard coach fare.
- Advertising and public relations.
- Alcoholic beverages.
- Bad debts.
- Entertainment costs.
- Fines and penalties.
- Goodwill.
- Lobbying.
- Losses on other contracts.

The FAR states that costs of amusement, diversion, social activities, and any directly associated costs such as tickets to shows or sports events, meals, lodging, rentals, transportation and gratuities are unallowable.

Unbillable hours are hours charged to a project that are costs to that project but are not reimbursable by the customer. Examples include hours charged above a contract ceiling, or hours related to project management that the customer is unwilling to reimburse. Costs that are for the benefit or convenience of the company such as the following may not be reimbursable. Care must be taken when including these type costs in your proposal.

- Relocation
- Travel and transportation incidental to employment
- Incentive awards
- Tools
- Uniforms
- Social functions, gifts, celebrations

In the preceding chapter the sources of income which are ordinarily open to a bank have been outlined, and one of them - the rate of interest or discount - has been analysed at some length. It is equally important to consider with care the various elements of cost which the bank is obliged to incur. Speaking generally, these elements of cost may be summarized as follows:

- Fixed expenses - rent (or the interest on invest-ment in building and equipment), insurance, surety bonds, taxes, light, heat, etc.
- Bad debts.
- Overhead expenses - salaries of president and general officers not assigned to any specific duty.
- Operating salaries.
- Stationery, printing, postage, etc.
- Allowance for interest on capital.
- Depreciation of equipment and building.

Most of these expenses are sufficiently obvious to require no description or explanation. The bank, of course, must have some definite quarters and it gets these either by hiring them from others or by purchas-ing or building them. In any case there is either an annual outlay or a capital sum on which interest must be allowed which represents the cost of the bank's quarters or offices.

In the same way the fixed expenses for lighting, heating, and caring for the offices of the bank must be provided for, and may be regarded as a fixed sum in a degree independent of the total amount of business the bank has to do and in a large measure independent of the amount of its capital.

The overhead expenses are in somewhat the same class as these fixed or plant expenses. Every bank has a certain number of salaried officers whose work when well done is of utmost importance to the institution, but whose pay cannot be assigned to any particular undertaking.

They are "overhead" in the sense that they belong to or must be charged against everything beyond bank debts in due proportion - that is to say, they are salaries which are practically incident to the doing of any business and which have only a secondary relationship to the amount of such business. We shall presently see how the cost of such salaries is usually distributed among the different factors or divisions of the organization.

IDENTIFYING COST ELEMENTS

The cost elements' classification of accounts is the very first structure in the internal accounting's chart of accounts.

From this first class of accounts (which will be identified with the number two), we shall begin.

Consequently we must use great care to correctly identify the different amounts that will be incorporated in internal accounting, which then will help us to accurately establish the specific cost of production and the important appraisal of the cost of goods sold.

Let us start with a very basic first approach: We shall establish the code structure of our internal accounting's chart of accounts.

Class of Accounts: This is expressed by the first digit of the code. The cost elements class will be designated with the number two.

Group of Accounts: This is the identification by the next digit of the code. I recommend the use of only one digit in this position, for a total of nine groups in each class of accounts.

Main Accounts: These numbers should have only two digits, which will make it possible to create a total of roughly 90 main accounts. In my experience, I believe it is adequate to designate up to 90 main accounts within each group of accounts.

Sub Accounts: These should have a total of three digits. With a capacity of up to 900 sub accounts for each of the 90 main accounts within each group of accounts, we have created an adequate quantity of sub accounts for the code structure of the internal chart of accounts.

Sub-Sub Accounts: In case there is a need to increase the chart of accounts, we may allocate four digits for these sub-sub accounts, which would then increase the capacity of each sub account with some 9,000 accounts.

The code structure within the internal chart of accounts will be identified in following way.

Class	Group	Main	Sub	Sub-Sub
X	X	XX	XXX	XXXX

With this planned structure, we will now develop the following group of accounts.

- 2-1-00-000 Salaries and Wages
- 2-2-00-000 Benefits
- 2-3-00-000 Stores Withdrawal
- 2-4-00-000 Depreciation and Amortization
- 2-5-00-000 Adm. & Sales Costs
- 2-6-00-000 Utilities - Services
- 2-7-00-000 Financial Costs
- 2-8-00-000 General Costs

Let us now consider some main accounts that could be incorporated under some specific groups of accounts.

- 2-1-01-000 Salaries for Management and Professionals
- 2-1-05-000 Hourly Wages — Direct
- 2-1-11-000 Hourly Wages — Indirect
- 2-3-01-000 Stores Withdrawal of Direct Materials
- 2-3-11-000 Stores Withdrawal of Indirect Materials
- 2-3-41-000 Stores Withdrawal of Supplies
- 2-3-51-000 Stores Withdrawal of Spare-Parts
- 2-5-11-000 Administrative Costs of Professional Fees
- 2-5-12-000 Travel and Representation

- 2-5-13-000 Telephone and Fax
- 2-5-51-000 Sales Commissions
- 2-5-53-000 Advertising
- 2-6-11-000 Outside Services
- 2-6-15-000 Facility Services
- 2-8-06-000 Postage and Mailing Services
- 2-8-11-000 Employee Relations
- 2-8-21-000 Lease and Rentals

These main accounts can then be complemented with all necessary sub accounts to create an ideal information structure about all cost elements that the company may have. All of these cost elements are accrued costs. They are accrued or "matched" costs of this accounting period and the company's functional activities.

We should not approve costs that do not belong to this accounting period and to the functional activities. Instead we shall proceed with the same attention as we do when matching expenses towards revenues.

This matching procedure is very important. Since the newly developed internal chart of accounts will correctly establish the cost of goods sold and compare it with the corresponding sales revenues, there is no longer a need for accounts such as prepaid expenses in the general accounting structure. These prepaid accounts were developed for the purpose of matching the expenses towards the sales revenues. This approach of matching costs is only necessary in internal accounting.

This is a very important statement: We have created an absolutely new approach in our accounting philosophy.

Until now, there have been mixed definitions in general accounting (financial accounting) that actually correspond only to managerial accounting. We had to use these mixed definitions because there was not a separate internal accounting structure. Therefore we had to use prepaid accounts to prevent mistakes in income statement presentations. Amounts for prepaid rent, prepaid insurance, etc. had to be included in the assets.

We now have internal accounting and the philosophy of matching expenses, which solves the cost elements accounts. We no longer need any prepaid accounts in our assets. An additional benefit to the internal accounting structure: Within the cost elements' class of accounts, we will open accounts that will register all necessary amounts regar-ding price, payment and efficiency variances.

These new details will be included in the stores withdrawal group of accounts to show management a clear structure of the variances that exist between actual price and standard price, actual labour hours and standard labour hours.

All these variations will be referring to the job orders that we worked with our new internal cost approach, we will be able to create absolutely new information that is as good as unthinkable with the old general accounting structure.

DIFFERENCE BETWEEN COST CONTROL AND COST REDUCTION

Cost reduction is a much wider concept than cost control. As stated earlier, cost control aims at controlling costs within prescribed limits with the help of budgets and standards. The following are the differences between the two:

	Cost Control		Cost Reduction
1.	Cost control process involves: – Setting targets and standards – Ascertaining actual performance – Comparing actual performance with – Investigating the variances and – Taking corrective action.	1.	Cost reduction is not concerned with setting targets and standards and maintaining performance according to standards. Cost targets reduction is the final result in the cost control process.
2.	Cost control aims at achieving standards,*i.e.* cost targets. It assumes existence of the standards.	2.	Cost reduction aims at improving It challenges standards and assumes existence of concealed potential savings in the standards.
3.	It follows a conservative procedure and lacks dynamic approach.	3.	It is continuous, dynamic and innovative in nature, looking always for measures and alternative to reduce costs.
4.	It is a preventive function.	4.	It is a corrective function.
5.	In cost control, costs are optimised before they are incurred.	5.	In cost reduction, there is always assumed a scope for reducing the incurred costs under controlled conditions.
6.	It is generally applicable to items whichhave standards.	6.	This is applicable to every activity of the business.
7.	It contains guidelines and directive of management as to how to do a thing.	7.	It adds thinking and analysis to action at all levels of management.

COST OF GOODS SOLD

Cost of goods sold refers to the inventory costs of those goods a business has sold during a particular period. Costs are associated with particular goods using one of several formulas, including specific identification, first-in-first-out (FIFO), or average cost. Costs include all costs of purchase, costs of conversion and other costs incurred in bringing the inventories to their present location and condition. Costs of goods made by the business include material, labour, and allocated overhead.

The costs of those goods not yet sold are deferred as costs of inventory until the inventory is sold or written down in value. Many businesses sell goods that they have bought or made. When the goods are bought or made, the costs associated with such goods are capitalized as part of inventory (or stock) of goods. These costs are treated as an expense in the period the business recognizes income from sale of the goods. Determining costs requires keeping records of goods or materials purchased and any discounts on such purchase. In addition, if the goods are modified, the business must determine the costs incurred in modifying the goods. Such modification costs include labour, supplies or additional material, supervision, quality control, use of equipment, and other overhead costs.

Principles for determining costs may be easily stated, but application in practice is often difficult due to a variety of consideration in the allocation of costs. Cost of goods sold may also reflect adjustments. Among the potential adjustments are decline in value of the goods (*i.e.,* lower market value than cost), obsolescence, damage, etc. When multiple goods are bought or made, it may be necessary to identify which costs relate to which particular goods sold. This may be done using an identification convention, such as specific identification of the goods, first-in-first-out (FIFO), or average cost. Alternative systems may be used in some countries, such as last-in-first-out (LIFO), gross profit method, retail method, or combinations of these. Cost of goods sold may be the same or different for accounting and tax purposes, depending on the rules of the particular jurisdiction.

IMPORTANCE OF INVENTORIES

Inventories have a significant effect on profits. A business that makes or buys goods to sell must keep track of inventories of goods under all accounting and income tax rules. An example shows why. Fred buys auto parts and resells them. In 2008, Fred buys 100 worth of parts. He sells parts for 80 that he bought for 30, and has 70 worth of parts left. In 2009, he sells the remainder of the parts for 180. If he keeps track of inventory, his profit in 2008 is 50, and his profit in 2009 is 110, or 160 in total. If he deducted all the costs in 2008, he would have a loss of 20 in 2008 and a profit of 180 in 2009. The total is the same, but the timing is much different. All countries' accounting and income tax rules (if the country has an income tax) require the use of inventories for all businesses that regularly sell goods they have made or bought.

COST OF GOODS FOR RESALE

Cost of goods purchased for resale includes purchase price as well as all other costs of acquisitions. This cost should reflect any discounts. Additional costs may include freight paid to acquire the goods, customs duties, sales or use taxes not recoverable paid on materials used, and fees paid for acquisition. For financial reporting purposes such period costs as purchasing department, warehouse, and other operating expenses are usually not treated as part of inventory or cost of goods sold.

For U.S. income tax purposes, some of these period costs must be capitalized as part of inventory. Costs of selling, packing, and shipping goods to customers are treated as operating expenses related to the sale. Both International and U.S.

accounting standards require that certain abnormal costs, such as those associated with idle capacity, must be treated as expenses rather than part of inventory. Value added tax is generally not treated as part of cost of goods sold if it may be used as an input credit or otherwise recoverable from the taxing authority.

COST OF GOODS MADE BY THE BUSINESS

The cost of goods produced in the business should include all costs of production. The key components of cost generally include:

- Parts, raw materials and supplies used,
- Labour, including associated costs such as payroll taxes and benefits, and
- Overhead of the business allocable to production.

Most business makes more than one of a particular item. Thus, costs are incurred for multiple items rather than a particular item sold. Determining how much of each of these components to allocate to particular goods requires either tracking the particular costs or making some allocations of costs. Parts and raw materials are often tracked to particular sets (*e.g.,* batches or production runs) of goods, and then allocated to each item. Labour costs include direct labour and indirect labour. Direct labour costs are the wages paid to those employees who spend all their time working directly on the product being manufactured.

Indirect labour costs are the wages paid to other factory employees involved in production. Costs of payroll taxes and fringe benefits are generally included in labour costs, but may be treated as overhead costs. Labour costs may be allocated to an item or set of items based on timekeeping records. Materials and labour may be allocated based on past experience, or standard costs. Where materials or labour costs for a period exceed the expected amount of standard costs, a variance.

Such variances are then allocated among cost of goods sold and remaining inventory at the end of the period. Determining overhead costs often involves making assumptions about what costs should be associated with production activities and what costs should be associated with other activities. Traditional cost accounting methods attempt to make these assumptions based on past experience and management judgement as to factual relationships. Activity based costing attempts to allocate costs based on those factors that drive the business to incur the costs.

Overhead costs are often allocated to sets of produced goods based on the ratio of labour hours or costs or the ratio of materials used for producing the set of goods. Overhead costs may be referred to as factory overhead or factory burden for those costs incurred at the plant level or overall burden for those costs incurred at the organization level.

Where labour hours are used, a burden rate or overhead cost per hour of labour may be added along with labour costs. Other methods may be used to associate overhead costs with particular goods produced. Overhead rates may be standard rates, in which case there may be variances, or may be adjusted for each set of goods produced.

Variable production overheads are allocated to units produced based on actual use of production facilities. Fixed production overheads are often allocated based on normal capacities or expected production. More or fewer goods may be produced than expected when developing cost assumptions (like burden rates). These differences in production levels often result in too much or too little cost being assigned to the goods produced. This also gives rise to variances.

IDENTIFICATION CONVENTIONS

In some cases, the cost of goods sold may be identified with the item sold. Ordinarily, however, the identity of goods is lost between the time of purchase or manufacture and the time of sale. Determining which goods have been sold, and the cost of those goods, requires either identifying the goods or using a convention to assume which goods were sold. This may be referred to as a cost flow assumption or inventory identification assumption or convention.

The following methods are available in many jurisdictions for associating costs with goods sold and goods still on hand:

- *Specific identification*: Under this method, particular items are identified, and costs are tracked with respect to each item. This may require considerable recordkeeping. This method cannot be used where the goods or items are indistinguishable or fungible.
- *Average cost*: The average cost method relies on average unit cost to calculate cost of units sold and ending inventory. Several variations on the calculation may be used, including weighted average and moving average.
- *First-In-First-Out*: (FIFO) assumes that the items purchased or produced first are sold first. Costs of inventory per unit or item are determined at the time made or acquired. The oldest cost (*i.e.,* the first-in) is then matched against revenue and assigned to cost of goods sold.
- *Last-In First-Out*: (LIFO) is the reverse of FIFO. Some systems permit determining the costs of goods at the time acquired or made, but assigning costs to goods sold under the assumption that the goods made or acquired last are sold first. Costs of specific goods acquired or made are added to a pool of costs for the type of goods. Under this system, the business may maintain costs under FIFO but track an offset in the form of a LIFO reserve. Such reserve (an asset or contra-asset) represents the difference in cost of inventory under the

FIFO and LIFO assumptions. Such amount may be different for financial reporting and tax purposes in the United States.

- *Dollar Value LIFO*: Under this variation of LIFO, increases or decreases in the LIFO reserve are determined based on dollar values rather than quantities.
- *Retail inventory method*: Resellers of goods may use this method to simplify recordkeeping. The calculated cost of goods on hand at the end of a period is the ratio of cost of goods acquired to the retail value of the goods times the retail value of goods on hand. Cost of goods acquired includes beginning inventory as previously valued plus purchases. Cost of goods sold is then beginning inventory plus purchases less the calculated cost of goods on hand at the end of the period.

EXAMPLE

Jane owns a business that resells machines. At the start of 2009, she has no machines or parts on hand. She buys machines A and B for 10 each, and later buys machines C and D for 12 each.

All the machines are the same, but they have serial numbers. Jane sells machines A and C for 20 each. Her cost of goods sold depends on her inventory method. Under specific identification, the cost of goods sold is 10 + 12, the particular costs of machines A and C. If she uses FIFO, her costs are 20 (10+10).

If she uses average cost, here costs are 22 ((10+10+12+12)/4 × 2). If she uses LIFO, her costs are 24 (12+12). Thus, her profit for accounting and tax purposes may be 20, 18, or 16, depending on her inventory method. After the sales, her inventory values are either 20, 22 or 24.

After year end, Jane decides she can make more money by improving machines B and D. She buys and uses 10 of parts and supplies, and it takes 6 hours at 2 per hour to make the improvements to each machine. Jane has overhead, including rent and electricity. She calculates that the overhead adds 0.5 per hour to her costs. Thus, Jane has spend 20 to improve each machines (10/2 + 12 + (6 × 0.5)).

She sells machine D for 45. Her cost for that machine depends on her inventory method. If she used FIFO, the cost of machine D is 12 plus 20 she spent improving it, for a profit of 13.

Remember, she used up the two 10 cost items already under FIFO. If she uses average cost, it is 11 plus 20, for a profit of 14. If she used LIFO, the cost would be 10 plus 20 for a profit of 15. In year 3, Jane sells the last machine for 38 and quits the business.

She recovers the last of her costs. Her total profits for the three years are the same under all inventory methods. Only the timing of income and the balance of inventory differ. Here is a comparison under FIFO, Average Cost, and LIFO:

		Cost of Goods Sold			------ Profit ------		
Year	**Sales**	**FIFO**	**Avg.**	**LIFO**	**FIFO**	**Avg.**	**LIFO**
1	40	20	22	24	20	18	16
2	45	32	31	30	13	14	15
3	38	32	31	30	6	7	8
Total	**123**	**84**	**84**	**84**	**39**	**39**	**39**

WRITE-DOWNS AND ALLOWANCES

The value of goods held for sale by a business may decline due to a number of factors. The goods may prove to be defective or below normal quality standards (subnormal). The goods may become obsolete. The market value of the goods may simply decline due to economic factors. Where the market value of goods has declined for whatever reasons, the business may chose to value its inventory at the lower or cost or market value, also known as net realizable value. This may be recorded by accruing an expense (*i.e.,* creating an inventory reserve) for declines due to obsolescence, etc.

Current period net income as well as net inventory value at the end of the period is reduced for the decline in value. Any property held by a business may decline in value or be damaged by unusual events, such as a fire. The loss of value where the goods are destroyed is accounted for as a loss, and the inventory is fully written off. Generally, such loss is recognized for both financial reporting and tax purposes. However, book and tax amounts may differ under some systems.

ALTERNATIVE VIEWS

Alternatives to traditional cost accounting have been proposed by various management theorists.

These include:

- Throughput Accounting, under the Theory of Constraints, under which only direct materials costs are included in cost of goods sold and inventory.
- Lean accounting, in which most traditional costing methods are ignored in favour of measuring weekly "value streams".
- Resource consumption accounting, which discards most current accounting concepts in favour of proportional costing based on simulations.

None of these views conform to U.S. Generally Accepted Accounting Principles or International Accounting Standards, nor are any accepted for most income or other tax reporting purposes.

3

Cost Accounting

INTRODUCTION

Industrialization and advent of factory system during the second half of 19th Century necessitating accurate cost information have led to the development of cost accounting. The growth of cost accounting was slow. To quote Eldons Handristen "Not until the last 20 years of the 19th Century was there much literature on the subject of cost accounting in England and even very little was found in the United States.

Most of the literature until this time emphasized the procedure for the calculation of prime costs only". Rapid development in cost accounting has taken place after 1914 with the growth of heavy industry and large scale production as a consequence of First World War when cost other than material and labour constituted a significant portion of total cost. The development of cost accounting in India is of recent origin and it is given importance after independence, when provision for Cost Audit under Sec.233 B of Companies Act was made.

Vivian Bose Enquiry Committee revealed the malpractices of manufacturing companies. It was felt that the financial audit falls short of expectations to reveal the malpractices. Therefore, under the Companies Act, the government was given the power to order for cost audit. This has given impetus to the development of cost accounting in India.

HISTORICAL COST

In accounting, historical cost is the original monetary value of an economic item. Historical cost is based on the stable measuring unit assumption. In some circumstances, assets and liabilities may be shown at their historical cost, as if there had been no change in value since the date of acquisition.

The balance sheet value of the item may therefore differ from the "true" value. While historical cost is criticised for its inaccuracy (deviation from "true" value), it remains in use in most accounting systems. Various corrections to historical cost are used, many of which require the use of management judgement and may be difficult to implement or verify. he trend in most accounting standards is a move to more accurate reflection of the fair or market value, although the historical cost principle remains in use, particularly for assets of little importance.

Depreciation affects the carrying value of an asset on the balance sheet. The historical cost will equal the carrying value if there has been no change recorded in the value of the asset since acquisition. Improvements may be added to the cost basis of an asset. Historical cost does not generally reflect current market valuation. Alternative measurement bases to the historical cost measurement basis, which may be applied for some types of assets for which market values are readily available, require that the carrying value of an asset (or liability) be updated to the market price (mark-to-market valuation) or some other estimate of value that better approximates the real value.

Accounting standards may also have different methods required or allowed (even for different types of balance sheet variable real value non-monetary assets or liabilities) as to how the resultant change in value of an asset or liability is recorded, as a part of income or as a direct change to shareholders' equity.

The Constant Item Purchasing Power Accounting model is an International Accounting Standards Board approved alternative basic accounting model to the traditional Historical Cost Accounting model.

HISTORICAL COST BASIS (ORIGINAL COST)

Under the historical cost basis of accounting, assets and liabilities are recorded at their values when first acquired. They are not then generally restated for changes in values. Costs recorded in the Income Statement are based on the historical cost of items sold or used, rather than their replacement costs.

For example:

- A company acquires an asset in year 1 for ₹100;
- The asset is still held at the end of year 1, when its market value is ₹120;
- The company sells the asset in year 2 for ₹115.

At the end year 1 the asset is recorded in the balance sheet at cost of ₹100. No account is taken of the increase in value from ₹100 to ₹120 in year 1. In year 2 the company records a sale of ₹115. The cost of sales is ₹100, being the historical cost of the asset. This gives rise to a profit of ₹15 which is wholly recognised in year 2.

MEASUREMENT UNDER THE HISTORICAL COST BASIS

Inventory

It is standard under the historical cost basis to write down the value of inventory (stock) to a lower cost and net realisable value.

As a result:

- A downward movement in the realisable value of inventory below cost is recognised immediately
- An upward movement in the realisable value of inventory is not recognised until the inventory is sold

Property, Plant and Equipment

Property, plant and equipment are recorded at cost under the historical cost basis.Cost includes:

- Purchase price, including import duties and non-refundable purchase taxes, after deducting trade discounts and rebates;
- Any costs directly attributable to bringing the asset to the location and condition necessary for it to be capable of operating. These can include site preparation, delivery and handling costs, installation, assembly, testing, professional fees and the costs of employees directly involved in these activities.

In IFRS, cost also includes the initial estimate of the costs of dismantling and removing the item and restoring it. Cost may include the cost of borrowing to finance construction if this policy is consistently adopted. Cost is then subject to depreciation with to write off the cost of the asset over its estimated useful life down to the recoverable amount. In most cases the method is "straight line", with the same depreciation charge from the date when an asset is brought into use until it is expected to be sold or no further economic benefits obtained from it, but other patterns of depreciation are used if assets are used proportionately more in some periods than others.

Assets and Liabilities Denominated in Foreign Currency

Monetary items such as cash balances, receivables and payables which are denominated in foreign currency are reported using the closing exchange rate under IFRS.

EXCEPTIONS TO THE HISTORICAL COST BASIS OF ACCOUNTING

REVALUATION OF PROPERTY, PLANT AND EQUIPMENT

Under IFRS it is acceptable, but not required, to restate the values of property, plant and equipment to fair value. 'Fair value' is the amount for which an asset could be exchanged, or a liability settled, between knowledgeable, willing parties in an arm's length transaction. Such a policy must be applied to all assets of a particular class. It would therefore be acceptable for an entity to revalue freehold properties every three years. The revaluations must be made with sufficient regularity to ensure that the carrying value does not differ materially from market value in subsequent years. A surplus on revaluation would be recorded as a reserve movement, not as income.

Derivative Financial Instruments

Under IFRS and US GAAP derivative financial instruments are stated at fair value ("mark-to-market") with movements recorded in the income statement.

Financial Reporting in Hyperinflationary Economies

IFRS requires a separate method of accounting in currencies deemed to be hyperinflationary. The characteristics of a hyperinflation include the population keeping its wealth in non-monetary assets or relatively stable foreign currencies, prices quoted in foreign currencies or widespread indexation of prices. This might arise if cumulative inflation reaches or exceeds 100 per cent over three years. An entity operating in a hyperinflationary economy:

- Records a gain or loss on its 'net monetary position' in its income statement.
- Records non-monetary items (for example, property, plant and equipment) in the balance sheet by applying indexation to their historical cost.

Management Accounting Techniques

In management accounting there are a number of techniques used as alternatives to historical cost accounting including:

- Measuring profit on sale of inventory by reference to its replacement cost. If inventory with a historical cost of ₹100 is sold for ₹115 when it costs ₹110 to replace it, the profit recorded would be ₹5 only based on replacement cost, not ₹15;
- Charging economic rent for assets, particularly property. If a business uses a 20-year old property which it owns, depreciation on a historical cost basis might be insignificant. However, the management accounts could show a notional rent payable, being perhaps opportunity cost—the amount the business could receive if it let the property to a third party.

ADVANTAGES AND DISADVANTAGES OF HISTORICAL COST ACCOUNTING

Advantages

- Historical cost accounts are straight forward to produce.
- Historical cost accounts do not record gains until they are realised.
- Historical cost accounts are still used in most accounting systems.

Disadvantages

- Historical cost accounts give no indication of current values of the assets of a business.
- Historical cost accounts do not record the opportunity costs of the use of older assets, particularly property which may be recorded at a value based on costs incurred many years ago.
- Historical cost accounts do not measure the loss of value of monetary assets as a result of inflation.

OBJECTIVES OF COST ACCOUNTING

These are the following important objectives of cost accounting:

- *Ascertainment of Cost*: The primary objectives of the cost accounting is to ascertain cost of each product, process, job, operation or service rendered.
- *Ascertainment of Profitability*: Cost accounting determines the profitability of each product, process, job, operation or service rendered. The statement of profit or losses and Balance Sheet also submitted to the management periodically.
- *Classification of Cost*: Cost accounting classifies cost in to different elements such as materials, laborer and expenses. It has further been divided as direct cost and indirect cost for cost control and recording.
- *Control of Cost:* Cost accounting aims at controlling cost by setting standards and compared with the actual, the deviation or variation between two is identified and necessary steps are taken to control them.
- Fixation or Selling Prices: Cost accounting guides management in regard to fixation of selling prices of the products. It is also helpful for preparing tender and quotations.

There is a relationship among information needs of management, cost accounting objectives, and techniques and tools used for analysis in cost accounting. Cost accounting has the following main objectives to serve:

- *Determining selling price:* The objective of determining the cost of products is of main importance in cost accounting. The total product cost and cost per unit of product are important in deciding selling price of product. Cost accounting provides information regarding the cost to make and sell product or services. Other factors such as the quality of product, the condition of the market, the area of distribution, the quantity which can be supplied etc., are also to be given consideration by the management before deciding the selling price, but the cost of product plays a major role.
- *Controlling cost:* Cost accounting helps in attaining aim of controlling cost by using various techniques such as Budgetary Control, Standard

costing, and inventory control. Each item of cost [*viz.* material, labour, and expense] is budgeted at the beginning of the period and actual expenses incurred are compared with the budget. This increases the efficiency of the enterprise.

- *Providing information for decision-making:* Cost accounting helps the management in providing information for managerial decisions for formulating operative policies. These policies relate to the following matters:
  - Determination of cost-volume-profit relationship.
  - Make or buy a component
  - Shut down or continue operation at a loss
  - Continuing with the existing machinery or replacing them by improved and economical machines.
- *Ascertaining costing profit:* Cost accounting helps in ascertaining the costing profit or loss of any activity on an objective basis by matching cost with the revenue of the activity. The financial statements are prepared generally once a year or half year to meet the needs of the management. In order to operate the business at high efficiency, it is essential for management to have a review of production, sales and operating results. Cost accounting provides daily, weekly or monthly statements of units produced, accumulated cost with analysis.
- *Facilitating preparation of financial and other statements:* Cost accounting helps to produce statements at short intervals as the management may require.

IMPORTANCE OF COST ACCOUNTING

The limitation of financial accounting has made the management to realize the importance of cost accounting. The importance of cost accounting is as follows:

- *Importance to Management:* Cost accounting provides invaluable help to management. It is difficult to indicate where the work of cost accountant ends and managerial control begins. The advantages are as follows:
- *Helps in ascertainment of cost:* Cost accounting helps the management in the ascertainment of cost of process, product, Job, contract, activity, etc., by using different techniques such as Job costing and Process costing.
- *Aids in Price fixation:* By using demand and supply, activities of competitors, market condition to a great extent, also determine the price of product and cost to the producer does play an important role. The producer can take necessary help from his costing records.

- *Helps in Cost reduction:* Cost can be reduced in the long-run when cost reduction programme and improved methods are tried to reduce costs.
- *Elimination of wastage:* As it is possible to know the cost of product at every stage, it becomes possible to check the forms of waste, such as time and expenses etc., are in the use of machine equipment and material.
- *Helps in identifying unprofitable activities:* With the help of cost accounting the unprofitable activities are identified, so that the necessary correct action may be taken.
- *Helps in checking the accuracy of financial account:* Cost accounting helps in checking the accuracy of financial account with the help of reconciliation of the profit as per financial accounts with the profit as per cost account.
- *Helps in fixing selling Prices:* It helps the management in fixing selling prices of product by providing detailed cost information.
- *Helps in Inventory Control:* Cost furnishes control which management requires in respect of stock of material, work in progress and finished goods.
- *Helps in estimate:* Costing records provide a reliable basis upon which tender and estimates may be prepared. The scope of cost accounting is very wide. There are lots of techniques, tools, procedures, processes; programmes are used in cost accounting for calculating cost and its control. But basically, we divide its scope within three major parts.

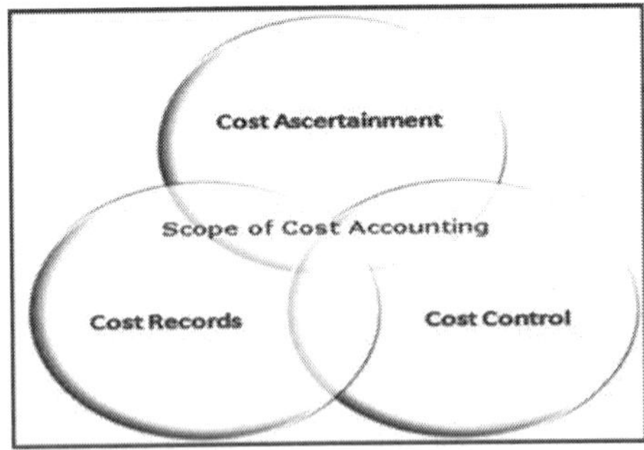

  - *Cost Ascertainment:* In this region of cost accounting, cost accounting collects product's material, labour and overhead cost and try to calculate total and per unit cost of product. This total cost calculation will be based on historical or standard or estimated basis. After this, cost accountant will use any method of costing like specific order costing, operation costing, and direct costing technique. These techniques and methods may be used for calculating different nature products in same organization.

- *Cost Records:* In this part of cost accounting, cost accountant maintains cost books, vouchers, ledgers, reports and other cost related documents for future comparison and reference. It will also be under the scope of cost accounting.
- *Cost Control:* This is the end boundary of cost accounting scope. In this division, cost accountant used different techniques and methods for controlling the cost. Save One Rupees in the cost of product means we have earned one rupees in the production of goods. So, Cost accountant uses budgetary control, standard costing, break even point analysis and many other techniques for controlling the cost.

The focus of cost accounting is different. In the modern days of cut throat competition, any business organization has to pay attention towards their cost of production. Computation of cost on scientic basis and thereafter cost control and cost reduction has become of paramount importance. Hence it has become essential to study the basic principles and concepts of cost accounting. These are discussed in the subsequent paragraphs.

- *Cost:* Cost can be dened as the expenditure (actual or notional) incurred on or attributable to a given thing. It can also be described as the resources that have been sacriced or must be sacriced to attain a particular objective. In other words, cost is the amount of resources used for something which must be measured in terms of money. For example – Cost of preparing one cup of tea is the amount incurred on the elements like material, labour and other expenses; similarly cost of offering any services like banking is the amount of expenditure for offering that service. Thus cost of production or cost of service can be calculated by ascertaining the resources used for the production or services.
- *Costing:* Costing may be dened as 'the technique and process of ascertaining costs'. According to Weldon, 'Costing is classifying, recording, allocation and appropriation of expenses for the determination of cost of products or services and for the presentation of suitably arranged data for the purpose of control and guidance of management. It includes the ascertainment of every order, job, contract, process, service units as may be appropriate. It deals with the cost of production, selling and distribution. If we analyze the above denitions, it will be understood that costing is basically the procedure of ascertaining the costs. As mentioned above, for any business organization, ascertaining of costs is must and for this purpose a scientic procedure should be followed. 'Costing' is precisely this procedure which helps them to nd out the costs of products or services.

- *Cost Accounting:* Cost Accounting primarily deals with collection, analysis of relevant of cost data for interpretation and presentation for various problems of management. Cost accounting accounts for the cost of products, service or an operation. It is dened as, 'the establishment of budgets, standard costs and actual costs of operations, processes, activities or products and the analysis of variances, protability or the social use of funds'.
- *Cost Accountancy:* Cost Accountancy is a broader term and is dened as, 'the application of costing and cost accounting principles, methods and techniques to the science and art and practice of cost control and the ascertainment of protability as well as presentation of information for the purpose of managerial decision making.' If we analyze the above denition, the following points will emerge.
  - Cost accounting is basically application of the costing and cost accounting principles.
  - This application is with specic purpose and that is for the purpose of cost control, ascertainment of protability and also for presentation of information to facilitate decision making.

COST CENTER

A cost centre or cost center is a division within a business which is financed from the profit margin adding to the cost of the organization, but contributing to its profit indirectly. Typical examples include research and development, marketing and customer service.

There are some significant advantages to classifying simple, straightforward divisions as cost centres, since cost is easy to measure.

However, cost centres create incentives for managers to underfund their units in order to benefit themselves, and this underfunding may result in adverse consequences for the company as a whole [for example, reduced sales because of bad customer service experiences].

Because the cost centre has a negative impact on profit (at least on the surface) it is a likely target for rollbacks and layoffs when budgets are cut. Operational decisions in a cost centre, for example, are typically driven by cost considerations. Investments in new equipment, technology and staff are often difficult to justify to management because indirect profitability is hard to translate to bottom-line figures.

Business metrics are sometimes employed to quantify the benefits of a cost centre and relate costs and benefits to those of the organization as a whole. In a contact centre, for example, metrics such as average handle time, service level and cost per call are used in conjunction with other calculations to justify current or improved funding. A cost center is often a department within a company. The manager and employees of a cost center are responsible for its costs but are not responsible for revenues or investment decisions. A manufacturer's cost centers include each of its production departments as well as the manufacturing service departments such as the maintenance department or quality control department. Other examples of cost centers include the human resource department, the IT department, the accounting department, and so on.

Cost centers are not limited to departments. There might be several cost centers within a department. For example, each assembly line could be a cost center. Even a special machine could be a cost center.

Cost centers are usually associated with the topic of decentralization, responsibility accounting, and planning and control.

COST ACCOUNTING AND FINANCIAL ACCOUNTING

- Financial accounting aims at finding out results of accounting year in the form of Profit and Loss Account and Balance Sheet. Cost Accounting aims at computing cost of production/service in a scientific manner and facilitate cost control and cost reduction.
- Financial accounting reports the results and position of business to government, creditors, investors, and external parties.
- Cost Accounting is an internal reporting system for an organization's own management for decision making.
- In financial accounting, cost classification based on type of transactions, *e.g.* salaries, repairs, insurance, stores etc. In cost accounting, classification is basically on the basis of functions, activities, products, process and on internal planning and control and information needs of the organization.
- Financial accounting aims at presenting 'true and fair' view of transactions, profit and loss for a period and Statement of financial position (Balance Sheet) on a given date. It aims at computing 'true and fair' view of the cost of production/services offered by the firm.

Now, we are explaining the differences between cost accounting and financial accounting in other sense of Accounting.

MEANING

- *Cost Accounting:* Cost accounting is that part of accounting which is helpful to calculate the cost and control the cost. In cost accounting, we deeply study the variable cost, fixed cost, overheads and capital cost.
- *Financial Accounting:* Financial Accounting is that part of accounting in which we record the transactions and we make the financial statements. Through making the financial statement, it provide information of profitability and financial position to the interested parties.

OBJECTIVE

- *Cost Accounting:* We cannot take all decisions on the basis of information which have been provided by financial accounting. After making the financial statements under financial accounting, we calculate the cost of each unit and use the techniques of cost accounting for better decision making.
- *Financial Accounting:* Main objective of financial accounting is to show the financial statement correctly.

Law

- *Cost Accounting:* There is not any restriction on the cost accounts. It can be made according to the need of company but some company must audit their cost accounts under cost audit.
- *Financial Accounting:* In financial accounting, there are lots of law restrictions. For example, company accounts and financial statements must be according to the format of company law. It should also follow the rules of IFRS and income tax law.

Controlling

- *Cost Accounting:* In cost accounting, we study the techniques of controlling the cost. All the costs are calculated for the purpose of controlling the cost. For example, Company produces product A, B and C. If product C is generating 30 per cent but product A and B is generating just 5 per cent. We will try to control the cost of A and B product through different techniques of cost control.
- *Financial Accounting:* In financial accounting, we just record the transactions correctly. We do not care to control the cost.

Profit Analysis

- *Cost Accounting:* In cost accounting, to find the profit per job or per batch or per service unit is possible.
- *Financial Accounting:* In financial accounting. We make the income statement which shows the net profit or loss or whole organization not one job or batch.

Record

- *Cost Accounting:* In cost accounting, both actual transactions record and estimations are used. For example budgetary control and variance analysis, we set the standard cost which is based on the estimations. These estimations may be differ from actual cost.
- *Financial Accounting:* In financial accounting, we use actual transaction for recording purpose. We do not use the estimation for preparing income statements and balance sheet.

Valuation of Inventory

- *Cost Accounting:* In cost accounting, inventory's valuation will be on cost.
- *Financial Accounting:* In financial accounting, inventory's valuation will be on the cost or market value which will be low.

Cycle

- *Cost Accounting:* In cost accounting, we first calculate the raw material cost. Then, we calculate the labour cost. Then, we calculate the direct material cost. After this, we calculate the overhead cost. All these cost are added. A profit margin is added. An estimated sale price is calculated. Its whole controlling cycle will be relating to control the cost of raw material, labour cost and overheads.
- *Financial Accounting:* In financial accounting, we pass the journal entries. Then, we make the ledger accounts. Then, we prepare the trial balance. Then, we make the final accounts.

BASIC COST CONCEPTS

Term cost is used in this very form. In reference to production/manufacturing of goods and services cost refers to sum total of the value of resources used like raw material and labour and expenses incurred in producing or manufacturing of given quantity.

Elements of Cost

Cost of production/manufacturing consists of various expenses incurred on production/manufacturing of goods or services. These are the elements of cost which can be divided into three groups: Material, Labour and Expenses.

Material

To produce or manufacture material is required. For example to manufacture shirts cloth is required and to produce flour wheat is required.

All material which becomes an integral part of finished product and which can be conveniently assigned to specific physical unit is termed as "Direct Material". It is also described as raw material, process material, prime material, production material, stores material, etc. The substance from which the product is made is known as material. It may be in a raw or manufactured state. Material is classified into two categories:

- Direct Material
- Indirect Material

Direct Material

Direct Material is that material which can be easily identified and related with specific product, job, and process. Timber is a raw material for making furniture, cloth for making garments, sugarcane for making sugar, and Gold/ silver for making jewelers, etc are some examples of direct material.

Indirect Material

Indirect Material is that material which cannot be easily and conveniently identified and related with a particular product, job, process, and activity. Consumable stores, oil and waste, printing and stationery etc, are some examples of indirect material. Indirect materials are used in the factory, the office, or the selling and distribution department.

Labour

Labour is the main factor of production. For conversion of raw material into finished goods, human resource is needed, and such human resource is termed as labour. Labour cost is the main element of cost in a product or service. Labour can be classified into two categories:

Direct Labour

Labour which takes active and direct part in the production of a commodity. Direct labour is that labour which can be easily identified and related with specific product, job, process, and activity.

Direct labour cost is easily traceable to specific products. Direct labour costs are specially and conveniently traceable to specific products. Direct labour varies directly with the volume of output.

Direct labour is also known as process labour, productive labour, operating labour, direct wages, manufacturing wages, etc. Cost of wages paid to carpenter for making furniture, cost of a tailor in producing readymade garments, cost of washer in dry cleaning unit are some examples of direct labour.

Indirect Labour

Indirect labour is that labour which cannot be easily identified and related with specific product, job, process, and activity. It includes all labour not directly engaged in converting raw material into finished product. It may or may not vary directly with the volume of output. Labour employed for the purpose of carrying out tasks incidental to goods or services provided is indirect labour. Indirect labour is used in the factory, the office, or the selling and distribution department. Wages of store-keepers, time-keepers, salary of works manager, salary of salesmen, etc, are all examples of indirect labour cost.

Basic Cost Concepts

- Insurance of factory building, plant, and machinery.
- Municipal taxes of factory building.
- Depreciation of factory building, plant and machinery, and their repairs and maintenance charges.

- Power and fuel used in factory.
- Factory telephone expenses.

Office and Administrative overheads

These expenses are related to the management and administration of the business. They are incurred for the direction and control of an undertaking. These represent the aggregate of the cost of indirect material, indirect labour, and indirect expenses incurred by the office and administration department of an organization.

Some examples are as follows: Office printing and stationery, Cost of brushes, dusters etc. for cleaning office building and equipments, Postage and stamps.

Salary of office manager, clerks, and other employees, Salary of administrative directors, Salaries of legal adviser, Salaries of cost accountants and financial accountants, Salary of computer operator.

Rent, insurance, rates and taxes of office building, Office lighting, heating and cleaning, Depreciation and repair of office building, furniture, and Equipment etc., Legal charges, Bank charges, Trade subscriptions, Telephone charges, Audit fee etc.

Selling and Distribution Overheads

Selling and distribution overheads are incurred for the marketing of a commodity, for securing order for the articles, dispatching goods sold or for making efforts to find and retain customers.

These expenses represent the aggregate of indirect material, indirect labour, and indirect expenses incurred by the selling and distribution department of the organization. These overheads have two aspects (i) procuring orders (ii) executing the order. Based upon this concept the selling and distributions are studied separately.

CLASSIFICATION OF COST

Cost may be classified into different categories depending upon the purpose of classification. Some of the important categories in which the costs are classified are as follows:

1. FIXED, VARIABLE AND SEMI-VARIABLE COSTS

The cost which varies directly in proportion with every increase or decrease in the volume of output or production is known as variable cost. Some of its examples are as follows:

- Wages of laborers
- Cost of direct material
- Power

The cost which does not vary but remains constant within a given period of time and a range of activity in spite of the fluctuations in production is known as fixed cost. Some of its examples are as follows:

- Rent or rates
- Insurance charges
- Management salary

The cost which does not vary proportionately but simultaneously does not remain stationary at all times is known as semi-variable cost. It can also be named as semi-fixed cost. Some of its examples are as follows:

- Depreciation
- Repairs

Fixed costs are sometimes referred to as "period costs" and variable costs as "direct costs" in system of direct costing. Fixed costs can be further classified into:

- Committed fixed costs
- Discretionary fixed costs

Committed fixed costs consist largely of those fixed costs that arise from the possession of plant, equipment and a basic organization structure. For example, once a building is erected and a plant is installed, nothing much can be done to reduce the costs such as depreciation, property taxes, insurance and salaries of the key personnel etc. without impairing an organization's competence to meet the long-term goals.

Discretionary fixed costs are those which are set at fixed amount for specific time periods by the management in budgeting process. These costs directly reflect the top management policies and have no particular relationship with volume of output. These costs can, therefore, be reduced or entirely eliminated as demanded by the circumstances. Examples of such costs are research and development costs, advertising and sales promotion costs, donations, management consulting fees etc. These costs are also termed as managed or programmed costs. In some circumstances, variable costs are classified into the following:

- Discretionary cost
- Engineered cost

The term discretionary costs are generally linked with the class of fixed cost. However, in the circumstances where management has predetermined that the organization would spend a certain percentage of its sales for the items like research, donations, sales promotion etc., discretionary costs will be of a variable character.

Engineered variable costs are those variable costs which are directly related to the production or sales level. These costs exist in those circumstances where specific relationship exists between input and output. For example, in an automobile industry there may be exact specifications as one radiator, two fan belts, one battery etc. would be required for one car. In a case where more than one car is to be produced, various inputs will have to be increased in the direct proportion of the output.

Thus, an increase in discretionary variable costs is due to the authorization of management whereas an increase in engineered variable costs is due to the volume of output or sales.

2. PRODUCT COSTS AND PERIOD COSTS

The costs which are a part of the cost of a product rather than an expense of the period in which they are incurred are called as "product costs." They are included in inventory values. In financial statements, such costs are treated as assets until the goods they are assigned to are sold. They become an expense at that time. These costs may be fixed as well as variable, *e.g.*, cost of raw materials and direct wages, depreciation on plant and equipment etc.

The costs which are not associated with production are called period costs. They are treated as an expense of the period in which they are incurred. They may also be fixed as well as variable. Such costs include general administration costs, salaries salesmen and commission, depreciation on office facilities etc. They are charged against the revenue of the relevant period.

Differences between opinions exist regarding whether certain costs should be considered as product or period costs. Some accountants feel that fixed manufacturing costs are more closely related to the passage of time than to the manufacturing of a product. Thus, according to them variable manufacturing costs are product costs whereas fixed manufacturing and other costs are period costs. However, their view does not seem to have been yet widely accepted.

3. DIRECT AND INDIRECT COSTS

The expenses incurred on material and labour which are economically and easily traceable for a product, service or jobs are considered as direct costs. In the process of manufacturing of production of articles, materials are purchased, laborers are employed and the wages are paid to them. Certain other expenses are also incurred directly. All of these take an active and direct part in the manufacture of a particular commodity and hence are called direct costs.

The expenses incurred on those items which are not directly chargeable to production are known as indirect costs. For example, salaries of timekeepers, storekeepers and foremen. Also certain expenses incurred for running the administration are the indirect costs. All of these cannot be conveniently allocated to production and hence are called indirect costs.

4. DECISION-MAKING COSTS AND ACCOUNTING COSTS

Decision-making costs are special purpose costs that are applicable only in the situation in which they are compiled. They have no universal application.

They need not tie into routine-financial accounts. They do not and should not conform the accounting rules. Accounting costs are compiled primarily from financial statements. They have to be altered before they can be used for decision-making. Moreover, they are historical costs

and show what has happened under an existing set of circumstances. Decision-making costs are future costs. They represent what is expected to happen under an assumed set of conditions. For example, accounting costs may show the cost of a product when the operations are manual whereas decision-making cost might be calculated to show the costs when the operations are mechanized.

5. RELEVANT AND IRRELEVANT COSTS

Relevant costs are those which change by managerial decision. Irrelevant costs are those which do not get affected by the decision.

For example, if a manufacturer is planning to close down an unprofitable retail sales shop, this will affect the wages payable to the workers of a shop. This is relevant in this connection since they will disappear on closing down of a shop. But prepaid rent of a shop or unrecovered costs of any equipment which will have to be scrapped are irrelevant costs which should be ignored.

6. SHUTDOWN AND SUNK COSTS

A manufacturer or an organization may have to suspend its operations for a period on account of some temporary difficulties, *e.g.*, shortage of raw material, non-availability of requisite labour etc. During this period, though no work is done yet certain fixed costs, such as rent and insurance of buildings, depreciation, maintenance etc., for the entire plant will have to be incurred. Such costs of the idle plant are known as shutdown costs.

Sunk costs are historical or past costs. These are the costs which have been created by a decision that was made in the past and cannot be changed by any decision that will be made in the future. Investments in plant and machinery, buildings etc. are prime examples of such costs. Since sunk costs cannot be altered by decisions made at the later stage, they are irrelevant for decision-making.

An individual may regret for purchasing or constructing an asset but this action could not be avoided by taking any subsequent action. Of course, an asset can be sold and the cost of the asset will be matched against the proceeds from sale of the asset for the purpose of determining gain or loss. The person may decide to continue to own the asset. In this case, the cost of asset will be matched against the revenue realized over its effective life. However, he/she cannot avoid the cost which has already been incurred by him/her for the acquisition of the asset. It is, as a matter of fact, sunk cost for all present and future decisions.

EXAMPLE

Jolly Ltd. purchased a machine for $. 30,000. The machine has an operating life of five yea$ without any scrap value. Soon after making the purchase, management feels that the machine should not have been purchased since it is not yielding the operating advantage originally contemplated. It is expected to result in savings in operating costs of $. 18,000 over a period of five years. The machine can be sold immediately for $. 22,000. To take the decision whether the machine should be sold or be used, the relevant amounts to be compared are $. 18,000 in cost savings over five yea$ and $. 22,000 that can be realized in case it is immediately disposed. $. 30,000 invested in the asset is not relevant since it is same in both the cases. The amount is the sunk cost. Jolly Ltd., therefore, sold the machinery for $. 22,000 since it would result in an extra profit of $. 4,000 as compared to keeping and using it.

7. CONTROLLABLE AND UNCONTROLLABLE COSTS

Controllable costs are those costs which can be influenced by the ratio or a specified member of the undertaking. The costs that cannot be influenced like this are termed as uncontrollable costs.

A factory is usually divided into a number of responsibility centers, each of which is in charge of a specific level of management. The officer incharge of a particular department can control costs only of those matte$ which come directly under his control, not of other matte$. For example, the expenditure incurred by tool room is controlled by the foreman incharge of that section but the share of the tool room expenditure which is apportioned to a machine shop cannot be controlled by the foreman of that shop. Thus, the difference between controllable and uncontrollable costs is only in relation to a particular individual or level of management. The expenditure which is controllable by an individual may be uncontrollable by another individual.

8. AVOIDABLE OR ESCAPABLE COSTS AND UNAVOIDABLE OR INESCAPABLE COSTS

Avoidable costs are those which will be eliminated if a segment of a business (*e.g.*, a product or department) with which they are directly related is discontinued. Unavoidable costs are those which will not be eliminated with the segment. Such costs are merely reallocated if the segment is discontinued. For example, in case a product is discontinued, the salary of a factory manager or factory rent cannot be eliminated. It will simply mean that certain other products will have to absorb a large amount of such overheads.

However, the salary of people attached to a product or the bad debts traceable to a product would be eliminated. Certain costs are partly avoidable and partly unavoidable.

For example, closing of one department of a store might result in decrease in delivery expenses but not in their altogether elimination.

It is to be noted that only avoidable costs are relevant for deciding whether to continue or eliminate a segment of a business.

9. IMPUTED OR HYPOTHETICAL COSTS

These are the costs which do not involve cash outlay. They are not included in cost accounts but are important for taking into consideration while making management decisions. For example, interest on capital is ignored in cost accounts though it is considered in financial accounts. In case two projects require unequal outlays of cash, the management should take into consideration the capital to judge the relative profitability of the projects.

PRODUCT COSTING

Product costing is the process of tracking and studying all the various expenses that are accrued in the production and sale of a product, from raw materials purchases to expenses associated with transporting the final product to retail establishments. It is widely regarded as an extremely important component in evaluating and planning overall business strategies. As John A. Lessner indicated in the Journal of Accountancy, "in today's hotly competitive business environment, accurate product costing has become critically important to a business's survival."

Product costing has undergone a dramatic meta-morphosis in America over the past 50 years, as Textile World's Frank Wilson noted: "In the 1940s, cost estimates normally included nothing more than total manufacturing costs. In the late '50s direct costing was implemented to separate variable [cost of materials, cost of transportation] and fixed [interest payments on equipment and facilities, rent, property taxes, executive salaries] costs." Indeed, Lessner remarked that "fifty years ago, when manufacturing was far less automated than it is today, the costs of materials, labour and overhead were just about evenly divided.

Now, production of a product's various components is often so synchronized on highly automated production lines that there is little or no need to maintain component inventories; thus, the old costing formulas, still used by many industries, are no longer applicable. Further complicating the costing equation is the trend in manufacturing to focus more attention on quality, flexibility and responsiveness, to meet customer needs. This makes production-line cost analysis more difficult because each line requires small, but significant, changes in production techniques." As a result, today's managers and business owners have found that the limited information available through older job costing methods is inadequate for making informed decisions in the contemporary business environment. With this in mind, companies have increasingly turned to detailed, long-range examinations that provide a more accurate representation of a product's true costs and benefits. "Companies are discovering that their competitiveness is enhanced when purchasing, manufacturing, logistics, and product design groups begin using total life cycle costing," wrote Joseph Cavinato in Chilton's Distribution. "Total life cycle cost recognizes that the purchase price of an item is only part of its total cost, just the beginning of a series of costs to be accumulated by the firm, its downstream customers, and users until the end of the product's life."

This analysis is further enhanced when companies include suppliers/ vendors in the process, because the costing process can help create a partnership relationship that enables both parties to move away from competitive stances on pricing, delivery dates, etc., towards cooperative initiatives that optimize the expense of creating and maintaining new products.

Costs Associated With Manufactured Products

As Chilton's Distribution observes, there are myriad potential costs associated with selling a product which may be directly or indirectly linked to the actual production process.

Possible costs include:

- Developing and maintaining supplier relationships.
- Transportation costs, including carrier payment terms; special charges in the realms of packaging, handling, and loading and unloading; and loss and damage expenses.
- Sales and freight terms that define payment terms, sales, and title transfers.
- Payment terms—options here range from 15 days to as many as 90 days in some industries, and letter of credit terms provide additional options. These options, stated Cavinato, "often are not considered by managers in purchasing, traffic, and sales. Instead, most firms mandate these terms and they become 'boiler plate' in purchase orders, carrier contracts, and invoices. It can be mutually beneficial to negotiate these terms with suppliers and carriers.
- Costs to receive, process, or make ready, including unloading, counting, inspection, and inventory costs, as well as expenses associated with disposal of packaging and other product protection/ transportation materials.
- Logistics expenses (warehousing, loading, unloading, handling, inventory control), which are typically lumped together under the catch-all title "Overhead," despite the fact that costs for each of these can vary significantly depending on the arrangement.
- Production costs accrued in actual manufacture of goods.
- Warranty costs.

- Quality costs, including costs associated with defective products (what percentage and how far down the production line), inspections, product returns, charge backs, cooperage, and storage.
- Lot size costs, including inventory and cash flow costs associated with lots of varying size.
- Supplier inventory.
- Overhead costs of supplier and customer transactions, including billing, collection, payment preparation, and receiving processes.
- Product improvement and modification, including costs of correcting defects and standardization of materials and packaging.
- Regulatory/environmental costs associated with meeting federal or state laws and community expectations on environmentally friendly production and packaging processes.

Product Costing in Multi-Product Environments

Some manufacturers distort true product costing results by evenly distributing costs for a certain aspect of production across all product lines, even though costs might vary with each specific product.

In some instances, this practice might have little or no impact on a business's well being; a company that is enjoying record growth and profits on all three of its product lines, for instance, is unlikely to be seriously harmed by accounting practices that evenly divide transportation costs three ways, even though one of the product lines may account for, say, half of the firm's transportation expenses.

Huge profits mask such inequities fairly well. But relatively few companies are in such a luxurious position.

Most companies—and especially most small businesses, which typically have less margin for error than their larger cousins—need to work hard to arrive at true product costing figures. "As national and global competition increase," wrote Lessner, "even tiny costing disparities can have an overwhelming impact on whether a product—or an entire company, for that matter—survives.

Over the longterm, product profitability analyses that use these distorted costs cause management to erroneously assume custom products generate better margins than they actually do," and top performing goods end up subsidizing other, less profitable, product lines.

Product Costing in Non-manufacturing Firms

Although product costing is primarily associated with manufacturing businesses, it also has applications in non-manufacturing industries. "Merchandising companies include the costs of buying and transporting merchandise in their product costs," observed Ronald W. Hilton in Managerial

Accounting. "Producers of inventoriable goods, such as mining products, petroleum, and agricultural products, also record the costs of producing their goods. The role of product costs in these companies is identical to that in manufacturing firms."

Business experts also note that while service-oriented companies (both service businesses and non-profit organizations) do not offer products that can be stored and sold in the manner of manufactured items, they nonetheless need to track the varied costs that they accrue in offering their services.

After all, the services that they offer are in essence, their "product" line. "Banks, insurance companies, restaurants, airlines, law firms, hospitals, and city governments all record the costs of producing various services for the purposes of planning, cost control, and decision making," wrote Hilton.

ASCERTAINMENT OF COST

It enables the management to ascertain the cost of product, job, contract, service or unit of production so as to develop cost standard. Costs may be ascertained, under different circumstances, using one or more types of costing principles-standard costing, marginal costing, uniform costing etc.

FIXATION OF SELLING PRICE

Cost data are useful in the determination of selling price or quotations. Apart from cost ascertainment, the cost accountant analyses the total cost into fixed and variable costs.

This will help the management to fix the selling price; sometimes, below the total cost but above the variable cost. This will increase the volume of salesmore sales than previously, thus leading to maximum profit.

COST CONTROL

The object is to minimize the cost of manufacturing. Comparison of actual cost with standards reveals the discrepancies–variances. It the variances are adverse, the management enters into investigation so as to adopt corrective action immediately.

MATCHING COST WITH REVENUE

The determination of profitability of each product, process, department etc. is the important object of costing.

SPECIAL COST STUDIES AND INVESTIGATIONS

It undertakes special cost studies and investigations and these are the basis for the management in decision-making or policies. This will also include pricing of new products, contraction or expansion programmes, closing down or continuing a department, product mix, price reduction in depression etc.

PREPARATION OF FINANCIAL STATEMENTS, PROFI AND LOSS ACCOUNT, BALANCE SHEET

To prepare these statements, the value of stock, work-in-progress, finished goods etc., are essential; in the absence of the costing department, when we have to close the accounts it rather takes too much time. But a good system of costing facilitates the preparation of the statements, as the figures are easily available; they can be prepared monthly or even weekly.

COST ACCOUNTING IS COSTLY TO OPERATE

One of the objections against cost accounting is that it involves heavy expenditure to operate.No doubt, expenses are involved in introduction and operation of cost accounting system. This is the case with any accounting system; the benefits derived by operating the system are more than the cost. Therefore an organization need not hesitate to install and operate the system.

COST ACCOUNTING IS UNNECESSARY

It is felt by a few that cost accounting is of recent origin and an enterprise can survive without cost accounting.No doubt financial accounting may be helpful to draw P & L Account and Balance Sheet but an enterprise can work efficiently with the help of cost accounting and it is necessary to increase efficiency and profitability in the long run.

COST ACCOUNTING INVOLVES MANY FORMS AND STATEMENTS

It is pointed against cost accounting that it involves usage of many forms and statements which leads to monotony in filling up of forms and increase of paper work. It is true that cost accounting is operated by introducing many forms and preparation of statements. This will become routine and as time passes the utility of forms is realized and the forms can be reviewed, revised, simplified and minimized.

COSTING MAY NOT BE APPLICABLE IN ALL TYPES OF INDUSTRIES

Existing methods of cost accounting may not be applicable in all types of industries. Cost accounting methods can be devised for all types of industries, and services.

IT IS BASED ON ESTIMATIONS

Some people claim that costing system relies on predetermined data and therefore it is not reliable. Costing system estimates costs scientifically based on past and present situations and with suitable modifications for the future.

This leads to accurate cost figures based on which management can initiate decisions. But for the predetermined costs, cost accounting also becomes another 'Historical Accounting'.

SCOPE OF COST ACCOUNTING

The term scope here refers to filed of activity. Cost accounting is concerned with ascertainment and control of costs. The information provided to the management is helpful for cost control and cost reduction through functions of planning, decision making and control. In the initial stages of evolution, cost accounting confined itself to cost ascertainment and presentation of the same with the main objective of finding the product cost. With the development of business activity and introduction of large scale production, the scope of cost accounting was broadened and providing information for cost control and cost reduction has assumed equal significance along with finding out cost of production. In addition to enlargement of scope, the area of application of cost accounting has also widened. Initially cost accounting was applied in manufacturing activities only. Now, it is applied in service organizations, government organizations, local authorities, farms, extractive industries, etc.

Cost accounting is the process of determining and accumulating the cost of product or activity. It is a process of accounting for the incurrence and the control of cost. It also covers classification, analysis, and interpretation of cost. In other words, it is a system of accounting, which provides the information about the ascertainment, and control of costs of products, or services. It measures the operating efficiency of the enterprise. It is an internal aspect of the organization. Cost Accounting is accounting for cost aimed at providing cost data, statement and reports for the purpose of managerial decision making. The Institute of Cost and Management Accounting, London defines "Cost accounting is the process of accounting from the point at which expenditure is incurred or committed to the establishment of its ultimate relationship with cost centres and cost units.

In the widest usage, it embraces the preparation of statistical data, application of cost control methods and the ascertainment of profitability of activities carried out or planned". Costing includes "the techniques and processes of ascertaining costs." The 'Technique' refers to principles which are applied for ascertaining costs of products, jobs, processes and services. The `process' refers to day to day routine of determining costs within the method of costing adopted by a business enterprise.

Costing involves "the classifying, recording and appropriate allocation of expenditure for the determination of costs of products or services; the relation of these costs to sales value; and the ascertainment of profitability".

The terms 'costing' and 'cost accounting' are many times used interchangeably. However, the scope of cost accounting is broader than that of costing. Following functional activities are included in the scope of cost accounting:

- Cost book-keeping: It involves maintaining complete record of all costs incurred from their incurrence to their charge to departments, products and services. Such recording is preferably done on the basis of double entry system.
- Cost system: Systems and procedures are devised for proper accounting for costs.
- Cost ascertainment: Ascertaining cost of products, processes, jobs, services, etc., is the important function of cost accounting. Cost ascertainment becomes the basis of managerial decision making such as pricing, planning and control.
- Cost Analysis: It involves the process of finding out the causal factors of actual costs varying from the budgeted costs and fixation of responsibility for cost increases.
- Cost comparisons: Cost accounting also includes comparisons between cost from alternative courses of action such as use of technology for production, cost of making different products and activities, and cost of same product/ service over a period of time.
- Cost Control: Cost accounting is the utilization of cost information for exercising control. It involves a detailed examination of each cost in the light of benefit derived from the incurrence of the cost. Thus, we can state that cost is analyzed to know whether the current level of costs is satisfactory in the light of standards set in advance.
- Cost Reports: Presentation of cost is the ultimate function of cost accounting. These reports are primarily for use by the management at different levels. Cost Reports form the basis for planning and control, performance appraisal and managerial decision making.

FUNCTIONS OF COST ACCOUNTING

Blocker and Weltemer, "Cost Accounting is to serve management in the execution of polices and in comparison of actual and estimated results in order that the value of each policy may be appraised and changed to meet the future conditions".

The main functions of cost accounting are:

- To serve as a guide to price fixing of products.
- To disclose sources of wastage in process of production.
- To reveal sources of economy in production process.
- To provide for an effective system of stores, materials etc.
- To exercise effective control on factors of production.
- To ascertain the profitability of each product.

- To suggest management of future expansion policies.
- To present and interpret data for management decisions.
- To organize cost reduction programmes.
- To facilitate planning and control of business activity.
- To supply timely information for various decisions.
- To organize the internal audit systems etc.

ADVANTAGES OF COST ACCOUNTING

HELPS IN DECISION MAKING

Cost accounting helps in decision making. It provides vital information necessary for decision making.

For instance, cost accounting helps in deciding:

- Whether to make a product buy a product?
- Whether to accept or reject an export order?
- How to utilize the scarce materials profitably?

HELPS IN FIXING PRICES

Cost accounting helps in fixing prices. It provides detailed cost data of each product which enables fixation of selling price. Cost accounting provides basis information for the preparation of tenders, estimates and quotations.

FORMULATION OF FUTURE PLANS

Cost accounting is not a post-mortem examination. It is a system of foresight. On the basis of past experience, it helps in the formulation of definite future plans in quantitive terms. Budgets are prepared and they give direction to the enterprise.

AVOIDANCE OF WASTAGE

Cost accounting reveals the sources of losses or inefficiencies such as spoilage, leakage, pilferage, inadequate utilization of plant etc. By appropriate control measures, these wastages can be avoided or minimized.

HIGHLIGHTS CAUSES

The exact cause of an increase or decrease in profit or loss can be found with the aid of cost accounting. For instance, it is possible for the management to know whether the profits have decreased due to an increase in labour cost or material cost or both.

REWARD TO EFFICIENCY

Cost accounting introduces bonus plans and incentive wage systems to suit the needs of the organization. These plans and systems reward efficient workers and improve productivity as well improve the morale of the workforce.

PREVENTION OF FRAUDS

Cost accounting envisages sound systems of inventory control, budgetary control and standard costing. Scope for manipulation and fraud is minimized.

IMPROVEMENT IN PROFITABILITY

Cost accounting reveals unprofitable products and activities. Management can drop those products and eliminate unprofitable activities. The resources released from unprofitable products can be used to improve the profitability of the business.

PREPARATION OF FINAL ACCOUNTS

Cost accounting provides for perpetual inventory system. It helps in the preparation of interim profit and loss account and balance sheet without physical stock verification.

FACILITATES CONTROL

Cost accounting includes effective tools such as inventory control, budgetary control and variance analysis. By adopting them, the management can notice the deviation from the plans. Remedial action can be taken quickly.

COST BEHAVIOUR

The most important building block of both microeconomic analysis and cost accounting is the characterization of how costs change as output volume changes. Output volume can refer to production, sales, or any other principle activity that is appropriate for the organization under consideration. The following discussion examines the volume of production in a factory, but the same principles apply regardless of the type of organization and the appropriate measure of activity. Costs can be variable, fixed, or mixed.

VARIABLE COSTS

Variable costs vary in a linear fashion with the production level. However, when stated on a per unit basis, variable costs remain constant across all production levels within the relevant range. The following two charts depict this relationship between variable costs and output volume.

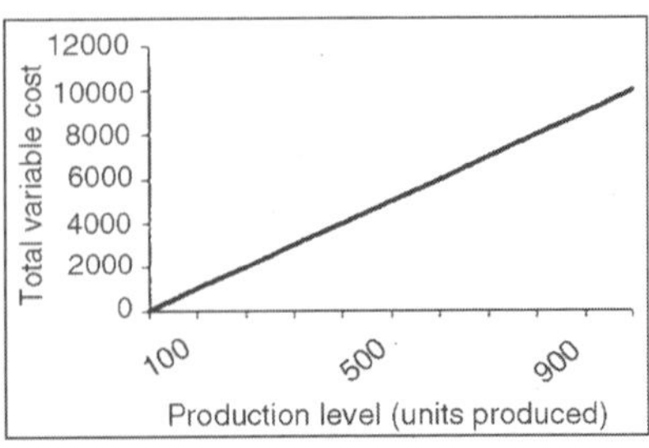

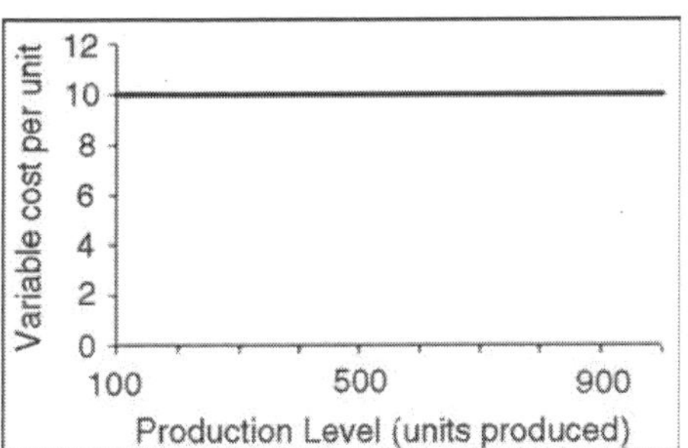

A good example of a variable cost is materials. If one pair of pants requires $10 of fabric, then every pair of pants requires $10 of fabric, no matter how many pairs are made. The fabric cost is $10 per unit at every level of production.

If one pair is made, the total fabric cost is $10; if two pairs are made, the total fabric cost is $20; and if 1,000 pairs are made, the total fabric cost is $10,000. Hence, the total cost is increasing and linear in the production level.

FIXED COSTS

Fixed costs do not vary with the production level. Total fixed costs remain the same, within the relevant range. However, the fixed cost per unit decreases as production increases, because the same fixed costs are spread over more units. The following two charts depict this relationship between fixed costs and output volume. In this example, fixed costs are $50,000. The first chart shows that fixed costs remain $50,000 at all production levels from 100 units to 1,000 units.

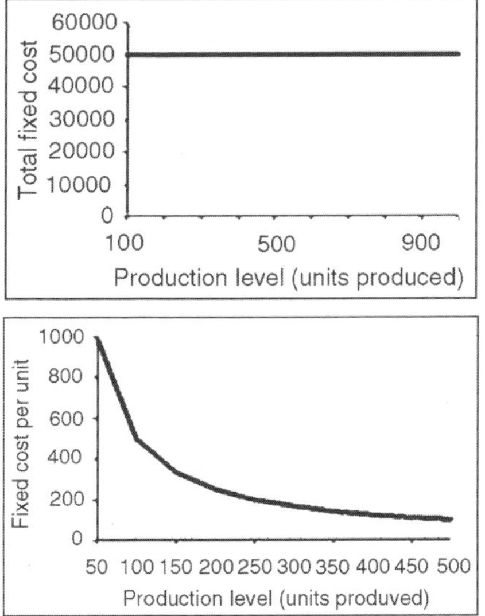

The second chart shows that the fixed cost per unit decreases as production increases. Hence, when 100 units are manufactured, the fixed cost per unit is $500 ($50,000 ÷ 100). When 500 units are manufactured, the fixed cost per unit is $100 ($50,000 ÷ 500).

RELEVANT RANGE

The relevant range is the range of activity over which these relationships are valid. For example, if the factory is operating at capacity, increasing production requires additional investment in fixed costs to expand the facility or to lease or build another factory. Alternatively, production might be reduced below a threshold at which point one of the company's factories is no longer needed, and the fixed costs associated with that factory can be avoided. With respect to variable costs, the company might qualify for a volume discount on fabric purchases above some production level. The relevant range for characterizing fabric as a variable cost ends at that production level, because the fabric cost per unit of output is different when the factory produces above that threshold than when the factory produces below that threshold.

MIXED COSTS

If, within a relevant range, a cost is neither fixed nor variable, it is called semi-variable or mixed. Following are two common examples of mixed costs.

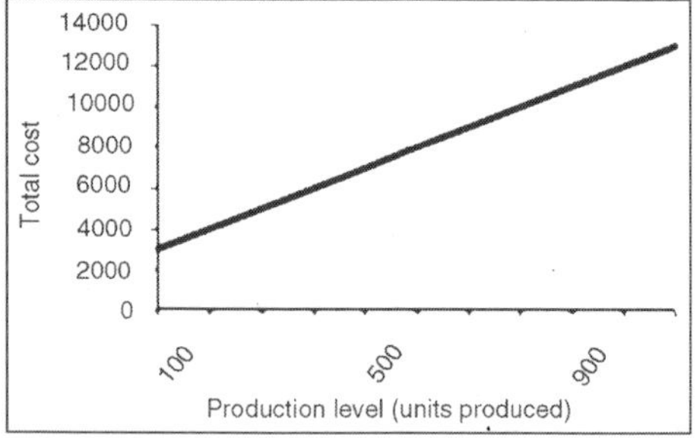

In this example, although the total cost line increases in production, it does not pass through the origin because there is a fixed cost component. An example of a cost that fits this description is electricity. A fixed amount of electricity is required to run the factory air conditioning, computers and lights. There is also a variable cost component related to running the machines on the factory floor. The fixed component in this example is $3,000 per month. The variable cost component is $10 per unit of output. Hence, at a production level of 500 units, the total electric cost is $8,000 [$3,000 + ($10 × 500)].

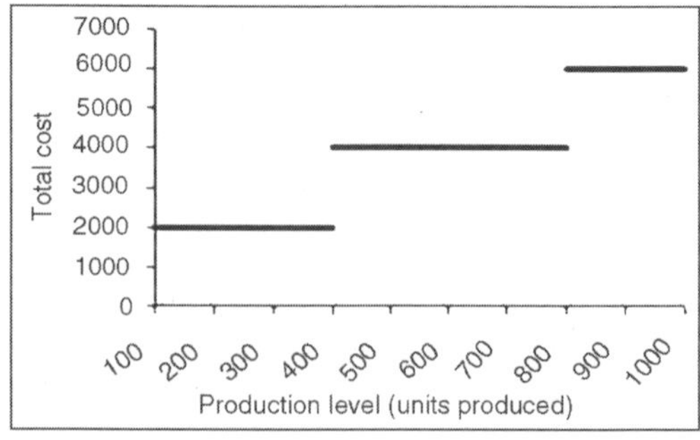

The mixed cost showed in the chart is called a step function. An example of such cost behaviour would be the total salary expense for shift supervisors. If the factory runs one shift, only one shift supervisor is required.

In order for the factory to produce the maximum capacity of a single shift, the factory must add a second shift and hire a second shift supervisor, so that total shift supervisor salary expense doubles. If the factory runs three shifts, three shift supervisors are required.

COST BEHAVIOUR ASSUMPTIONS IN MANAGEMENT ACCOUNTING VERSUS MICROECONOMICS

Microeconomic analysis usually assumes decreasing marginal costs of production, sometimes followed by increasing marginal costs of production beyond a certain production level. Hence, economists' graphs of the total cost of production and the average per-unit cost of production show smooth, curved functions. Management accountants usually assume the linear relationships depicted in the graphs. Linearity is a more accurate description of many situations encountered by management accountants than the economists' curves, and even when linearity constitutes a simplifying assumption it is almost always sufficiently descriptive for the task at hand.

SOCIAL RESPONSIBILITY ACCOUNTING

THE PURSUIT OF JUSTICE

Francis de Sales, controller of the Genesee Cable Company, was not pleased with the way the meeting of the management group had gone. At the meeting, the sales manager Teresa Avila had given a brilliant presentation, at the end of which she had recommended that cable service from the Casual Network be offered as part of their regular package in order to boost cable subscriptions. What disturbed Francis was that Casual's fare was widely regarded as soft pornography, a type of television to which Francis was opposed on moral grounds.

At first, John Cross, the president, had seemed to object. John recalled that when Genesee had been competing for the franchise in this community he had stated at a public hearing that Genesee had no intention of offering pornographic material of any type over the cable service. He wondered aloud whether taking on the Casual station wouldn't be breaking a promise to the community.

Yet Teresa had persisted. She noted that a statement made at a public hearing was not legally binding. She also cited her market research, which showed demand for Casual from many people in the community who were not currently subscribers.

What galled Francis most was the fact that Teresa was able to use accounting numbers properly developed in his department to show that by adopting her recommendation Genesee would improve its profits dramatically. At the end of the meeting John seemed to be swayed by the profitability argument, although he did say he wanted to reflect on the recommendation a bit further.

After returning to his office, Francis mused: "Surely there must be more to business than just the bottom line. It seems so irresponsible to break our promise to the community for the sake of making more money. I wonder if accounting, as an information system, might not assign some sort of value to the old-fashioned notion of keeping a promise."

INFORMATION ABOUT RESPONSIBILITY

During the 1970s substantial discussion was available in accounting literature about social responsibility accounting. In recent years this topic has been placed on the back burner. Yet, with increasing attention being given to business ethics, we can expect social responsibility accounting to re-emerge as a "hot" topic.

After all, once society decides that ethical behaviour is a desired trait to be expected of businesses and business personnel, the logical question will follow: Who is and who is not acting ethically or responsibly? This question creates a demand for information, and accounting is one place to which we turn for information about business enterprise.

ETHICS AND ACCOUNTING REPORTS

A leading proponent of social responsibility accounting, defines it as "the process of selecting firm-level social performance variables, measures, and measurement procedures; systematically developing information useful for evaluating the firm's social performance; and communicating such information to concerned social groups, both within and outside the firm." A key accounting role seems apparent here.

Accounting, as the language of business, is a primary provider of information. Traditional accounting concerns itself with financial information. In expanding the purview of providing information, we may be going beyond data and interpretation that are clearly financial. Yet ethical process and content may also be "accounted for."

Social responsibility accounting must somehow transform ethical information, which accountants may find "squishy," into financial information, or at least information in financial terms, so that accountants preparing and interpreting the reports are within their professional sphere.

The task here is a formidable one. Accountants must work with identified users of information to ascertain what sort of information is required. Then management must decide whether such information should be reported and, if so, in what form. Once these two barriers are surmounted, the accounting profession will be better able to satisfy the need by coming up with the "how" of reporting.

Much debate has occurred about the desirability of even having social responsibility accounting. Its proponents have suggested several models as starting points for developing this kind of accounting. Our intention is to examine the notion of social responsibility from the point of view of ethics. Two major ethical theories, utilitarianism and deontologism. Utilitarianism can and has been used to create a good case for accountants not to engage in social responsibility accounting. Following that as suggested, present a deontological case in favour of social responsibility accounting.

UTILITARIAN ARGUMENTS

Opponents of social responsibility accounting argue in an analytical rather than descriptive fashion. That is, they approach the entire issue from the standpoint of cost/benefit analysis. Most accountants are quite comfortable with this type of analysis. Cost/benefit analysis is a concept that is deeply rooted in utilitarian ethics. In this analysis the utility defined—that is, the good we maximize—is material wealth expressed in terms of dollars. Simply stated, we sum the cost of an action and compare it with the sum of the economic benefits expressed in financial terms. Under a utilitarian criterion we should undertake a project where the economic benefits exceed the costs.

As an example of this kind of utilitarian reasoning, let's return to the Genesee Cable Company. As part of her research concerning the Casual Network, Teresa asked Francis to provide her a differential cost schedule. This kind of managerial report is a common one in accounting.

The differential cost schedule clearly points to the decision to accept Casual Network programming. The operating income with this option exceeds operating income without it by $162,000. Using the terminology of cost/benefit analysis, we can say that the benefits exceed the costs. This is a straightforward case, since both the benefits and the costs may be clearly identified when the utility that we seek to maximize is monetary wealth measured in dollars.

A careful analysis of the social responsibility accounting issue on this utilitarian ground provides disappointing results for its proponents. From the standpoint of the corporation, the costs of placing any new accounting system into place are substantial. Here the company must consider more than the immediate costs of designing and implementing such an accounting system. Also included should be the possible consequences (costs) of publicly reporting the company's actions in the social responsibility arena.

An honest reporting of these matters could bring consequences that are not in the best interests of the owners or managers of the corporation. These might come in the form of possible calls for increased government action in the affairs of the company, possible action against the company from special interest groups, or lawsuits from parties who believe they have sustained injury from the company's actions. Moreover, these costs of implementing social responsibility accounting are fairly easy to measure using conventional business forecasting methods. We may thus be fairly certain about the magnitude of the costs. Against these costs we should weigh the benefits of social responsibility accounting. Here we run into problems, particularly as far as the accountant is concerned. Accounting tends to deal with information that is specific in nature. Within accounting certain types of information are sanctioned as real and true. Accountants therefore focus their attention upon this type of information to the exclusion of other kinds.

The benefits of reporting social responsibility information fall into a category of information that is not currently sanctioned by accounting. Much of the benefit of ethical behaviour is not obviously financial in nature. Accountants are therefore understandably uncomfortable with attempts to measure this information, let alone report upon it.

The benefits of going through this effort are therefore elusive and difficult to express in financial terms. By way of example, let's return to the Genesee Cable Company. Certainly utilitarian arguments may be made to reject Teresa's plan to schedule Casual's programming. In the long run the public, in perceiving that Genesee is a company that keeps its promises and is concerned with community values, will be anxious to have increased business contact with Genesee. In accounting terms we might be tempted to call this goodwill. Yet accountants have recognized the problems associated with measuring goodwill for years.

Today this task is not even attempted unless the goodwill is demonstrated by a purchase transaction on the open market. The economically rational manger would be hard pressed not to offer Casual's programming, especially if he attempted to use cost/benefit analysis in arriving at a decision. The possible benefits of a future good name in the community seem somewhat smaller than the prospect of an increase in profit of $162,000 when we take the cost/benefit point of view. Thus the use of cost/benefit analysis as a criterion for the desirability of social responsibility accounting usually leaves us with heavy, easy-to-measure costs on one hand balanced against vague and seemingly small benefits on the other.

Many accounting writers who have looked at the issue of social responsibility accounting from this utilitarian perspective have been quite pessimistic about its future in accounting. Indeed, the practical application of socially responsible actions themselves finds nearly insurmountable hurdles from a cost/benefit point of view. Yet there are underlying weaknesses in attempts to use cost/benefit analysis or any other utilitarian system in a practical way. These have been identified by Alasdair MacIntyre:

Utilitarian tests must presuppose the application of some prior non-utilitarian principle that sets limits on the range of activities to be considered. Utilitarian tests must presuppose some method of rank ordering the values of good and evil. This method must be non-utilitarian. Different agents will make different assessments of harms and benefits. The question of what is to count as a consequence of a given action must be answered. Boundaries must be placed upon responsibility for consequences.

A time scale must be used in assessing consequences. The question of how far the present should be sacrificed for the future requires a non-utilitarian answer. These weaknesses of the practical application of utilitarianism readily appear in the use of cost/benefit analysis to assess the usefulness of social responsibility accounting.

As we have discussed, the weakness of a non-utilitarian principle is encountered in the fact that accounting has traditionally dealt solely with financial information. The ethical benefits in cost/benefit analysis are often difficult to translate into financial terms. Thus, many accountants are uncomfortable entering into this realm.

Cost/benefit analysis presupposes that material wealth is the sole good to be considered. Thus an arbitrary, non-utilitarian method is assumed at the beginning of the utilitarian reasoning process. Yet reasonable people do not really believe that the accumulation of wealth is the only criterion to look at with respect to good and evil.

The final three weaknesses of practical utilitarianism are particularly evident in examining the benefit side of cost/benefit analysis.

Hence the frustration with social responsibility accounting among so many accountants. Different agents translate the benefits into financial terms at different amounts. To many accountants this appears to violate the principle of verifiability.

Which consequence of an action is the subject of measurement for the accountant also arises. Finally, the entire matter of comparing the present value of probable future benefits with the costs incurred now is a particularly sticky one in cost/benefit analysis.

We see that the deck seems stacked against not only social responsibility accounting but also socially responsible action when we attempt to apply utilitarian arguments. Yet the economic system in which corporations and their managers operate motivates them to take a utilitarian perspective. Compounding this are forces in the business community that encourage managers to look to short-term rather than long-term results.

A change in the underlying way we view the role of the corporation in society can enable us to more realistically assess not only the need for socially responsible action but also the ways accounting can assist managers and outside readers of accounting reports in the tough choices with respect to these actions. This change is to move towards a deontological perspective.

THE DEONTOLOGICAL VIEW

The use of deontologism for the professions in general and for accounting in particular is not new. Lawyers who defend clients' interests irrespective of the general consequences use deontological reasons to justify this behaviour. Scientists frequently make enquiry into areas where an answer may lead to bad consequences (atomic power, for example). In medicine the doctrine of informed consent, whereby a patient is not subjected to an experiment without his full knowledge and approval, is well entrenched.

Many accountants agree that the Financial Accounting Standards Board should use representative faithfulness (a deontological perspective) over economic consequences (a utilitarian perspective) as a criterion for standard setting. Moreover, the accounting profession in general and certified public accountants in particular have taken great pains to present their field to society as a profession.

Among them are that each is governed by ethical principles that emphasize the virtues of self-subordination, honesty, probity, and devotion to the welfare of those served. CPAs have obligations not only to those served but also to third parties. In fact, the obligations to third parties may supersede the obligation to the party about which the CPA issues a report.

DEONTOLOGICAL FRAMEWORK

Deontological ethics can be applied to situations only if an obligation can be satisfied. The ideas of W. D. Ross, a prominent philosopher of the twentieth century. He provided specific criteria to be used as tests for the existence of an obligation and suggested a set of prima facie duties that represent the main moral convictions of the "plain man."

- Fidelity
- Reparation
- Gratitude
- Justice
- Beneficence
- Self-improvement
- Non-maleficence

We suggest that this list may serve as a starting point for discussion about whether corporations have reporting responsibilities with respect to social responsibility. Two questions must be addressed at the outset. First, do organizations such as corporations have duties that apply to the "plain man?" Second, how shall we know whether a specific duty applies to a particular organization?

Some modern ethicists argue that corporations are moral persons. This is true because people are behind the corporate veil and these people make decisions with moral implications. Society therefore cannot condone as amoral corporate actions that would be considered immoral for the individuals who actually make decisions for the corporation. Portions of the Foreign Corrupt Practices Act that hold corporate officers personally responsible for corporate actions serve as an example of this premise. P. H. Werhane convincingly takes the issue of corporate social responsibility a step farther in Persons, Rights, and Corporations. She argues that corporations have responsibilities apart from the individual responsibilities of persons behind the corporate veil.

She demonstrates that corporations argue for legal rights that must have a moral basis if they are justified. An example of this is the enforcement of contracts, which depends upon the moral duty of fidelity. Moreover, "If corporations have moral rights, then they have the obligations connected with such rights, and they can be held accountable, morally accountable."

If the prima facie duties apply correctly to individuals, including individuals who manage corporations, then they apply to corporations themselves. We may therefore turn to the second question of how to ascertain whether a specific duty applies to a corporation.

S. E. Toulmin has provided a test that may be applied to the prima facie duties: In any particular community, certain principles are current-that is to say, attention is paid to certain types of argument as appealing to accepted criteria of "real goodness," "real rightness," "real obligation," etc. From these the members of the community are expected to regulate their lives and judgements. And such a set of principles of "prima facie obligations" of "categorical imperatives" is what we call the "moral code" of the community.

As citizens, readers of financial reports should be concerned about the actions a company is taking or failing to take in the realm of social responsibility. The socially responsible corporation should therefore report upon how it is meeting or failing to meet its duties to the public. Research among investors and other stakeholders indicates that they are in fact interested in corporate activities that fall within the scope of the prima facie duties. We now explain each of these in terms of the business and accounting community.

Fidelity

Fidelity is the first of two duties that rest upon previous acts. Fidelity is simply the keeping of promises. The promises to be kept may be explicit or implicit.

Many explicit promises are already recognized and reported by corporations. Warranties, for example, are accounted for as contingency liabilities with a corresponding expense. Duties stemming from explicit promises may also raise ethical questions that are not so easily recognized in financial terms.

Let us return to the cable television company case. Management here is faced with a hard choice between its often-stated duty to maximize return for stockholders and the moral duty to keep the corporation's promise. We have demonstrated how the accounting system through the commonly used differential cost schedule uses utilitarian reasoning to report upon future consequences of managerial action.

We have shown that such purely utilitarian reasoning, when used alone, would rarely motivate a manager to choose the socially responsible course of action. Yet Francis, and perhaps John, believe that a duty exists here because of the statements made at the public hearing. The duty that they recognize is fidelity.

From the accountant's viewpoint, can a report be developed to assist the decision-making process from a deontological perspective? Moreover, once the choice is made, can it be reported to interested stakeholders in an accounting context?

Reparation

Duties of reparation rest upon a previous wrongful act of the one who has the duty. Examples of duties of reparation in business are quite common and well publicized. The poison gas leak at the Union Carbide plant in Bhopal, India, and Manville's asbestos-related problems provide recent examples. In both cases the victims of actions taken by the company have received monetary compensation.

A clear reporting problem appears to exist in both the Union Carbide and Manville cases; yet, the wrongful act need not be so dramatic for a duty to arise. Suppose our cable television enterprise decides to proceed with the soft pornography offering. Later Francis learns that a father accused of sexually abusing his four-year-old daughter claims that he was motivated to do so after watching a show on Genesee Cable.

Clearly no legal liability exists here under current law. Yet, ethics are usually considered to be on a higher plane than the law. Therefore a duty with corresponding social responsibility accounting implications may arise when no legal liability is present.

Suppose John, Teresa, and Francis are struck with conscience in this matter and therefore are considering paying for the treatment of the little girl. Their consideration might arise from a sense of duty of reparation. Should they later decide to have Genesee make these payments, a social responsibility accounting implication may have been created.

The management of a particular corporation would have the responsibility of deciding the corporation's ethical standards with respect to reparation. The accountant's role would be to report upon the financial implications of meeting those standards. Such reporting might be internal or external. A corporate decision not to accept a reparation duty could also be a reportable event under social responsibility accounting.

Gratitude

Duties of gratitude arise from services done by others for the one who has the duty of gratitude. At first the notion of corporate gratitude may seem questionable, yet official communication from corporations often express gratitude. Annual reports of companies frequently express corporate appreciation for a job well done by employees. Gratitude can be more specific. When Frank Cary retired as the chairman of the board of International Business Machines, the new chairman stated that the company was "indebted" to him "for the wisdom and skill with which he led the company."

The duty of gratitude is not only owed employees. A company might have reason to be grateful to a community, to suppliers, to customers, or to others who interact with it. The duty arises because of the previous actions of the other entities. A question of interest with respect to social responsibility accounting is whether the gratitude expressed by corporations has an associated duty, and whether there is a future cost associated with the duty. If a corporation appreciates efforts by its loyal employees, has a duty been created for the corporation to those employees when economic times are not so good? Does indebtedness of IBM imply that a duty exists? Moreover, if the answers to these questions are yes, what are the costs of fulfilling these duties or not fulfilling them?

On the other hand, a company need not express gratitude for the duty to exist. From the standpoint of ethics an unrecognized duty might exist. Social responsibility accounting may be one vehicle that could assist managers and others in recognizing this duty.

Justice

Duties of justice rest on the fact or possibility of a distribution of pleasure or happiness (or the means thereto) that is not in accordance with the merit of the persons concerned. A duty may arise in such cases to upset or prevent such a distribution. Corporations are frequently confronted with duties that arise from justice. Such duties would create reporting implications under social responsibility accounting.

Suppose that a large corporation is headquartered in a maturing city that contains a ghetto. The youth of the ghetto are unable to attain employment at the corporation because, due to circumstances beyond their control, they are unqualified. In such circumstances enlightened management may believe that it is their duty, and by connection the corporation's, to overturn this state of affairs by providing job training programmes. Such a sense of duty would arise from a concern for justice.

Notice that in this case the sense of duty did not arise from any previous action or promise of the corporation or its management. Duties of justice arise simply because an observed situation is wrong per se. If the corporation recognizes such a duty, a cost may ensue in the future should the corporation create a training programme, for example.

Of interest here is that the corporation does not internalize an externality that it created, an often heard reason for socially responsible action, nor does the corporation take action because it believes that the training programme will benefit it in the long run (a utilitarian argument). Rather the action is undertaken due to a sense of duty.

The duty arises from a concept of justice, perhaps best stated by John Rawls. "Justice is the virtue of practices where there are assumed to be competing interests and conflicting claims and where it is supposed that persons will press their rights on each other.

That persons are mutually self-interested in certain situations and for certain purposes is what gives rise to the questioning of justice in practices couching those circumstances." Rawls argues that every person may be supposed to have a concept of justice. This proposition is true because each person is involved in some relationships with others. In the context of these relationships each person forms a concept of justice for herself as well as for others. Corporate persons would be among those under this societal umbrella.

Beneficence

Like duties of justice, duties of beneficence do not arise because of any culpability on the part of the corporation. Duties of beneficence rest upon the mere fact that there are other beings in the world whose condition can be made better. If the corporation recognizes these beings and is able to improve their condition, then a duty of beneficence arises.

The fact that duties of beneficence are recognized by managers of corporations is demonstrated by the fact that they cause the corporations to make charitable contributions. One is hard pressed to swallow utilitarian reasoning that such contributions may in the long run improve profitability by the creation of goodwill. In fact, the best arguments against such action are utilitarian in nature. Milton Friedman represents perhaps the best-known proponent of this utilitarian point of view.

The Philip Morris Company is well known in some circles as a supporter of the arts. Yet this company does not have a great deal of goodwill in general. Contributions to the ballet are not made in the hope of generating cigarette sales. They are made because people who work for this company believe that society will benefit from having the arts more widely available to the public. In other words, the donations are made because of a sense of duty, the duty of beneficence.

Duties of beneficence on the part of corporations are recognized in the tax laws, in that amounts spent for charity are deductible for tax purposes. They provide an interesting twist in that the duty recognized by the corporation is externalized. Persons who may not recognize the duty become partners in fulfilling the duty in the sense that the government receives less revenue from the corporate source.

Self-Improvement

Duties of self-improvement are the most difficult of Ross's duties of individuals to translate to a corporation. Duties of self-improvement rest on the fact that one can improve her own condition with respect to virtue or intelligence. Interestingly, Ross includes pleasure in the improvement of another's condition but omits it in the improvement of one's own condition. The difficulty with respect to duties of self-improvement lies in defining the corporation when viewing it as something where virtue or knowledge warrant improvement. However, if we accept the notion a priori that a corporation improves itself when it improves its management, duties of self-improvement may be found. An example is the practice of companies paying the cost of sending managers to universities to improve their education. Utilitarians would undoubtedly argue that such action is taken to improve profits through lower costs generated from the better management the corporation expects to receive from better-educated managers. Corporations would undeniably justify this practice on such utilitarian grounds.

However, the imagination must truly be stretched to translate an individual manager's education to the bottom line. A more plausible explanation for such things as classes in human relations might be found in the desire to fulfill a duty for self-improvement. If this is true, does the public bear costs when a corporation does not recognize such a duty? For example, one could argue that by failure to improve managers' knowledge of business ethics, a corporation has caused the public to incur greater risk of unethical conduct by the corporation.

The duty of self-improvement becomes one we may more easily associate with business enterprise if we expand upon Ross's definition a bit. A commonly held and frequently cited belief is that business corporations have the duty to make profits. We may easily accept this notion by stating that the company has the duty to improve itself by improving its financial position. As we do this we agree with Ross that the duty of self-improvement should be subordinated to the other duties.

Non-Maleficence

This is the only duty that is stated in a negative way. Non-maleficence is the duty not to injure others. Duties of non-maleficence are clearly the most compelling; violations of these duties create debate about corporate irresponsibility.

Pollution can serve as an example of how deontological ethics is superior to utilitarian ethics in solving dilemmas. A utilitarian argument for pollution may be made on the basis that those who pollute will generate more profit than those who incur costs to avoid pollution. Yet, reasonable men and women view pollution as undesirable. The utilitarian solution to this dilemma is to argue that the externalities created by the pollution involve more bad than the good created by the profits. The logical conclusion to the utilitarian view is that the responsible corporation should pollute just up to the point where the pollution will not exceed the good generated by the profit and no further. These arguments do not represent the attitudes of plain-thinking people. Indeed, most reasonable people could agree that pollution of the air and water is a prima facie wrong. It is wrong because it is injurious to others irrespective of utility. Because pollution is wrong, members of society, including corporate members, have a duty not to engage in the practice. This is the duty of non-maleficence.

The implications for social responsibility accounting are perhaps most clear under duties of non-maleficence. In the pollution example, those companies that internalize the cost of pollution by purchasing anti-pollution equipment have done their duty and would so report. Those who do not incur these costs will make higher profits, but should be required to report as a social cost the damage the pollution has done or will do.

The duty of non-maleficence could also apply in the Genesee Cable case. As part of his consideration of Teresa's proposal, John might recall an article that asserts that men who watch pornographic material on television develop an attitude towards women that views them as objects to be exploited rather than persons to be respected. John may decide against accepting Teresa's proposal on the grounds that he does not desire Genesee to be a party to fostering such attitudes in the community. In this case he would be acting out of the duty of non-maleficence.

4

Cost Analysis

COST

In business, retail, and accounting, a cost is the value of money that has been used up to produce something, and hence is not available for use anymore. In economics, a cost is an alternative that is given up as a result of a decision. In business, the cost may be one of acquisition, in which case the amount of money expended to acquire it is counted as cost. In this case, money is the input that is gone in order to acquire the thing. This acquisition cost may be the sum of the cost of production as incurred by the original producer, and further costs of transaction as incurred by the acquirer over and above the price paid to the producer. Usually, the price also includes a mark-up for profit over the cost of production. Costs are often further described based on their timing or their applicability.

ACCOUNTING VS OPPORTUNITY COSTS

In accounting, costs are the monetary value of expenditures for supplies, services, labour, products, equipment and other items purchased for use by a business or other accounting entity. It is the amount denoted on invoices as the price and recorded in bookkeeping records as an expense or asset cost basis. Opportunity cost, also referred to as economic cost is the value of the best alternative that was not chosen in order to pursue the current endeavour-*i.e.*, what could have been accomplished with the resources expended in the undertaking. It represents opportunities forgone. In theoretical economics, cost used without qualification often means opportunity cost.

COMPARING PRIVATE, EXTERNAL, SOCIAL, AND PSYCHIC COSTS

When a transaction takes place, it typically involves both private costs and external costs. Private costs are the costs that the buyer of a good or service pays the seller. This can also be described as the costs internal to the firm's production function. External costs in contrast, are the costs that people other than the buyer are forced to pay as a result of the transaction. The bearers of such costs can be either particular individuals or society at large. Note that external costs are often both non-monetary and problematic to quantify for comparison with monetary values.

They include things like pollution, things that society will likely have to pay for in some way or at some time in the future, but that are not included in transaction prices. Social costs are the sum of private costs and external costs. For example, the manufacturing cost of a car reflects the private cost for the manufacturer. The polluted waters or polluted air also created as part of the process of producing the car is an external cost borne by those who are affected by the pollution or who value unpolluted air or water. Because the manufacturer does not pay for this external cost and does not include this cost in the price of the car they are said to be external to the market pricing mechanism. The air pollution from driving the car is also an externality produced by the car user in the process of using his good. The driver does not compensate for the environmental damage caused by using the car. A psychic cost is a subset of social costs that specifically represent the costs of added stress or losses to quality of life.

COST ESTIMATES AND COST OVERRUN

When developing a business plan for a new company, product, or project, planners typically make cost estimates in order to assess whether revenues/ benefits will cover costs. This is done in both business and government. Costs are often underestimated resulting in cost overrun during implementation. Main causes of cost underestimation and overrun are optimism bias and strategic misrepresentation. Reference class forecasting was developed to curb optimism bias and strategic misrepresentation and arrive at more accurate cost estimates. Cost Plus, is where the Price = Cost plus or minus X per cent, where x is the percentage of built in overhead or profit margin.

EXPENSE

In common usage, an expense or expenditure is an outflow of money to another person or group to pay for an item or service, or for a category of costs. For a tenant, rent is an expense. For students or parents, tuition is an expense. Buying food, clothing, furniture or an automobile is often referred to as an expense. An expense is a cost that is "paid" or "remitted", usually in exchange for something of value. Something that seems to cost a great deal is "expensive". Something that seems to cost little is "inexpensive". "Expenses of the table" are expenses of dining, refreshments, a feast, etc. In accounting, expense has a very specific meaning. It is an outflow of cash or other valuable assets from a person or company to another person or company. This outflow of cash is generally one side of a trade for products or services that have equal or better current or future value to the buyer than to the seller. Technically, an expense is an event in which an asset is used up or a liability is incurred. In terms of the accounting equation, expenses reduce owners' equity.

The International Accounting Standards Board defines expenses as:

- ...Decreases in economic benefits during the accounting period in the form of outflows or depletions of assets or incurrences of liabilities that result in decreases in equity, other than those relating to distributions to equity participants.

BOOKKEEPING FOR EXPENSES

In double-entry bookkeeping, expenses are recorded as a debit to an expense account and a credit to either an asset account or a liability account, which are balance sheet accounts. An expense decreases assets or increases liabilities. Typical business expenses include salaries, utilities, depreciation of capital assets, and interest expense for loans. The purchase of a capital asset such as a building or equipment is not an expense.

CASH FLOW

In a cash flow statement, expenditures are divided into operating, investing, and financing expenditures:

- Operational expense (OPEX)—salary for employees
- Capital expenditure (CAPEX)—buying equipment
- Financing expense—interest expense for loans and bonds

An important issue in accounting is whether a particular expenditure is classified as an expense, which is reported immediately on the business's income statement; or whether it is classified as a capital expenditure or an expenditure subject to depreciation, which is not an expense. These latter types of expenditures are reported as expenses when they are depreciated by businesses that use accrual-basis accounting, which is most large businesses and all C corporations.

The most common interpretation of whether an expense is of capital or income variety depends upon its term. Viewing an expense as a purchase helps alleviate this distinction. If, soon after the "purchase", that which was expensed holds no value then it is usually identified as an expense. If it retains value soon and long after the purchase, it will be viewed as capital with life that should be amortized/depreciated and retained on the Balance Sheet.

DEDUCTION OF BUSINESS EXPENSES UNDER THE US TAX CODE

For tax purposes, the Internal Revenue Code permits the deduction of business expenses in the taxable year in which those expenses are paid or incurred. This is in contrast to capital expenditures that are paid or incurred to acquire an asset. Expenses are costs that do not acquire, improve, or prolong the life of an asset. For example, a person who buys a new truck for a business would be making a capital expenditure because they have acquired a new business-related asset.

This cost could not be deducted in the current taxable year. However, the gas the person buys during that year to fuel that truck would be considered a deductible expense.

The cost of purchasing gas does not improve or prolong the life of the truck but simply allows the truck to run. Even if something qualifies as an expense, it is not necessarily deductible. As a general rule, expenses are deductible if they relate to a taxpayer's trade or business activity or if the expense is paid or incurred in the production or collection of income from an activity that does not rise to the level of a trade or business.

Section 162(a) of the Internal Revenue Code is the deduction provision for business or trade expenses. In order to be a trade or business expense and qualify for a deduction, it must satisfy 5 elements in addition to qualifying as an expense. It must be ordinary and necessary. Expenses paid to preserve one's reputation do not appear to qualify. In addition, it must be paid or incurred during the taxable year. It must be paid in carrying on a trade or business activity. To qualify as a trade or business activity, it must be continuous and regular, and profit must be the primary motive.

Section 212 of the Internal Revenue Code is the deduction provision for investment expenses. In addition to being an expense and satisfying elements 1-4 above, expenses are deductible as an investment activity under Section 212 of the Internal Revenue Code if they are for the production or collection of income, for the management, conservation, or maintenance of property held for the production of income, or in connection with the determination, collection, or refund of any tax. In investing, one controversy that mounted throughout 2002 and 2003 was whether companies should report the granting of stock options to employees as an expense on the income statement, or should not report this at all in the income statement, which is what had previously been the norm.

COSTS FOR DECISION-MAKING AND PLANNING

OPPORTUNITY COST

Scarcity of resources is one of the more basic concepts of economics. Scarcity necessitates trade-offs, and trade-offs result in an opportunity cost. While the cost of a good or service often is thought of in monetary terms, the opportunity cost of a decision is based on what must be given up (the next best alternative) as a result of the decision. 4Any decision that involves a choice between two or more options has an opportunity cost. Opportunity cost contrasts to accounting cost in that accounting costs do not consider forgone opportunities. Consider the case of an MBA student who pays $30,000 per year in tuition and fees at a private university. For a two-year MBA programme, the cost of tuition and fees would be $60,000. This is the monetary cost of the education.

However, when making the decision to go back to school, one should consider the opportunity cost, which includes the income that the student would have earned if the alternative decision of remaining in his or her job had been made.

If the student had been earning $50,000 per year and was expecting a 10 per cent salary increase in one year, $105,000 in salary would be foregone as a result of the decision to return to school.

Adding this amount to the educational expenses results in a cost of $165,000 for the degree. Opportunity cost is useful when evaluating the cost and benefit of choices. It often is expressed in non-monetary terms

For example, if one has time for only one elective course, taking a course in microeconomics might have the opportunity cost of a course in management. By expressing the cost of one option in terms of the foregone benefits of another, the marginal costs and marginal benefits of the options can be compared.

As another example, if a shipwrecked sailor on a desert island is capable of catching 10 fish or harvesting 5 coconuts in one day, then the opportunity cost of producing one coconut is two fish (10 fish/5 coconuts). Note that this simple example assumes that the production possibility frontier between fish and coconuts is linear.

Relative Price

Opportunity cost is expressed in relative price, that is, the price of one choice relative to the price of another. For example, if milk costs $4 per gallon and bread costs $2 per loaf, then the relative price of milk is 2 loaves of bread.

If a consumer goes to the grocery store with only $4 and buys a gallon of milk with it, then one can say that the opportunity cost of that gallon of milk was 2 loaves of bread (assuming that bread was the next best alternative). In many cases, the relative price provides better insight into the real cost of a good than does the monetary price.

Applications of Opportunity Cost

The concept of opportunity cost has a wide range of applications including:

- Analysis of comparative advantage
- Career choice
- Consumer choice
- Cost of capital
- Production possibilities
- Time management

SUNK COSTS

In economics and business decision-making, sunk costs are retrospective (past) costs that have already been incurred and cannot be recovered. Sunk costs are sometimes contrasted with prospective costs, which are future costs that may be incurred or changed if an action is taken. Both retrospective and prospective costs may be either fixed (that is, they are not dependent on the volume of economic activity, however measured) or variable (dependent on volume).

In traditional microeconomic theory, only prospective (future) costs are relevant to an investment decision. Traditional economics proposes that an economic actor not let sunk costs influence one's decisions, because doing so would not be rationally assessing a decision exclusively on its own merits. The decision-maker may make rational decisions according to their own incentives; these incentives may dictate different decisions than would be dictated by efficiency or profitability, and this is considered an incentive problem and distinct from a sunk cost problem.

Evidence from behavioural economics suggests this theory fails to predict real-world behaviour. Sunk costs greatly affect actors' decisions, because humans are inherently loss-averse and thus normally act irrationally when making economic decisions.

Sunk costs should not affect the rational decision-maker's best choice. However, until a decision-maker irreversibly commits resources, the prospective cost is an avoidable future cost and is properly included in any decision-making processes. For example, if you are considering pre-ordering movie tickets, but have not actually purchased them yet, the cost remains avoidable. If the price of the tickets rises to an amount that requires you to pay more than the value you place on them, the change in prospective cost should be figured into the decision-making, and the decision should be reevaluated.

Description

The sunk cost is distinct from the economic loss. For example, when a car is purchased, it can subsequently be resold; however, it will probably not be resold for the original purchase price. The economic loss is the difference (including transaction costs). The sum originally paid should not affect any rational future decision-making about the car, regardless of the resale value: if the owner can derive more value from selling the car than not selling it, it should be sold, regardless of the price paid. In this sense, the sunk cost is not a precise quantity, but an economic term for a sum paid, in the past, which is no longer relevant to decisions about the future; it may be used inconsistently in quantitative terms as the original cost or the expected economic loss. It may also be used as shorthand for an error in analysis due to the sunk cost fallacy, non-rational decision-making or, most simply, as irrelevant data.

Economists argue that sunk costs are not taken into account when making rational decisions. In the case of the movie ticket, the ticket-buyer can choose between the following two end results:

- Having paid the price of the ticket and having suffered watching a movie that he does not want to see, or;
- Having paid the price of the ticket and having used the time to do something more fun.

In either case, the ticket-buyer has"paid the price of the ticket" so"that part" of the decision no longer affects the future. If the ticket-buyer regrets buying the ticket, the current decision should be based on whether he wants to see the movie at all, regardless of the price, just as if he were to go to a free movie. The economist will suggest that, since the second option involves suffering in only one way (spent money), while the first involves suffering in two (spent money plus wasted time), option two is obviously preferable.

Sunk costs may cause cost overrun. In business, an example of sunk costs may be investment into a factory or research that now has a lower value or no value whatsoever. For example, $20 million has been spent on building a powerplant; the value at present is zero because it is incomplete (and no sale or recovery is feasible). The plant can be completed for an additional $10 million, or abandoned and a different but equally valuable facility built for $5 million. It should be obvious that abandonment and construction of the alternative facility is the more rational decision, even though it represents a total loss of the original expenditure-the original sum invested is a sunk cost. If decision-makers are (economically) irrational or have the wrong incentives, the completion of the project may be chosen. For example, politicians or managers may have more incentive to avoid the appearance of a total loss. In practice, there is considerable ambiguity and uncertainty in such cases, and decisions may in retrospect appear irrational that were, at the time, reasonable to the economic actors involved and in the context of their own incentives.

Behavioural economics recognizes that sunk costs often affect economic decisions due to loss aversion: the price paid becomes a benchmark for the value, whereas the price paid should be irrelevant. This is considered non-rational behaviour (as rationality is defined by classical economics). Economic experiments have shown that the sunk cost fallacy and loss aversion are common; hence economic rationality-as assumed by much of economics-is limited. This has enormous implications for finance, economics, and securities markets in particular. Daniel Kahneman won the Nobel Prize in Economics in part for his extensive work in this area with his collaborator, Amos Tversky.

Features Characterizing the Sunk Cost Heuristic

Two specific features characterizing the sunk cost heuristic worth mentioning are:

- An overly optimistic probability bias, whereby after an investment the evaluation of one's investment reaping dividends is increased.
- The requisite of personal responsibility. Sunk cost appears to operate chiefly in those who feel personal responsibility for the investments that are to be viewed as sunk.

Overly Optimistic Probability Bias

In 1968 Knox and Inkster, in what is perhaps the classic sunk cost experiment, approached 141 horse bettors: 72 of the people had just finished placing a $2.00 bet within the past thirty seconds, and 69 people were about to place a $2.00 bet in the next thirty seconds. Their hypothesis was that people who had just committed themselves to a course of action (betting $2.00) would reduce post-decision dissonance by believing more strongly than ever that they had picked a winner. Knox and Inkster asked the bettors to rate their horse's chances of winning on a 7 point scale.

What they found was that people who were about to place a bet rated the chance that their horse would win at an average of 3.48 which corresponded to a"fair chance of winning" whereas people who had just finished betting gave an average rating of 4.81 which corresponded to a"good chance of winning."

Their hypothesis was confirmed: after making a $2.00 commitment, people became more confident their bet would pay off. Knox and Inkster performed an ancillary test on the patrons of the horses themselves and managed (after normalization) to repeat their finding almost identically. Additional evidence of inflated probability estimations can be found in Arkes and Blumer and Arkes and Hutzel.

Requisite of Personal Responsibility

In a study of 96 business students in 1976 Staw and Fox gave the subjects a choice between making an R&D investment in either an underperforming company department, or in other parts of the hypothetical company. Staw and Fox divided the participants into two groups; a low responsibility condition and a high responsibility condition. In the high responsibility condition the participants were told that they as manager had made an earlier, disappointing R&D investment.

In the low responsibility condition, subjects were told that a former manager had made a previous R&D investment in the underperforming division and were given the same profit data as the other group.

In both cases subjects were then asked to make a new $20 million investment. There was a significant interaction between assumed responsibility and average investment, with the high responsibility condition averaging $12.97 million and the low condition averaging $9.43 million. Similar results have been obtained in earlier studies by Staw and by Arkes and Blumer and Whyte.

Loss Aversion and the Sunk Cost Fallacy

Many people have strong misgivings about "wasting" resources. This is called "loss aversion". In the example, involving a non-refundable movie ticket, many people, for example, would feel obliged to go to the movie despite not really wanting to, because doing otherwise would be wasting the ticket price; they feel they passed the point of no return. This is sometimes called the sunk cost fallacy. Economists would label this behaviour "irrational": it is inefficient because it misallocates resources by depending on information that is irrelevant to the decision being made.

Colloquially, this is known as "throwing good money after bad". This line of thinking, in turn, may reflect a non-standard measure of utility, which is ultimately subjective and unique to the consumer. A ticket-buyer who purchases a ticket to a bad movie in advance, makes a semi-public commitment to watching it. To leave early is to make this lapse of judgement manifest to strangers, an appearance he may rationally choose to avoid.

Alternatively, he may take pride in having recognized the opportunity cost of the alternative use of time. The idea of sunk costs is often employed when analyzing business decisions. A common example of a sunk cost for a business is the promotion of a brand name. This type of marketing incurs costs that cannot normally be recovered. It is not typically possible to later "demote" one's brand names in exchange for cash. A second example is research and development costs.

Once spent such costs are sunk and should have no effect on future pricing decisions. So a pharmaceutical company's attempt to justify high prices because of need to recoup research and development expenses is fallacious.

The company will charge the same price whether R&D were one dollar or one million dollars. R&D cost do count when deciding whether to spend the money on research and development but once spent they have no effect on firm decisions. The sunk cost fallacy is in game theory sometimes known as the "Concorde Fallacy", referring to the fact that the British and French governments continued to fund the joint development of Concorde even after it became apparent that there was no longer an economic case for the aircraft. The project was regarded privately by the British government as a "commercial disaster" which should never have been started, and was almost cancelled, but political and legal issues ultimately made it impossible for either government to pull out.

The Sunk cost Dilemma

The economic approach that sunk costs should not be considered when decisions are being made can lead to a situation where the sum of a number of good decisions can lead to one big disaster. This dilemma situation can be described using a game theory approach for 1-player games. The sunk cost dilemma with its sequence of good decisions should not be confused with the sunk cost fallacy, where a misconception of sunk costs can lead to bad decisions.

Bygones Principle

The bygones principle is an economic theory used in business. Economists stress the "extra" or "marginal" costs and benefits of every decision. The idea is to not look backwards when making decisions and stresses the importance of ignoring past costs in future decision-making. The bygones principle states that when making a decision, one should make a hard-headed calculation of the extra costs one will incur and weigh these against its extra advantages. It emphasizes the importance of only taking into account the future costs and benefits when making decisions.

Example

An important example of this is related to nuclear power. In the late 1980s, about two dozen partially complete nuclear power plants dotted the USA's landscape. Some had already absorbed billions of dollars of investment but were not yet ready to operate.

One particularly difficult case was the Shoreham plant on Long Island Sound, New York. By 1987 the owner had spent $5.5 billion on bricks, mortar, fuel rods, and interest, but the operating license had not been granted. From an economic point of view, the $5.5 billion of past investments should not be weighed in decision-making processes. The bygones principle would state that the $5.5 billion of past cost is irrelevant. From an economic point of view, the only relevant issue concerns future costs and benefits. That is, the economic benefits of the electricity that Shoreham would produce.

The key to observe in making this calculation is that the sunk cost of $5.5 billion is irrelevant to future costs and benefits. Studies indicated that, if the $5.5 billion were ignored, the future costs of the nuclear power plant would be slightly less than the next-best alternative, even though the total cost was far higher than the alternative. A purely economic analysis would conclude that the most efficient outcome would be to finish the construction and open the Shoreham Nuclear Power Plant. However, citing many reasons, including the sunk costs, the plant was closed by protests in 1989 without generating any commercial electrical power.

RELEVANT COSTS

Relevant costs are those costs that will make a difference in a decision. Relevant costs are future costs that will differ among alternatives. We can demonstrate relevant costs with the following situation. A company is deciding whether or not to eliminate a product line. The product line accounts for approximately 4 per cent of the company's activities. If the product line is eliminated, the officers of the corporation will continue to receive the same salaries and the central office expenses will not change. The product line managers and other employees working directly on the product line will be terminated. Hence, their salaries will be eliminated. The salaries of the product line managers and other employees whose salaries will be eliminated are relevant to the decision.

If these salaries are $700,000 with the product line and $0 without the product line, the $700,000 of savings is relevant. Those cost savings and other possible cost savings will be considered along with the loss of sales revenues. On the other hand, the officers' salaries are not relevant in the decision. In other words, it doesn't matter if the officers' salaries are $500,000 or $5,000,000. The officers' salaries will be the same with or without the product line. Similarly, the decision maker does not need to know the amount of its central office expenses, since they will be the same with or without the product line. Expenses from previous years are also irrelevant. To recap, relevant costs are the future costs that will differ among alternatives. You might use the past costs to help you predict those future costs, but the past costs are otherwise irrelevant to the decision. Accountants refer to the past costs as sunk costs.

DIFFERENTIAL COST

Differential cost is a business term that refers to the difference in costs for a business when choosing between two alternatives. It is an important tool in the decision-making process for businesses looking to make possible changes to a business model. Closely associated with marginal cost, a term favoured by economists, differential cost can refer to either fixed or variable costs. The relevance of these costs is obvious when judged alongside of differential revenue to give businesses a perspective on the positives or negatives of a decision. In any decision-making process, a choice is made between alternatives. When it comes to the business world, those choices include costs and benefits that must be weighed in order to assess what decision to ultimately make. Differential cost is the difference in costs, either negative or positive, between two or more alternatives. This cost must be taken in tandem with the difference in revenue generated by these alternatives in order to come to a significant conclusion. For example, a company has decided to make a change in its advertising approach, doing away with its radio advertising in favour of advertising on television. Due to the increased production costs and the higher rate charged by television stations, the weekly advertising budget rises by $100 US Dollars, which would be the differential cost. If the company gets a significant boost in weekly sales of the product higher than the $100 USD cost difference, then the change was worth it, because the net operating revenue will have increased.

Businesses can encounter differential costs that are either fixed, meaning that they don't change, or variable, which means that they can vary depending on certain circumstances. Marginal cost is a closely associated term used by economists for a similar calculation. The difference with marginal cost is that it refers to the cost associated with making just one more unit of product, as opposed to differential cost, which is more useful for business accounting purposes. Two other types of costs are often discussed along with differential cost. Opportunity costs are costs incurred when taking on an alternative that might produce no immediate benefit.

For example, a business owner chooses to shut down his or her business for a week to attend a marketing seminar that might ultimately improve the business, but in the short term he or she incurs the loss of any income the business might have generated for that week, which would represent the opportunity cost. Sunk costs are costs incurred in the past which may not be recouped. These costs should never factor into the decision-making process if they bear no relevance to the alternatives available in the present decision.

IMPUTED COST

- In accounting, the expense of unreimbursed goods and services provided by one entity to another entity.
- An expense that is borne indirectly. For example, paying cash for a car avoids the direct cost of interest payments to a lender, but it entails the imputed cost of lost income from having funds invested in the car rather than a more productive asset.

OUT-OF-POCKET COST

The out of pocket cost is the total of all costs you must pay for service.

This includes the annual deductible, the co-pay amount, and any fees in excess of the approved maximum charges for a service.

COST VOLUME PROFIT ANALYSIS

Conceptually, conventional linear cost-volume-profit (CVP) analysis is a simplified, short term planning technique that evolved as a practical version of the theoretical model of the firm described in economics textbooks. From an accounting perspective it is compatible with the direct, or variable costing method of inventory valuation.

To use the CVP model, a company must separate total costs into fixed and variable categories using one of the methods. Recall from our earlier discussions of these terms that variable costs are those costs that vary with changes in the level of activity. The only activities that are allowed to affect variable costs in traditional cost-volume-profit analysis are production output and sales. Remember that fixed costs are those costs that do not vary with changes in the activity level.

Conceptually, fixed costs are not constant. By definition, fixed simply means that these costs are not driven by short run changes in production or sales volume. Although explicit recognition of non- production volume related cost drivers is a key concept in activity based costing, the idea is ignored in the conventional linear CVP model. Finally, it is important to recognize that the concept of fixed and variable costs is a short run concept. All costs tend to vary in the long run as the company adds to its' capacity to produce and distribute products and services.

Therefore, the short run emphasis of CVP analysis tends to conflict with the long run emphasis of activity based costing and the lean enterprise concepts of JIT and TOC. This creates another thought provoking controversial issue.

The purpose of this chapter is to describe the assumptions and techniques of the conventional linear cost-volume-profit approach as well as the controversy concerning the compatibility of CVP analysis with ABC and the continuous improvement concepts.

The chapter is divided into five main sections. The first section addresses the underlying assumptions of the conventional linear model and the implications of relaxing these assumptions. This section is mainly conceptual and is illustrated with a series of graphs.

The second section illustrates the basic planning techniques for a single product company that provide the foundation for more realistic problems. The third section extends the basic analysis to multiproduct companies. Both sections two and three are more mechanical than conceptual and are mainly illustrated with a series of related equations.

The fourth section is fairly short, but illustrates how to convert the analysis to a cash flow basis. The last section introduces the controversy associated with the CVP approach as it relates to the newer concepts of ABC, JIT and TOC. Since the CVP methodology is closely related to direct or variable costing, this chapter helps provide a better foundation for the more detailed comparison of direct and absorption costing presented in.

ASSUMPTIONS OF CONVENTIONAL LINEAR CVP ANALYSIS

Constant Sales Price

To assume that the sales price is constant implies that the company is facing a horizontal demand function as illustrated in Figure below. The implications of a horizontal demand function are that the company can sell any number of units at a constant sales price. Another way to describe this is to say that consumers are willing and able to buy any quantity the company offers for sale at a constant price. Average revenue (AR) is constant and equal to the sales price, (*i.e.*, AR = PX÷X = P) as illustrated in Figure.

The slope of the total revenue function is equal to the sales price. When the company sells one additional unit, total revenue increases by an amount equal to the sales price of that unit.

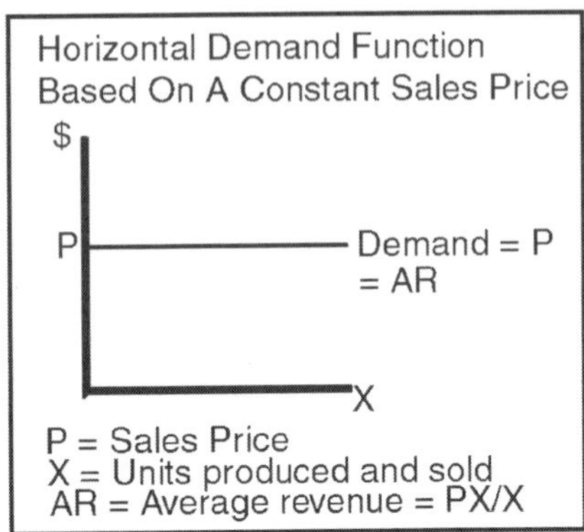

The fact that the sales price is constant causes the slope of the total revenue function to be constant which results in a linear total revenue function. Another way to describe this is to say that total revenue increases at a constant rate as additional units are sold.

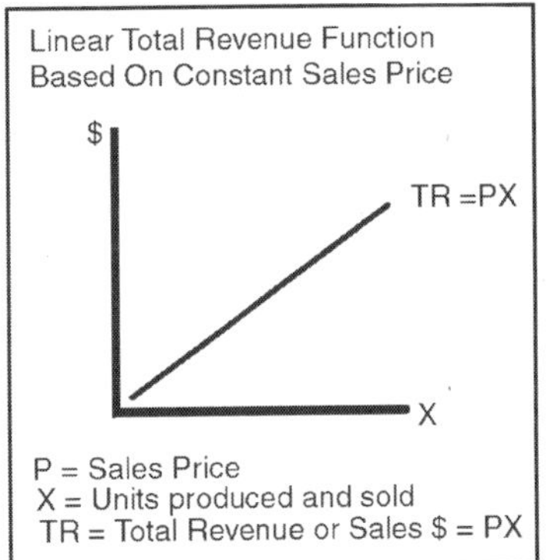

A more realistic down sloping demand function illustrates what economists refer to as the law of demand. This law describes the fundamental idea that consumers are willing and able to buy more at a lower price than a higher price.

When the price is decreased from P1 to P2, the quantity purchased, or demanded, increases from X1 to X2. The total revenue function based on the law of demand is non-linear as illustrated in Figure. Total revenue increases at a decreasing rate as additional units are sold. This is because the sale of additional units requires that the company reduce the sales price. Each price corresponds to a specific sales quantity. Thus, average revenue (AR) will be decreasing, rather than constant.

Although the assumption of a constant sales price is not realistic, it is defended as a practical way to expedite the planning process within a fairly narrow range of sales activity. The idea that most products are subject to a down sloping demand curve is intuitively obvious, but applying the concept is simply not practical. Most companies sell too many products in a constantly changing economic environment. Today's demand curve is very likely to be obsolete tomorrow.

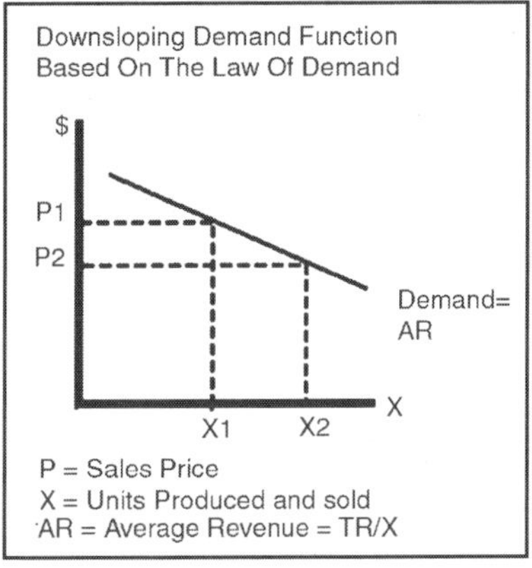

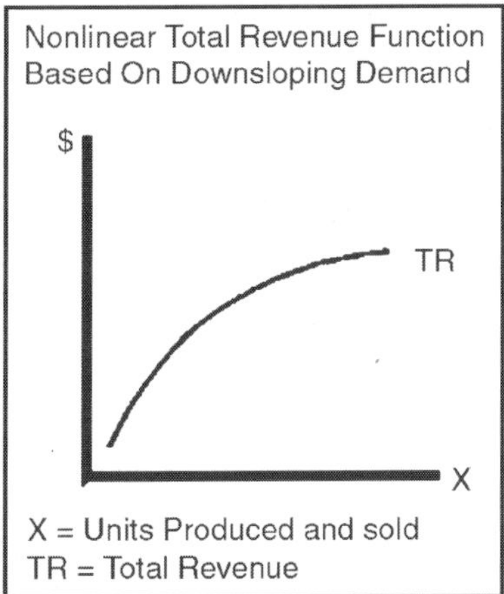

Constant Sales Mix and Inventory Level

The last two assumptions of the conventional linear cost-volume-profit model are more easily understood than the previous assumptions. The fourth assumption is that the sales mix will remain constant during the planning period for a multiproduct company. Sales mix proportions may be stated in terms of either units or dollars as explained in the illustrations below.

The fifth and last assumption is that units produced are equal to units sold. This means that there will be no changes in beginning or ending inventory levels to complicate the analysis. This assumption along with the assumption concerning constant fixed cost will be relaxed in the following chapter where we will use the conventional linear CVP model to consider the differences between direct costing and full absorption costing.

CONVENTIONAL AND THEORETICAL MODELS

Graphic summaries of the two models are presented in Figures below. In the linear model there is one break-even point (BEP) where total revenue is equal to total cost. Since the total revenue and total cost functions are linear, the profit function is also linear. This is because the slope of the profit function is equal to contribution margin per unit which is automatically constant when the sales price and variable cost per unit are constant.

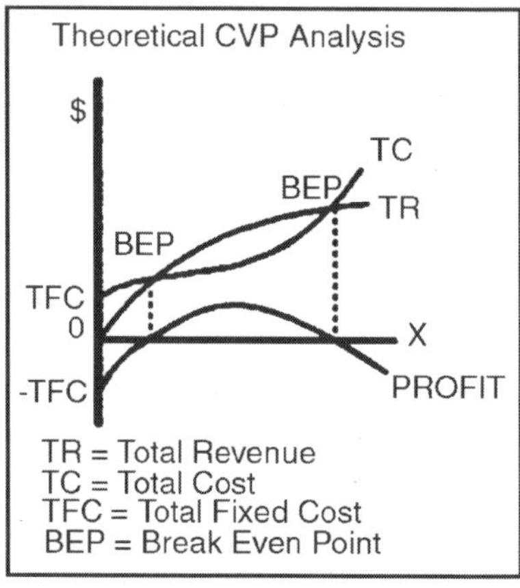

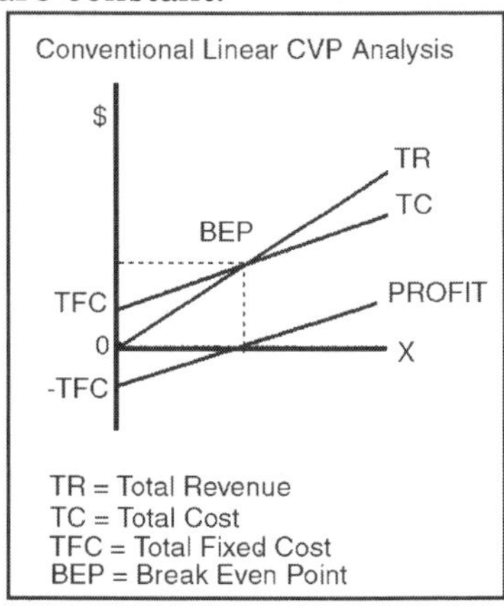

The theoretical model summarized in Figure above conveys a very different picture. There are two break-even points where total revenue and total cost are equal. The theoretical profit function intersects the horizonal axis at the two break-even points and reaches a maximum level at the point where the vertical distance between TR and TC is the greatest.

In the linear model illustrated in Figure, the area to the left of the break-even point represents a loss area and the area to the right of this point represents a profit area that continuously grows larger as additional units are produced and sold. In the linear model the company maximizes profit where production and sales are at maximum capacity. However, in the theoretical model, there are two loss areas, one to the left of the first BEP and one to the right of the second BEP. The profit area is between the two break-even points, thus trying to achieve the maximum level of production and sales will produce losses rather than increased profits. For this reason, some critics of the conventional linear model argue that it represents a naive and dangerous view of a firm's economic environment.

On the other hand, advocates of the linear model contend that short term planning does not require a theoretical model of the entire range of production possibilities. Although the concepts underlying the theoretical model are important, the model does not provide a practical approach for short term planning. However, the linear model is a practical and adequate alternative for planning within the normal relevant range of production and sales alternatives.

Analysis Versus Changing the Model

For any given linear CVP analysis, we can ask a whole set of "what-if" questions about how increases and decreases in the sales price, unit variable costs, sales mix and fixed costs would affect the outcome. However, when we do that we are simply changing from one set of static assumptions to another set. This means that we are changing from one conventional linear problem to a somewhat different conventional linear problem. If the first two assumptions are relaxed to allow the sales price and unit variable costs to change continuously in response to the forces of supply and demand, we are not asking a "what if" question, we are changing the analysis from the practical linear approach to the theoretical non-linear approach.

TECHNIQUES FOR SOLVING CVP PROBLEMS

The following symbols are used below to illustrate the various techniques used in cost-volume-profit analysis.

P = Sales price.

V = Variable costs per unit.

Note: This is not inventory cost because it includes both variable manufacturing costs as well as variable selling and administrative expenses.

X	The number of units produced and sold. A unit is a common way to describe an output, but an output may be expressed in pounds, gallons, board feet, cubic feet, etc.
TR	S = Total revenue, or sales dollars.
TVC	Total variable costs = VX
TFC	Total fixed costs.
TC	Total costs = TFC + TVC.
P-V	Contribution margin per unit. This is the amount of sales revenue that each unit provides towards covering the fixed costs and providing a profit, *i.e.*, what's left over after the variable costs associated with the unit have been covered.
TCM	Total contribution margin = (P – V)(X).

$$CMR = (P\text{-}V) \div P = (TR - TVC) \div TR = (PX - VX) \div PX = 1 - (V \div P)$$

These are just different ways to define the contribution margin ratio. They all work because the functions are linear.

There are many algebraic equations illustrated on the next several pages that may appear to require memorization. However, every equation is simply a variation of the following basic concepts:

$$\text{Total Revenue} = \text{Total Cost} + \text{Profit}$$

$$TR = TC + NIBT$$

$$TR = TFC + TVC + NIBT$$

$$TR - TVC = TFC + NIBT$$

$$TCM = TFC + NIBT$$

Total revenue, or sales dollars, less total variable costs equals total contribution margin. Contribution margin is the revenue over and above the variable costs that contributes towards covering the fixed costs and also towards providing a profit after the fixed costs have been covered. Practically any cost-volume-profit problem can be solved with the last equation stated above and an understanding of the concepts involved.

Solving Single Product CVP Problems in Units

A summary of the cost volume profit equations for single product problems is presented below. All five equations are variations of the basic conceptual equation stated above. To reinforce the concept, each equation is developed and illustrated below. Single product CVP problems in units number equation used to determine:

- Units needed to break-even.

$$(P\text{-}V)X = TFC$$

- Units needed to generate a target net income before taxes.

$$(P\text{-}V)X = TFC + NIBT$$

- Units needed to generate a target net income after taxes.

$$(P\text{-}V)X = TFC + [NIAT \div (1\text{-}T)]$$

- Units needed to generate a target NIBT stated as a proportion (R) of sales dollars (PX).

$$(P\text{-}V)X = TFC + (R)(PX)$$

- Units needed to generate a target NIAT stated as a proportion (R) of sales dollars (PX).

$$(P\text{-}V)X = TFC + [(R)(PX) \div (1\text{-}T)]$$

UNITS NEEDED TO BREAK-EVEN

We can derive the break-even equation by starting with the fact that total revenue equals total cost at the break-even point. Then the equation is restated in terms of unit sales, unit prices and unit cost and then rearranged into the more convenient format presented in Equation.

$$TR = TC$$

$$TR = TFC + TVC$$

$$PX = TFC + VX$$

$$PX - VX = TFC$$

$$(P - V)X = TFC \text{ or } TCM = TFC$$

$$X = TFC \div (P - V)$$

Equation above shows that the break-even point is where total contribution margin (P – V)(X) is equal to total fixed costs, *i.e.*, this level of production and sales provides just enough revenue to cover all the cost.

UNITS NEEDED FOR TARGET NET INCOME BEFORE TAXES

This equation can be derived from scratch in the same manner used to develop Equation 1. Notice however that Equation 2 may be obtained by simply adding the desired amount of net income to the right hand side of Equation.

$$TR = TFC + TVC + \text{TARGET NIBT}$$

$$PX = TFC + VX + NIBT$$

$$PX - VX = TFC + NIBT$$

$$(P - V)X = TFC + NIBT$$

$$X = (TFC + NIBT) \div (P - V)$$

Equations simply indicates that total contribution margin is equal to the total fixed costs plus the desired net income before taxes. These relationships are illustrated graphically in Figure below which is similar to present.

Figure below shows that the break-even point is where the two lines representing total revenue and total cost intersect. To the left of this intersection, the vertical difference between the total revenue and total cost functions represents a net loss.

To the right of the break-even point, the vertical difference between the two functions represents net income before taxes. The lower part of the graph shows that the break-even point can also be found by plotting the before tax profit function.

When the number of units produced and sold equals zero, the loss is equal to total fixed costs. When the firm produces a positive number of units, the loss is reduced by an amount equal to the contribution margin per unit multiplied by the number of units produced and sold. The slope of NIBT is contribution margin per unit. When enough units are produced and sold to cover the fixed costs, the company reaches the break-even point. This is the point on the graph where the profit function intersects the horizontal axis and it is directly below the point where the total revenue and total cost functions intersect.

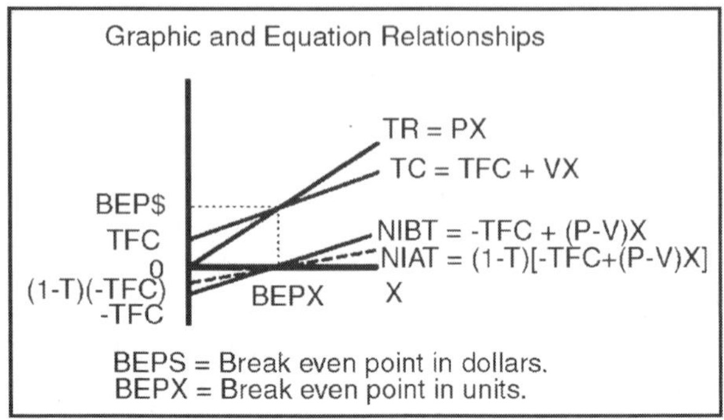

UNITS NEEDED FOR NET INCOME

If,

T = the tax rate, and

NIAT = desired net income after taxes, then

$$(1\text{-}T)(NIBT) = NIAT \text{ therefore } NIBT = NIAT \div (1\text{-}T)$$

Substituting NIAT÷(1-T) for NIBT in Equation 2, provides Equation 3, which allows us to solve for units needed to generate a desired amount of net income after taxes.

$$(P - V)\,X = TFC + [NIAT \div (1 - T)]$$

$$X = [TFC + [NIAT \div (1 - T)]] \div (P - V)$$

The after tax relationships are also illustrated graphically in Figure above. The after tax profit function begins at a point equal to (1 – T)(–TFC) assuming the tax benefits of a loss can be used in a prior period or perhaps in some other segment of the company. The slope of the after tax profit function is (1 – T)(P – V), therefore the function is not as steep as the before tax profit function. The break-even point is the same however, and the vertical difference between the two profit functions is equal to the amount of the tax involved.

When target net income before taxes is stated as a per cent of sales $. If we use R to define the desired rate of return on sales, *i.e.*, R = NIBT/TR, then we can substitute R(PX) for the desired net income before taxes in Equation.

$$(P - V)X = TFC + (R)(PX)$$

$$X = [TFC + (R)(PX)] \div (P - V)$$

Since PX equals sales dollars, then R multiplied by PX will provide the desired profit before taxes. Although the desired profit is often stated as a percentage, R is a proportion, i.e, it ranges from 0 to 1.

When target net income after taxes is stated as a percentage of sales \$. If the target rate of return is stated as an after tax rate, *i.e.*, R = NIAT/TR, then the following approach is used. Substituting R(PX)÷(1-T) for R(PX) in Equation.

$$(P - V)X = TFC + [(R)(PX) \div (1 - T)]$$

$$X = [TFC + [(R)(PX) \div (1 þ T)]] \div (P - V)$$

When solving CVP problems, it is less confusing visually and more convenient for computational purposes to leave (P – V) on the left-hand side of the equations initially. It is best to simplify the expressions on both sides of the equation first, rather than attempt to divide every element on the right-hand side by P – V. The Cal Company produces pocket size calculators that are sold for \$10 per unit.

The costs associated with each unit are as follows:

- Direct material = \$3.00,
- Direct labour = \$.25,
- Variable overhead = \$2.00,
- Variable selling and administrative cost = \$.75.

Total fixed costs are \$100,000 for manufacturing and \$20,000 for the selling and administrative functions.

The company's tax rate is 40 per cent. In a recent meeting, the board of directors asked the following questions. How many calculators do we need to produce and sell to accomplish each of the following requirements?

- Break-even.
- Earn net income before taxes of \$40,000.
- Earn net income after taxes of \$24,000.
- Earn a 20 per cent return on sales before taxes.
- Earn a 12 per cent return on sales after taxes.

To answer these questions, we start by calculating the contribution per unit as follows:

Contribution margin per unit,

$$= P - V = 10\ 2\ (3 + .25 + 2 + .75) = 10 - 6 = 4.$$

Then, the five questions are answered by using the equations in Exhibit 11-1.

Break-even. Using Equation [1]

$$4X = 120{,}000$$

$$X = \$120{,}000 \div 4 = 30{,}000 \text{ units.}$$

Earn net income before taxes of \$40,000. Using Equation [2]

$$4X = 120{,}000 + 40{,}000$$

$$X = 160{,}000 \div 4 = 40{,}000 \text{ units.}$$

Earn net income after taxes of $24,000. Using Equation [3]

$$4X = 120{,}000 + [24{,}000 \div (1-.4)]$$

$$4X = 120{,}000 + 40{,}000$$

$$X = 160{,}000 \div 4 = 40{,}000 \text{ unit.}$$

Earn a 20 per cent return on sales before taxes. Using Equation [4]

$$4X = 120{,}000 + .2(10X)$$

$$4X = 120{,}000 + 2X$$

$$2X = 120{,}000$$

$$X = 120{,}000 \div 2 = 60{,}000 \text{ units.}$$

Earn a 12 per cent return on sales after taxes. Using Equation [5]

$$4X = 120{,}000 + [.12(10X) \div (1-.4)]$$

$$4X = 120{,}000 + .2(10X)$$

$$4X = 120{,}000 + 2X$$

$$2X = 120{,}000$$

$$X = 120{,}000 \div 2 = 60{,}000 \text{ units.}$$

A graphic solution to Example is illustrated in Figure below.

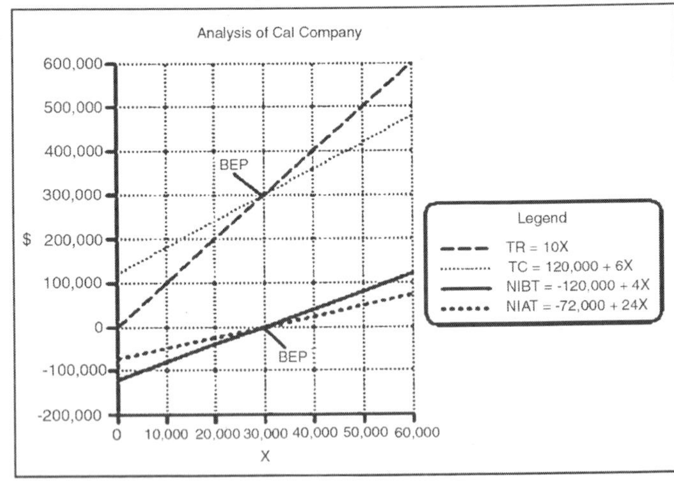

After Tax Equations the equation for NIAT that appears in the graph is found by multiplying the equation for NIBT by (1-T), *i.e.*, (1-.4)(-120,000 + 4X) = -72,000 + 2.4X. Rearranging this equation we have 2.4X = 72,000 + NIAT.

This revised equation indicates that the contribution margin after taxes ($2.4X) is equal to fixed costs after taxes ($72,000) plus the desired after tax income. It provides an alternative way to find the answers to questions 3 and 5 as illustrated below.

Earn net income after taxes of $24,000.

$$-\ 2.4X = 72{,}000 + \text{NIAT desired}$$

$$-\ 2.4X = 72{,}000 + 24{,}000$$

$$-\ 2.4X = 96{,}000$$

$$-\ X = 96{,}000 \div 2.4 = 40{,}000 \text{ units.}$$

Earn a 12 per cent return on sales after taxes.

$$-\ 2.4X = 72{,}000 + \text{NIAT desired}$$

$$-\ 2.4X = 72{,}000 + .12(10X)$$

$$-\ 2.4X = 72{,}000 + 1.2X$$

$$-\ 1.2X = 72{,}000$$

$$-\ X = 72{,}000 \div 1.2 = 60{,}000 \text{ units.}$$

Checking the Solutions

The accuracy of linear cost-volume-profit calculations can be verified easily. For example, the answers to the questions above can be verified as follows:

- Is 30,000 units the break-even point? Yes, since total contribution margin is equal to total fixed cost of 120,000, *i.e.*, (4)(30,000) = $120,000.
- Will 40,000 units generate a before tax profit of $40,000? Yes, because total contribution margin is (4)(40,000) = $160,000 and this amount is 160,000 - 120,000 = $40,000 above total fixed costs.
- Will 40,000 units generate an after tax profit of $24,000? Yes, since (1-.4)($40,000 NIBT) = $24,000.
- Will 60,000 units provide a 20 per cent return on sales before taxes? Yes, since the NIBT is TCM - TFC or (4)(60,000) - 120,000 = $120,000. Sales equals PX or ($10)(60,000) = $600,000. R = 120,000 ÷ 600,000 =.20 or 20 per cent.
- Will 60,000 units provide a 12 per cent return on sales after taxes. Yes, (1-.4)(.2) =.12 or 12 per cent. For an alternative check (1-.4)(120,000) = $72,000 NIAT. Therefore, the after tax rate of return is 72,000 ÷ 600,000 =.12 or 12 per cent.

SINGLE PRODUCT CVP PROBLEMS

A summary of the cost volume profit equations for solving single product problems in dollars is presented.

These five equations are also variations of the basic conceptual equation stated in the first part of this chapter. Each of these equations is developed and illustrated below.

Table. Single Product Cvp Problems In Dollars.

S.no	Equation	Used to Determine
1.	(CMR)(S) = TFC	Sales $ at break-even point.
2.	(CMR)(S) = TFC + NIBT	Sales $ for target NIBT.
3.	(CMR)(S) = TFC + [NIAT ÷ (1 – T)]	Sales $ for target NIAT.
4.	(CMR)(S) = TFC + (R)(S)	Sales $ for target NIBT stated as a proportion (R) or sales $.
5.	(CMR)(S) = TFC + [(R)(S) ÷ (1 – T)]	Sales $ for target NIAT stated as a proportion (R) of sales $.

BREAK-EVEN POINT

The equation for the break-even point in sales dollars may also be derived by equating total revenue and total cost. It is more convenient to use the single symbol S for sales dollars, rather than TR for total revenue.

$$TR = TC$$

$$S = TFC + TVC$$

Since the variable cost ratio (V÷P) multiplied by sales dollars (S) equals total variable cost, we can substitute (V ÷ P)(S) for variable cost in the equation above as follows.

$$S = TFC + (V \div P)(S)$$

Then subtracting variable cost from both sides of the equation provides the basic break-even point equation in sales dollars.

$$S - (V \div P)(S) = TFC$$

Stated in words, the equation indicates that total revenue, less total variable costs, equals total contribution margin, and the break even point is where total contribution margin is equal to total fixed cost. Since the contribution margin ratio (CMR = 1- V÷P) multiplied by total revenue equals total contribution margin, it is more convenient for computational purposes to state the equation in the following manner.

$$(1 - V \div P)(S) = TFC$$

$$(CMR)(S) = TFC$$

$$S = TFC \div CMR$$

Total revenue needed for target net income before taxes: Although we could derive this equation from scratch, the fact that total contribution margin must be equal to the total fixed costs plus the desired net income before taxes allows us to develop.

$$(CMR)(S) = TFC + NIBT$$

$$S = (TFC+NIBT) \div CMR$$

Total revenue needed for target net income after taxes: Solving for total revenue needed to generate a target net income after taxes involves substituting NIAT ÷ (1 – T) for NIBT in the equation for Sales dollars needed before taxes (*i.e.*, Equation). This provides Equation 3.

$$(CMR)(S) = TFC + [NIAT \div (1 - T)]$$

$$S = [TFC + [NIAT \div (1 - T)]] \div CMR$$

Total revenue needed when target nibt is stated as a percentage of sales $: To solve a problem in sales dollars, when the desired net income is stated as a percentage of sales dollars, substitute (R)(S) into Equation for NIBT as follows.

$$(CMR)(S) = TFC + (R)(S)$$

$$S = [TFC + (R)(S)] \div CMR$$

Total revenue needed when target niat is stated as a percentage of sales $: When the desired net income is stated as an after tax rate (R), the equation needed is developed by simply dividing (R)(S) in Equation by (1 – T).

$$(CMR)(S) = TFC + [(R)(S) \div (1 - T)]$$

$$S = [TFC + [(R)(S) \div (1 - T)]] \div CMR$$

To emphasize a point made earlier, it is less confusing visually and also more convenient for computational purposes to leave CMR on the left-hand side of each of the 5 equations initially. Simplify the expressions first, rather than attempting to divide every element on the right-hand side by CMR.

The Cal Company example can be restated in the following manner. Variable costs (including both manuf-acturing and selling and administrative costs) represent sixty per cent of sales dollars. Total fixed costs are $120,000. Assume the board of directors wants the answers to their questions provided in sales dollars rather than units. What amount of sales in dollars does the company need to accomplish each of the following requirements? 1. Break-even. 2. Earn net income before taxes of $40,000. 3.

Earn net income after taxes of $24,000. 4. Earn a 20 per cent return on sales before taxes. 5. Earn a 12 per cent return on sales after taxes. To answer these questions, we need the contribution margin ratio.

The ratio is,

$$CMR = 1 - V/P = 1 -.6 =.4$$

Then, the answers to the five questions are easily obtained as follows. Break even.Using Equation.

$$.4S = 120,000$$

$$S = 120,000 \div .4 = \$30,000$$

Earn net income before taxes of $40,000. Using Equation.

$$.4S = (120,000 + 40,000)$$

$$S = 160,000 \div .4 = \$400,000$$

Earn net income after taxes of $24,000. Using Equation.

$$.4S = 120,000 + (24,000 \div .60)$$

$$.4S = 120,000 + 40,000$$

$$S = 160,000 \div .4 = \$400,000$$

Earn a 20 per cent return on sales before taxes. Using equation

$$.4S = 120,000 + .2S$$

$$.2S = 120,000$$

$$S = 120,000 \div .2 = \$600,000$$

Earn a 12 per cent return on sales after taxes. Using equation

$$.4S = 120,000 + (.12S \div .6)$$

$$.4S = 120,000 + .2S$$

$$.2S = 120,000$$

$$S = 120,000 \div .2 = \$600,000$$

A graphic analysis of this example is also illustrated in Figure since we are simply solving the problem in dollars rather than units. The graph is also useful for comparing the two approaches. Example 11 – 1 places emphasis on the horizontal axis (units) while Example 11 – 2 places emphasis on the vertical axis (dollars).

BREAK-EVEN POINT FOR MULTIPLE PRODUCTS

The same logic used to solve single product problems is applicable to multiple product problems. At the break-even point, total contribution margin is equal to total fixed costs. However, in multiple product situations, total contribution margin is found by multiplying the weighted average contribution margin per unit by the total number of mixed units produced and sold.

The weighted average contribution margin per unit is calculated by multiplying each product's contribution margin per unit (Pi – Vi) by the mix ratio applicable to that product (Mi) and then summing the results. The mix ratios (Mi's) represent the weights. The equation is,

$$W = E\,[(Pi\text{-}Vi)(Mi)]$$

The break-even equation for mixed units (X) is stated in the following manner.

$$WX = TFC$$

After the total mixed units (X) have been determined, then the number of units of the individual products are found by multiplying the total mixed units by each product's mix ratio.

$$Xi = X(Mi)$$

Units Needed For Target Net Income Before Taxes: The equation for mixed units needed to generate a desired amount of net income before taxes is developed by simply adding NIBT to the right hand side of Equation.

$$WX = TFC + NIBT$$

Units needed for target net income after taxes: The equation for mixed units needed to generate a desired after tax profit is developed by substituting NIAT ÷ (1 – T) for NIBT.

$$WX = TFC + [NIAT \div (1 - T)]$$

When Target Net Income Before Taxes Is Stated As A Percentage Of Sales $

Using R to represent the target rate of return on sale dollars before taxes, *i.e.*, R = NIBT÷TR, the following equation can be used to find the mixed units needed.

$$WX = TFC + (R)(YX)$$

Sales dollars are represented by the term YX. Since total sales dollars are mixed, we must multiply the total mixed units (X) by a weighted average price (Y) to find the total mixed sales dollars. Then, multiplying the term YX by R represents the desired NIBT. The weighted average price (Y) is found by multiplying the price of each product (Pi) by the product mix ratios (Mi) and then summing the results, *i.e.*, Y = E (Pi)(Mi).

When Target Net Income After Taxes Is Stated As A Percentage Of Sales $ The appropriate equation for after tax net income is found by dividing the term [(R)(YX], in Equation 4, by 1 – T.

$$WX = TFC + [(R)(YX) \div (1 - T)]$$

Remember that it is usually best for computational purposes to leave the amount represented by W on the left hand side in each of the equations until the expression on the right hand side has been simplified. Also remember that the units for individual products (Xi) are always found by multiplying the total mixed units (X) by the mix ratios (Mi) for each product.

The Sandlot Cap Company produces baseball caps in two categories referred to as regular logo and special logo. Caps in the regular logo category are high volume products that display familiar names of universities and professional sports teams. Caps in the special design category are typically created for a particular customer to promote special events such as the Olympics, or the opening of a unique museum exhibit. For convenience we will refer to the regular logo caps as product X1 and the special logo caps as product X2. Sales prices and variable costs are provided below.

Product	Price	Variable Cost PerUnit	Mix Ratio Based on Units
X1	$4	$3	.75
X2	8	5	.25

The variable costs for each product include direct materials and conversion costs of $2. Marketing costs account for an additional $1 for regular logo caps and $3 for special logo caps. As indicated above, three quarters of the company's unit sales are represented by regular logo caps, while the other one quarter represents special logo caps. The company's total fixed costs are $300,000. Sandlot Cap Company management wants to know how many caps need to be produced and sold to accomplish the following:

- Break even.
- Earn desired net income before taxes of $60,000.
- Earn desired net income after taxes of $36,000 given the tax rate is 40 per cent.
- Earn desired net income before taxes equal to 15 per cent of sales dollars.
- Earn a desired net income after taxes equal to 9 per cent of sales dollars.

To solve this problem we need to calculate the weighted average contribution margin per unit, *i.e.*, the contribution margin per mixed unit.

$$W = (4\text{-}3)(.75) + (8 - 5)(.25) = 1.5$$

The mix ratios (.75 and.25) are used as the weights to reflect the fact that the company normally sells three times as many X1's as X2's. After obtaining the weighted average contribution of $1.50, then 1.5X represents the total contribution margin on the lefthand side of each equation. To break-even. Using Equation

$$1.5X = 300,000$$

$$X = 300,000 \div 1.5 = 200,000 \text{ Total mixed units.}$$

$$X1 = (200,000)(.75) = 150,000 \text{ units}$$

$$X2 = (200,000)(.25) = 50,000 \text{ units}$$

To earn $60,000 net income before taxes. Using Equation

$$1.5X = 300,000 + 60,000$$

$$1.5X = 360,000$$

$$X = 360,000 \div 1.5 = 240,000 \text{ mixed units}$$

$$X1 = (240,000)(.75) = 180,000 \text{ units}$$

$$X2 = (240,000)(.25) = 60,000 \text{ units}$$

To earn \$36,000 net income after taxes. Using Equation

$$1.5X = 300{,}000 + (36{,}000 \div .6)$$

$$1.5X = 300{,}000 + 60{,}000$$

$$X = 360{,}000 \div 1.5 = 240{,}000 \text{ mixed units}$$

$$X1 = (240{,}000)(.75) = 180{,}000 \text{ units}$$

$$X2 = (240{,}000)(.25) = 60{,}000 \text{ units}$$

In the last two requirements, income is stated as a percentage of sales dollars. Therefore, we need the YX measure of total mixed sales dollars to indicate the desired amount of income. Total mixed sales dollars is the weighted average price Y, multiplied by the mixed units X. To calculate Y we must use the unit mix ratios as weights to reflect the importance of each product in the price.

$$Y = 4(.75) + 8(.25) = \$5$$

Then, \$5 represents the weighted average price and 5X represents the total mixed sales dollars. To earn before tax net income equal to 15 per cent of sales dollars, we substitute.15(5X) in the equation for desired income, *i.e.*, R(YX). Then using Equation

$$1.5X = 300{,}000 + .15(5X)$$

$$1.5X = 300{,}000 + .75X$$

$$.75X = 300{,}000$$

$$X = 300{,}000 \div .75 = 400{,}000 \text{ mixed units}$$

$$X1 = .75(400{,}000) = 300{,}000 \text{ units}$$

$$X2 = .25(400{,}000) = 100{,}000 \text{ units}$$

To earn after tax net income equal to 9 per cent of sales dollars, the desired income is,

$$(R)(YX) \div 1 - T, \text{ or } (.09)(5X) \div (1 - .4).$$

Then using Equation

$$1.5X = 300{,}000 + [(.09)(5X) \div (1 - .4)]$$

$$1.5X = 300{,}000 + [.45X \div .6]$$

$$1.5X = 300{,}000 + .75X$$

$$.75X = 300{,}000$$

$$X = 300{,}000 \div .75 = 400{,}000 \text{ mixed units}$$

$$X1 = .75(400{,}000) = 300{,}000 \text{ units}$$

$$X2 = .25(400{,}000) = 100{,}000 \text{ units}$$

After Tax Equations As An Alternative

A graphic analysis of the Sandlot Cap Company example appears in Figure.

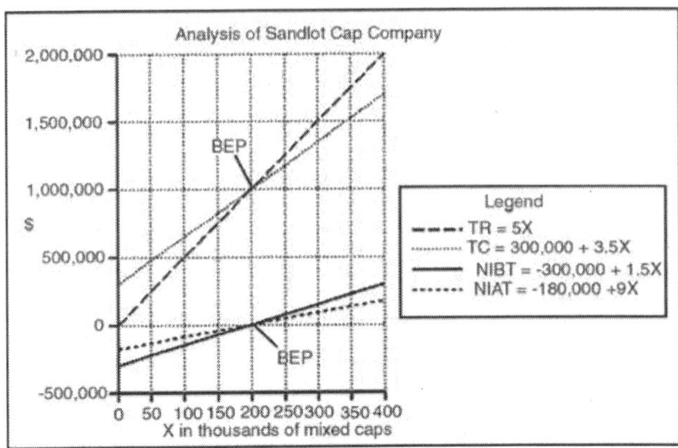

The equation for NIAT illustrated in the graph is found by multiplying the equation for NIBT by (1-T), *i.e.*, (1-.4)(-300,000) + (1-.4)(1.5X) = -180,000 +.9X. Rearranging this equation we have.9X = 180,000 + NIAT where.9X is the weighted average contribution margin after taxes. We can use this equation as an alternative way to find the answers to question as follows.

Earn desired net income after taxes of $36,000.

$$.9X = 180,000 + 36,000$$

$$.9X = 216,000$$

$$X = 216,000 \div .9 = 240,000 \text{ mixed units}$$

Earn desired net income after taxes equal to 9 per cent of sales dollars.

$$.9X = 180,000 + .09(5X)$$

$$.9X = 180,000 + .45X$$

$$.45X = 180,000$$

$$X = 180,000 \div .45 = 400,000 \text{ mixed units}$$

Solving Multiple Product CVP Problems in Dollars

Number	Equation	Used To Determine
[1]	WCMR(S) = TFC	Sales $ at break-even point.
[2]	WCMR(S) = TFC + NIBT	Sales $ for target NIBT.
[3]	WCMR(S) = TFC + [NIAT ÷ (1-T)]	Sales $ for target NIAT.
[4]	WCMR(S) = TFC + (R)(S)	Sales $ for target NIBT stated as a proportion (R) of sales $.
[5]	WCMR(S) = TFC + [(R)(S) ÷ (1-T)]	Sales $ for target NIAT stated as a proportion (R) of sales $.
	Si = S(M$i)	Sales dollars for each product after S is obtained.

The following additional symbols are used to develop this section:

- S = Total mixed sales dollars.
- Si = Sales dollars for product i.
- CMRi = Contribution margin ratio for product i.
- M$i = The mix ratio for product i based on sales dollars. Note, these ratios are not equal to the mix ratio based on units.
- WCMR = The weighted average contribution margin ratio.

$$WCMR= E(CMRi)(M\$i)$$

Break-even Point In Sales Dollars For Multiple Products: The same basic conceptual logic used in the previous sections is used to develop the equations in this section. The firm breaks even when total contribution margin is equal to total fixed costs.

$$(WCMR)(S) = TFC$$

The difference between the equations for single product and multiproduct situations is that we must use a weighted average contribution margin ratio, WCMR = E(CMRi)(M$I) to find the total mixed sales dollars. Then sales dollars for the individual products are found by multiplying the total mixed sales dollars (S) by the mix ratios for each product, Si = (S)(M$I)

Total Revenue Needed For Target Net Income Before Taxes Equation is developed in the usual manner by simply adding the desired amount of NIBT to the right hand side of Equation.

$$(WCMR)(S) = TFC + NIBT$$

Total Revenue Needed For Target Net Income After Taxes Revising the previous equation to include after tax profit we have:

$$(WCMR)(S) = TFC + [NIAT \div (1 - T)]$$

When Target Net Income Before Taxes Is Stated As A Percentage Of Sales $ If R is used as the before tax target rate of return on sales, *i.e.*, NIBT÷S, then the equation needed to achieve the target return before taxes is:

$$(WCMR)(S) = TFC + (R)(S)$$

When Target Net Income After Taxes Is Stated As A Percentage Of Sales $ If R is used as the after tax target rate of return on sales, *i.e.*, NIAT÷S, the equation becomes,

$$(WCMR)(S) = TFC + [(R)(S) \div (1 - T)]$$

Suppose the Sandlot Cap Company information is provided to you in the following format.

Product	**Contribution Margin Ratios**	**Mix Ratios Based on Sales Dollars**
X1	.25	.6
X2	.375	.4

TFC = \$300,000. Sandlot Cap Company management wants to know the amount of sales dollars needed for each product to accomplish the same five objectives.

- Break even.
- Earn desired net income before taxes of \$60,000.
- Earn desired net income after taxes of \$36,000. Assume the tax rate is 40 per cent.
- Earn desired net income before taxes equal to 15 per cent of sales dollars.
- Earn a desired net income after taxes equal to 9 per cent of sales dollars.

To find the answers we need to start by calculating the weighted average contribution margin ratio.

$$\text{WCMR} = (.25)(.60) + (.375)(.40) = .30$$

The mix ratios stated in dollars are used as the weights. Then the solutions are obtained as follows: To break even. Using Equation

$$.3S = 300,000$$

$$S = 300,000 \div .3 = \$1,000,000$$

$$S1 = (1,000,000)(.6) = \$600,000$$

$$S2 = (1,000,000)(.4) = 400,000$$

To earn \$60,000 before taxes. Using Equation

$$.3S = 300,000 + 60,000$$

$$S = 360,000 \div .3 = \$1,200,000$$

$$S1 = (1,200,000)(.6) = \$720,000$$

$$S2 = (1,200,000)(.4) = 480,000$$

To earn \$36,000 after taxes. Using Equation

$$.3S = 300,000 + (36,000 \div .6)$$

$$S = 360,000 \div .3 = \$1,200,000$$

$$S1 = (\$1,200,000)(.6) = \$720,000$$

$$S2 = (\$1,200,000)(.4) = 480,000$$

To earn desired NIBT of 15 per cent of sales dollars. Using Equation

$$.3S = 300,000 + .15S$$

$$.15S = 300,000$$

$$S = 300,000 \div .15 = \$2,000,000$$

$$S1 = (\$2,000,000)(.6) = \$1,200,000$$

$$S2 = (\$2,000,000)(.4) = 800,000$$

To earn desired NIAT of 9 per cent of sales dollars. Using Equation

$$.3S = 300{,}000 + (.09S \div .6)$$
$$.15S = 300{,}000$$
$$S = 300{,}000 \div .15 = \$2{,}000{,}000$$
$$S1 = (\$2{,}000{,}000)(.6) = \$1{,}200{,}000$$
$$S2 = (\$2{,}000{,}000)(.4) = 800{,}000$$

The solutions to these five questions are also illustrated in Figure since we simply changed our emphasis from the horizontal axis (units) to the vertical axis (dollars).

The mix ratios determine whether the emphasis is on units or dollars and the manner in which the answers must be obtained.

If the mix ratios are stated in units, as in Example 11-4, then the solutions must be obtained in units.

If the mix ratios are stated in dollars, as in Example 11-5, then the solutions must be obtained in dollars. Why? To see why we cannot use the mix ratios interchangeably, suppose the Sandlot Cap Company data were stated in the following manner.

Product	Price	Variable Cost per Unit	Mix Ratios Based on Sales Dollars
X1	$4	$3	.6
X2	8	5	.4

Total fixed costs = $300,000. Now, find the break-even point in units. Try this, at least mentally before you look at the solution in the footnote below. Now suppose Sandlot Cap Company management gave you following information and asks for the break-even point. TFC is still $300,000. What would you do?

Product	Contribution MarginRatios	Mix Ratios Based on Units
X1	.25	.75
X2	.375	.25

Think about it and then consult the footnote below. *The Cash Flow Break-even Point*: Since some of the fixed costs do not require cash payments (*e.g.*, depreciation), the cash flow break-even point will be below the conventional accrual accounting break-even point. The following

Cash Flow Break-even Before Taxes: The cash flow break-even point is where the cash inflows before taxes are equal to the cash outflows before taxes. This is presented in equation form below.

$$PX = TFC + VX - \text{Non cash Fixed Costs}$$

$$PX - VX = TFC - \text{Non- cash Fixed Costs}$$

$$(P - V)\,X = TFC - \text{Non- cash Fixed Costs}$$

The equation above is based on the assumption that all other costs are paid for during the period and that all sales dollars are collected during the period.

Cash Flow Break-even After Taxes: The cash flow break-even point after taxes is where the cash inflows after taxes are equal to the cash outflows after taxes. We simply convert the contribution margin and total fixed costs to an after tax basis by multiplying by 1-T. The equation is as follows:

$$(1 - T)(P - V)X = (1\ 2\ T)(TFC) - \text{Non- cash Fixed Costs}$$

Example: Cal Company's specifics from Example 11-1 are P = \$10, V = \$6, total fixed costs = \$120,000 and the tax rate is 40 per cent. If depreciation is \$24,000 and there are no other non- cash fixed costs, then the cash flow break-even point after taxes is:

$$(1 - .4)(4X) = (1 - .4)(120,000) - 24,000$$

$$2.4X = 72,000 - 24,000$$

$$X = 48,000 \div 2.4 = 20,000 \text{ units}$$

The solution is verified in Figure below.

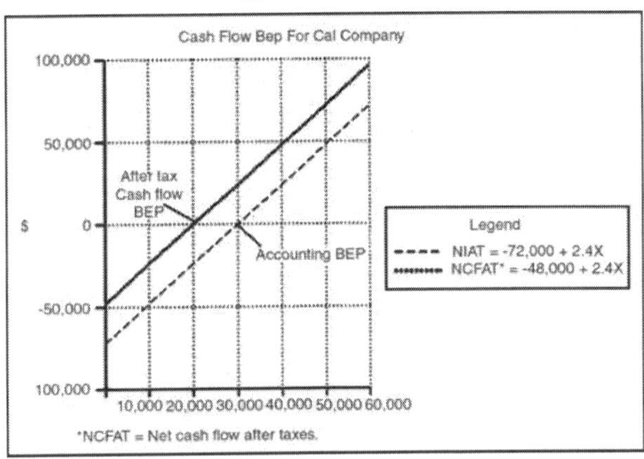

Table. Income Statement Showing Calculation of Company's Cash Flow Break-even Point.

Sales	₹
(20,000)(\$10)	\$200,000
Variable Costs (20,000)(\$6)	120,000
Contribution Margin	80,000
Less Total Fixed Costs	120,000
Net Loss	(40,000)
Add Tax Reduction(.4)(40,000)	16,000
Add back Depreciation	24,000
Cash Flow after taxes	0

We can also use the equation above to calculate the number of units needed to generate a desired amount of net cash inflow after taxes. Just add the desired amount and solve for X. For example, suppose management desires a net cash inflow after taxes of $36,000.

$$2.4X = 48{,}000 + 36{,}000$$

$$X = 84{,}000 \div 2.4 = 35{,}000 \text{ units}$$

Check: (35,000units)($4) = 140,000 contribution margin. Subtract fixed cost of $120,000, then multiply by.6 and we have $12,000 NIAT. Add back depreciation of 24,000 to obtain $36,000.

The Controversy Over The Contribution Margin Approach. There are two issues that involve the contribution margin approach and the closely related direct (or variable) costing inventory valuation method. The first issue is a relatively old controversy over whether direct costing or full absorption costing is the most useful way to present accounting information. The second issue questions the compatibility of the contribution margin approach to activity based costing and the lean enterprise concepts of just-in-time and the theory of constraints.

The second issue questions the wisdom of separating costs into fixed and variable categories. The following discussion concentrates on the second controversy. We will return to the first issue in the next chapter.

The Case Against

From the activity based costing perspective, critics of the contribution margin approach argue that the costs traditionally defined as fixed costs have been increasing faster than the costs traditionally defined as variable costs. As a result, the CVP model does not reflect the cost structure of complex, multiproduct organizations.

Although the CVP model may be useful for some short term forecasting and optimization decisions, it is misleading for decisions such as product introduction, product pricing, product mix and make versus buy. The so-called fixed costs are not explained by output volume, but by the diversity and complexity of the company's products, services, customers, distribution channels and product lines. The CVP approach is flawed because it assumes that the volume of production is the only cost driver. As a result, the model motivates managers to produce as much as possible to lower total unit cost. It encourages managers to add new products and services ignoring the "overhead creep" that inevitably results It supports the misguided view that the company should never drop a part of the business as long as that part generates a positive contribution margin.

But this signal to constantly expand is a trap because the costs that are assumed to be constant, increase rapidly instead, in response to the greater demands that are placed on the various support activities. As the so-called fixed costs rise, the manager attempts to add more volume to lower unit cost again. The process is somewhat analogous to a dog chasing it's tail.

From the lean enterprise, or continuous improvement perspective, the contribution margin approach emphasizes maximizing output with a static set of constraints, rather than emphasizing the continuous improvement of the company's value creating processes and activities. The contribution margin approach has the same basic defect as any other constrained optimization technique. It promotes short run optimization within a static system.

However, from the viewpoint of the lean enterprise concepts of just-in-time and the theory of constraints, becoming competitive and maintaining competitiveness in the long run requires a dynamic learning organization. The emphasis should be on relentlessly eliminating waste, removing constraints, re-engineering processes when necessary and increasing customer value, not on maximizing output in an attempt to minimize short run unit costs.

MARGIN OF SAFETY

Table. Summary Equations For Solving Multiple Product Cvp Problems In Units

Number	Equation	Used To Determine
[1]	WX = TFC	Total mixed units at the BEP.
[2]	WX = TFC + NIBT	Total mixed units for target NIBT.
[3]	WX = TFC + [NIAT ÷ (1-T)]	Total mixed units for target NIAT.
[4]	WX = TFC + (R)(YX)	Total mixed units for target NIBT stated as a proportion (R) of sales $.
[5]	WX = TFC + [(R)(YX) ÷ (1-T)]	Total mixed units for target NIAT stated as a proportion (R) of sales $.
	Xi = X(Mi)	The number of units of each product after X is obtained.

Before we move on to multiproduct companies, there is a handy concept referred to as the margin of safety that you might find useful. The margin of safety (MS) for any sales level represents the amount of sales dollars above or below the break-even point. Mathematically, the margin of safety is:

$$MS = Sales\$ - Break\text{-}even\ sales\$$$

When sales are above the break-even point, the margin of safety is positive. When sales are below the break-even point, the margin of safety is negative. After determining the MS for a particular sales level, Equations can be used to make some quick calculations.

$$NIBT = (MS)(CMR)$$

Solving Equation 6 provides the amount of contribution margin above the break-even point (when MS is positive) and this amount represents the net income (or loss if the MS is negative) before taxes.

Why? Because after the total fixed costs have been covered, additional contribution margin represents the before tax profit.

Before the fixed cost have been covered the additional contribution needed represents the before tax loss.

The equation for after tax profit is,

$$NIAT = (MS)(CMR)(1 - T)$$

Suppose we are in a board of directors meeting and a board member asks how much income would Cal Company generate at a particular sales level. For convenience let's say $1,000,000.

Using the margin of safety we can answer this question quickly. Since we already know the break-even point is $300,000, then the margin of safety is 1,000,000 - 300,000 = $700,000.

Using Equation,

$$NIBT = (700{,}000)(.4) = \$280{,}000.$$

Using Equation,

$$NIAT = (700{,}000)(.4)(.6) = \$168{,}000.$$

To show that the margin of safety calculations work on either side of the break-even point, consider another example. Suppose someone ask, how much income would Cal Company generate when total revenue is only $200,000?

MS = 200,000 – 300,000 = –100,000, *i.e.*, $100,000 below the BEP

Using Equation

$$NIBT = (-100{,}000)(.4) = -40{,}000 \text{ net loss before taxes,}$$

or Using Equation

$$NIAT = (-40{,}000)(.6) = -24{,}000 \text{ net loss after taxes.}$$

Solving Multiple Product Cvp Problems In Units Some additional symbols are needed to illustrate the algebraic techniques applicable to multiple product problems. The following symbols are used below:

- i = The number designating a particular product.
- Pi = The price of product i.
- Vi = The variable cost per unit of product i.
- X = Total mixed units sold, *i.e.*, includes all products.
- Xi = Units of product i sold.
- Mi = The mix ratio for product i, *i.e.*, the proportion that product i represents out of the total number of units sold.
- E = Sigma or summation sign which means "the sum of".
- W = Weighted average contribution margin per unit = E [(Pi-Vi)(Mi)]
- Y = The weighted average price = E (Pi)(Mi)

A summary of the cost volume profit relationships for multiproduct problems is presented in Exhibit 11-3. The five equations are comparable to the single product equations presented in Exhibit 11-1, but are somewhat more involved. Each equation is developed and illustrated below,

COST-EFFECTIVENESS ANALYSIS

Cost-effectiveness analysis (CEA) is a technique for selecting among competing wants wherever resources are limited. Developed in the military, CEA was first applied to health care in the mid-1960s and was introduced with enthusiasm to clinicians by Weinstein and Stason in 1977:

- "If these approaches were to become widely understood and accepted by the key decision makers in the health-care sector, including the physician, important health benefits or cost savings might be realised."

Regardless of whether this hope was realised, CEA has since become a common feature in medical literature.

THE BASICS OF CEA

CEA is a technique for comparing the relative value of various clinical strategies. In its most common form, a new strategy is compared with current practice in the calculation of the cost-effectiveness ratio:

$$\text{CE ratio} = \frac{\cos t_{\text{new strategy}} - \cos t_{\text{currentpractice}}}{\text{effect}_{\text{new strategy}} - \text{effect}_{\text{current pratice}}}$$

The result might be considered as the "price" of the additional outcome purchased by switching from current practice to the new strategy. If the price is low enough, the new strategy is considered "cost-effective." It's important to carefully consider exactly what that statement means. If a strategy is dubbed "cost-effective" and the term is used as its creators intended, it means that the new strategy is a good value. Note that being cost-effective does not mean that the strategy saves money, and just because a strategy saves money doesn't mean that it is cost-effective.

Also note that the very notion of cost-effective requires a value judgement—what you think is a good price for an additional outcome, someone else may not. It's also worthwhile to recognize that CEA is only relevant to certain decisions. The various way a new strategy might compare with an existing approach. Note that a CEA is relevant only if a new strategy is *both* more effective and more costly.

TRANSACTION COSTS

Transaction costs are commissions and processing charges incurred as part of a business transaction. In some cases, this transaction cost is a percentage of the total sale. In other cases, it may be a flat fee. In general, the money spent on the transaction costs is often referred to as a *spread*. Understanding transaction costs is very important for anyone who is looking to buy or sell any financial product, whether it is stocks, bonds, currency or valuable metals. It does not matter whether you are buying or selling assets, transaction costs can be incurred in a number of different situations. It is important to read all policies and agreements of the company executing the transaction in order to have full awareness of which transaction costs you may incur. One of the most common types of transaction costs is the buy/sell spread.

While they can go by several different names, spreads are the costs that an investment manager charges to execute a transaction. To provide a real-world example, let's assume the currency exchange rate is $2 US Dollar for every 1 Euro. Though someone may expect to get 5 Euros if they pay $10 USD, it is likely that he will receive somewhat less than that. Why is it that a trader may get less than the published rate? Because of the buy/sell spread. The person or agency executing the trade takes out a cut in order to provide the service. The amount charged for that service will likely be different, depending on the person or firm.

Some firms will actually use their transaction costs as an incentive to attract customers. If an investment firm has a competitive rate in their transaction costs, this can lead to a substantial cost savings for an investor, especially if that investor executes a large number of trades as a general practice. Though it is not as prevalent as it once was, several trading firms specializing in online trades advertise their transaction costs regularly.

TOTAL COST

In economics, and cost accounting, total cost describes the total economic cost of production and is made up of variable costs, which vary just as to the quantity of a good produced and include inputs such as labour and raw materials, plus fixed costs, which are independent of the quantity of a good produced and include inputs that cannot be varied in the short term, such as buildings and machinery. Total cost in economics includes the total opportunity cost of each factor of production in addition to fixed and variable costs. The rate at which total cost changes as the amount produced changes is called marginal cost. This is also known as the marginal unit variable cost. If one assumes that the unit variable cost is constant, as in cost-volume-profit analysis developed and used in cost accounting by the accountants, then total cost is linear in volume, and given by: total cost = fixed costs + unit variable cost * amount.

SUNK COSTS

Sunk costs are sums that have already been spent and can not be recovered. The concept is important because sunk costs are irrelevant to financial decisions. Many people tend to feel instinctively that because an investment has been made it is necessary to get a return on it. This can lead to people rejecting one course of action in favour of another that actually generates smaller cash flows.

This can happen to business, portfolio investment and personal decisions. Suppose a hotel has calculated that their cost for providing a room is £100 per night, of which £50 covers their rental of the building and £20 covers their other fixed costs and £30 covers the costs that result from having an extra guest. Now suppose the market rate for hotel rooms goes down and they are only able to charge £50 per night.

The hotel is committed to remaining open. It appears that the hotel will make a £50 loss on each night per guest so they should not accept bookings until prices rise. Of course this is wrong as the rent and other fixed costs are already committed to and have to be paid anyway.

The hotel should accept bookings at any price it can get above £30, as these make a positive contribution. A common mistake made by investors is reluctance to sell securities at a loss. It does not matter what you paid for shares, if the market price has fallen you have already made that loss. It is a sunk cost and should be forgotten about. What matters is whether the shares are worth holding or not at the current market price. A key question is whether the shares would still be worth buying at current prices. If not, they are probably not worth holding.

SEMI-VARIABLE COSTS

Semi-variable costs are those that have both fixed cost and variable cost elements. For example, a manufacturer's electricity bill may include elements that are fixed and elements that are variable.

SEARCH COST

Search costs are one facet of transaction costs or switching costs. Rational consumers will continue to search for a better product or service until the marginal cost of searching exceeds the marginal benefit. Search theory is a branch of microeconomics that studies decisions of this type. The costs of searching are divided into external and internal costs. External costs include the monetary costs of acquiring the information, and the opportunity cost of the time taken up in searching.

External costs are not under the consumer's control. All they can do is choose whether or not to incur them. Internal costs include the mental effort given over to undertaking the search, sorting the incoming information, and integrating it with what the consumer already knows. Internal costs are determined by the consumer's ability to undertake the search, and this in turn depends on intelligence, prior knowledge, education and training. These internal costs are the background to the study of bounded rationality. The Internet was expected to eliminate search costs. For example, electronic commerce was predicted to cause disintermediation as search costs become low enough for end-consumers to incur them directly instead of employing retailers to do this for them. This would in turn lead to lower prices and less variation between prices quoted by different sellers.

ABSORPTION COSTING

Absorption costing is a method for appraising or valuing a firm's total inventory by including all the manufacturing costs incurred to produce those goods. These manufacturing costs include.

Product Costs

- *Direct Materials*: These are the raw materials such as wood, metal, bricks, etc that are used in order to create a finished usable good which will be demanded by the market.
- *Direct Labour*: Direct Labour is the manwork and total factory hours put behind assembling the raw materials, creating the finished good, etc.
- *Fixed Manufacturing Overhead*: This includes expenses such as rent of factory where the raw materials are turned into finished goods, amortization of factory building, utilities, etc.
- *Variable Manufacturing Overhead*: These are the general and administrative expenses in the manufacturing process.

Absorption costing is different from the other costing methods because it takes into account fixed manufacturing overhead. It is hard to factor in the fixed manufacturing overhead expenses into calculating the per unit price of goods, therefore other methods such as Variable Costing do not take it into account. One drawback of absorption costing is that managers can increase production levels without taking into account total sales. With higher production levels, this year's expenses can be deferred to next year, thus lowering this year's costs. What does this mean? The managers get a fat bonus and pay raises thanks to more "profits."

Inventory Production and Absorption Costing

When beginning inventory and ending inventory levels are different, profit calculations using the Absorption costing can be difficult. Here are the effects of fluctuating inventory levels:

- If Beginning Inventory = Ending Inventory, then Absorption Costing = Variable Costing.
- If Inventory Levels = Low, then Variable Costing Profit > Absorption Costing Profit.

- If Inventory Levels = High, then Absorption Costing Profit >Variable Costing Profit.

REPUGNANCY COSTS

Repugnancy costs are costs borne by an individual or entity as a result of a stimulus that goes against that individual or entity's cultural mores. The cost could be emotional, physical, mental or figurative. The stimulus could be anything from food to people to an idea. These costs are perspective-dependent and individual. These costs may be different for different groups of people; countries, states, ethnicities, etc. The term allows for a clear and understandable way of representing the concept of contextual stigma in a literal and applicable sense.

QUALITY COST

Quality cost is the sum of all costs a company invests into the release of a quality product. When developing a software product, there are four types of quality costs: prevention costs, appraisal costs, internal failure costs, and external failure costs.

- Prevention costs represent everything a company spends to prevent software errors, documentation errors, and other product-related errors. These include requirements and usability analysis, for example. Dollars spent on prevention costs are the most effective quality dollars, because preventing errors from getting into the product is much cheaper than fixing errors later. If there is an error in a requirement or the intended usability, and money is spent on developing the software to the erroneous requirement, the costs of identifying the error, determining how to fix it, and then developing new code to correct it will arise later.
- Appraisal costs include the money spent on the actual testing activity. Any and all activities associated with searching for errors in the software and associated product materials falls into this category. This includes all testing: by the developers themselves, by an internal test team, and by an outsourced software test organization. This also includes all associated hardware, software, labour, and other costs. Once a product is in the coding phases, the goal is to do the most effective appraisal job, so that internal failure work is streamlined and well-managed and prevents skyrocketing external failure costs.
- Internal failure costs are the costs of coping with errors discovered during development and testing. These are bugs found before the product is released. The further in the development process the errors are discovered, the more costly they are to fix. So the later the errors are discovered, the higher their associated internal failure costs will be.

- External failure costs are the costs of coping with errors discovered after the product is released. These are typically errors found by your customers. These costs can be much higher than internal failure costs, because the stakes are much higher. These costs include post-release customer and technical support. Errors at this stage can also be costly in terms of your company's reputation and may lead to lost customers.

The Four Categories of Quality Costs

All the costs can be effectively reduced through smarter test efforts that include a high degree of test automation. Test automation when done right leads to greater test coverage, resulting in higher-quality products. Higher-quality products require less technical support, fewer patches, and lead to greater customer satisfaction. Smarter automated testing also speeds up the release process and incrementally reduces the manual test costs.

But most of all, more test coverage gives you and your customers more confidence in your product. You will feel more comfortable knowing that there are not bugs lurking in your software that have not been exposed yet because of insufficient test coverage.

You will also not have to scramble at the last minute to deal with a problem and fix it to your customer's satisfaction in a rush. The solution to quality cost problems is to get a better understanding of your investment in product quality and manage your costs better. The first place most organizations look for a better understanding is in the highest cost area: the software test effort or lack thereof. For example, if you do not test at all, your testing or appraisal cost is low.

You will ship on time but your external failure costs will skyrocket. Your prevention and appraisal costs will result in finding errors that can be corrected while they are still internal failures, where they are cheaper to deal with than when they are external failures. The goal of understanding quality costs is to analyse where you spend your time and money to get the most bang for the buck.

It is well known that it is faster and cheaper to find and fix a bug during unit testing done by developers early in the development cycle. Should we then spend most of our time/budget on unit testing? No. here are many limitations to unit testing. Unit testing is not capable of finding many varieties of bugs, including graphical user interface (GUI) bugs, usability problems, end-to-end bugs, and configuration bugs.

For most organizations, getting a better unit test effort will help you release a better product sooner. It is not a replacement for the test effort done by skilled software testers, but it may reduce the time that test effort takes. Understanding quality costs will hopefully help you shift some of your test effort to the most cost-effective places.

The total quality cost is shown in the upper bathtub-shaped curve. On the bottom axis is the quality of performance, ranging from totally defective to zero defects. On the left axis is the cost per good unit of product. You can see that with highly defective software, your prevention and appraisal costs are very low, but your failure costs are very high, yielding a high total quality cost. With zero defect software, likewise, your failure costs are very low, but your prevention and appraisal costs are very high. To optimize your total quality costs, you want to be between these extremes, at the bottom of the bathtub curve.

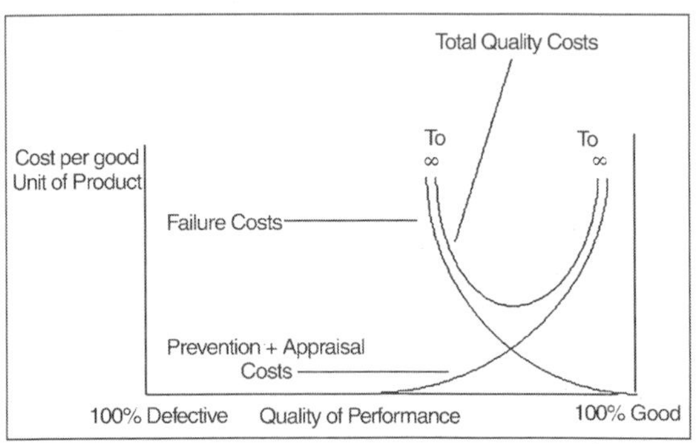

The Oretical Model of Optimum Quality Cost

This offers two challenges: First, a sufficiently sophisticated accounting system allowing a typical mid-sized company to track the total cost of quality has yet to be developed. To optimize total quality cost, you need to have the appropriate categories in your accounting system and keep track of the related costs. Second, you need to be able to track your external quality costs. You may not even have enough information from customers on why the software is not working for them.

How are you going to know what to book into your accounting system for external failure costs? The point here is that while capturing this data is difficult and expensive, you know that the benefit is reducing your overall cost of quality. You need to determine if the benefits of tracking your total quality cost will give you enough of a return on investment to make setting up the appropriate accounting system and paying for the implementation of the programme worthwhile.

ECONOMIC COST

The economic cost of a decision depends on both the cost of the alternative chosen and the benefit that the best alternative would have provided if chosen. Economic cost differs from accounting cost because it includes opportunity cost. As an example, consider the economic cost of attending college. The accounting cost of attending college includes tuition, room and board, books, food, and other incidental expenditures while there. The opportunity cost of college also includes the salary or wage that otherwise could be earning during the period. So for the two to four years an individual spends in school, the opportunity cost includes the money that one could have been making at the best possible job.

The economic cost of college is the accounting cost plus the opportunity cost. Thus, if attending college has a direct cost of $20,000 dollars a year for four years, and the lost wages from not working during that period equals $25,000 dollars a year, then the total economic cost of going to college would be $180,000 dollars ($20,000 x 4 years + $25,000 x 4 years).

ISOCOST

In economics an isocost line represents a combination of inputs which all cost the same amount. Although similar to the budget constraint in consumer theory, the use of the isocost pertains to cost-minimization in production, as opposed to utility-maximization. The typical isocost line represents the ratio of costs of labour and capital, so the formula is often written as.

$$rK + wL = C$$

Where w represents the wage of labour, and r represents the rental rate of capital. The slope is:

$$-w/r$$

or the negative ratio of wages divided by rental fees.

The isocost line is combined with the isoquant line to determine the optimal production point.

The Cost Function for a Firm with Two Variable Inputs

Consider a firm that uses two inputs and has the production function F. This firm minimizes its cost of producing any given output y if it chooses the pair (z1, z2) of inputs to solve the problem Min z1,z2w1s conditional input demand functions. The firm's minimal cost of producing the output y is w1z1*(y,w1, w2) + w2z2*(y,w1, w2) (the value of its total cost for the values of z1 and z2 that minimize that cost). The function TC defined by

$$TC(y,w1,w2) = w1z1 * (y,w1,w2) + w2z2 * (y,w1,w2)$$

Which is called the firm's (total) cost function. (Note that the hard part of the problem is finding the conditional input demands; once you have found these, then finding the cost function is simply a matter of adding the conditional input ogether with the weights w1 and w2.). An Isocost line shows all the combinations of capital and labour that can be bought for a given total cost"

LOCK-IN (DECISION-MAKING)

Lock-in can be seen as the escalating commitment of decision-makers to an ineffective course of action. It concerns institutional lock-in as compared to technical lock-in of which the QWERTY keyboard is a famous example. The decision-making process is characterised by various informal and formal decision-making moments and decision-makers can become committed to the project before the formal decision to build was taken.

The formation of commitment is not necessarily bad, but when commitment turns into lock-in, it has by definition a negative influence on the project performance. Lock-in can occur at the decision-making level or at the project level. There are possibilities to avoid lock-in when decision-makers can be made aware of this phenomenon. However, lock-in can also be used intentionally, in which case, it is much more difficult to prevent and hence manage cost overruns.

Decision Making Process

The decision-making process of large infrastructure projects is marked by the formal decision to build the project. However, there are several possible moments in the decision-making process before the formal decision is taken at which decision-makers are committed to the project.

The extent of which decision-makers are committed to the project is of importance here. Early commitment, commitment to the project before the formal decision to build has been taken, is in itself not necessarily negative. It could be advantageous to the decision-making process as it could enforce a decision.

This eventually could limit delay and contribute to the projects' performance. Early commitment can result in negative outcomes once the commitment turns into escalating commitment and lock-in. As lock-in is based on escalating commitment, it has, by definition, a negative influence on project performance. Lock-in has the potential to explain the large cost overruns in large scale transportation infrastructure projects.

Formation

Lock-in with respect to decision-making is created when sub-optimal policies are used as a consequence of *e.g.* path dependency, even though a better alternative is present. The term refers to the escalating commitment of decision-makers to an ineffective course of action. Escalating commitment itself refers to the style of psychological coping associated with the inability to withdraw from obligations. The process of escalating commitment is also known as "entrapment", the "sunk-cost effect", the "knee-deep in the big muddy" effect, and the "too-much-invested-to-quit" effect.

Occurrence

Lock-in can occur both at the decision-making level and can influence the extent of overruns in two ways:

- The first involves the "methodology" of calculating cost overruns just as to the "formal decision to build". Due to lock-in, however, the "real decision to build" is made much earlier in the decision-making process and the costs estimated at that stage are often much lower than those that are estimated at a later stage in the decision-making process, thus increasing cost overruns.

- The second way that lock-in can affect cost overruns is through "practice". Although decisions about the project need to be made, lock-in can lead to inefficient decisions that involve higher costs. Sunk costs in terms of both time and money, the need for justification, escalating commitment, and inflexibility and the closure of alternatives are indicators of lock-in.

Prevention

There are different types of lock-in; conscious/unconscious and intentional/ unintentional lock-in. Some of these types of lock-in can be avoided. Decision-makers can be made conscious about their behaviour, for example by confronting them with the lack of sufficient alternatives. When these decision-makers are willing to change their behaviour and consider other alternatives, they are less likely to become committed to one project alternative and hence, the chance for lock-in can be partly avoided. However, other types of lock-in are more difficult to control, especially intentional lock-in. Intentional lock-in is the result of specific behaviour of parties that act deliberately in the interest of their project. Cost overruns may thus be partly unnecessary or avoidable if such deliberate creation of lock-in had not taken place, and be partly unavoidable due to the incapacity of decision-makers to make optimal decisions.

EXPLICIT COST

An explicit cost is an easily accounted cost, such as wage, rent and materials. It can be transacted in the form of money payment and is lost directly, as opposed to monetary implicit costs. Explicit cost are those which the entrepreneur has to pay from his own pocket. Explicit costs require an outlay of money by the firm.

Implicit Costs, Explicit Costs, and Total Costs

Implicit cost + explicit cost = total cost. Implicit cost is not equal to total cost, but a component of it. A simple example: Sean builds a cabinet. He spends 2 hours building the cabinet. He could have been working instead and normally makes $25/hour at his job. Since he was building a cabinet he wasn't paid for this time.

The materials to make the cabinet cost him $20;

- His Explicit Costs are: $20 in materials
- His Implicit Costs are: $25/hr x 2 hrs= $50 of foregone pay
- His Total Costs are: $20 in materials + $50 of foregone pay = $70 Total Costs

INDIRECT COSTS

Indirect costs are costs that are not directly accountable to a cost object. Indirect costs may be either fixed or variable. Indirect costs include taxes, administration, personnel and security costs, and are also known as overhead.

Indirect vs. Direct Costs

Direct costs are those for activities or services that benefit specific projects, *e.g.*, salaries for project staff and materials required for a particular project. Because these activities are easily traced to projects, their costs are usually charged to projects on an item-by-item basis. Indirect costs are those for activities or services that benefit more than one project. Their precise benefits to a specific project are often difficult or impossible to trace. For example, it may be difficult to determine precisely how the activities of the director of an organization benefit a specific project.

It is possible to justify the handling of almost any kind of cost as either direct or indirect. Labour costs, for example, can be indirect, as in the case of maintenance personnel and executive officers; or they can be direct, as in the case of project staff members. Similarly, materials such as miscellaneous supplies purchased in bulk—pencils, pens, paper—are typically handled as indirect costs, while materials required for specific projects are charged as direct costs.

MARGINAL COST OF CAPITAL SCHEDULE

Marginal Cost of Capital (MCC) Schedule is a graph that relates the Cost of Capital (MCC) Schedule is a graph that relates the firm's weighted average cost of each dollar of capital to the total amount of new capital raised. The WACC is the minimum rate of return allowable, and still meeting financial obligationts such as debt, interest payments, dividends etc... Therefore, the WACC averages the required returns from all long-term financing sources. The WACC is based on cash flows, which are after-tax. By the same notion then, the WACC should be calculated on an after-tax basis.

MARGINAL COST

In economics and finance, marginal cost is the change in total cost that arises when the quantity produced changes by one unit. That is, it is the cost of producing one more unit of a good. Mathematically, the marginal cost (MC) function is expressed as the first derivative of the total cost (TC) function with respect to quantity (Q). Note that the marginal cost may change with volume, and so at each level of production, the marginal cost is the cost of the next unit produced.

$$MC = \frac{dTC}{dQ}$$

In general terms, marginal cost at each level of production includes any additional costs required to produce the next unit. If producing additional vehicles requires, for example, building a new factory, the marginal cost of those extra vehicles includes the cost of the new factory. In practice, the analysis is segregated into short and long-run cases, and over the longest run, all costs are marginal.

At each level of production and time period being considered, marginal costs include all costs which vary with the level of production, and other costs are considered fixed costs. A number of other factors can affect marginal cost and its applicability to real world problems. Some of these may be considered market failures. These may include information asymmetries, the presence of negative or positive externalities, transaction costs, price discrimination and others.

Cost Functions and Relationship to Average Cost

In the simplest case, the total cost function and its derivative are expressed as follows, where Q represents the production quantity, VC represents variable costs, FC represents fixed costs and TC represents total costs.

$$MC = \frac{dTC}{dQ} = \frac{d(FC + VC)}{dQ} = \frac{dVC}{dQ}$$

Since fixed costs do not vary with production quantity, it drops out of the equation when it is differentiated. The important conclusion is that marginal cost is not related to fixed costs. This can be compared with average total cost or ATC, which is the total cost divided by the number of units produced and does include fixed costs.

$$ATC = \frac{FC + VC}{Q}$$

For discrete calculation without calculus, marginal cost equals the change in total cost that comes with each additional unit produced. For instance, suppose the total cost of making 1 shoe is \$30 and the total cost of making 2 shoes is \$40. The marginal cost of producing the second shoe is \$40 - \$30 = \$10.

Economies of Scale

Production may be subject to economies of scale. Increasing returns to scale are said to exist if additional units can be produced for less than the previous unit, that is, average cost is falling. This can only occur if average cost at any given level of production is higher than the marginal cost. Conversely, there may be levels of production where marginal cost is higher than average cost, and average cost will rise for each unit of production after that point.

This type of production function is generally known as diminishing marginal productivity: at low levels of production, productivity gains are easy and marginal costs falling, but productivity gains become smaller as production increases; eventually, marginal costs rise because increasing output becomes more expensive. For this generic case, minimum average cost occurs at the point where average cost and marginal cost are equal; this point will not be at the minimum for marginal cost if fixed costs are greater than zero.

Externalities

Externalities are costs that are not borne by the parties to the economic transaction. A producer may, for example, pollute the environment, and others may bear those costs. A consumer may consume a good which produces benefits for society, such as education; because the individual does not receive all of the benefits, he may consume less than efficiency would suggest. Alternatively, an individual may be a smoker or alcoholic and impose costs on others. In these cases, production or consumption of the good in question may differ from the optimum level.

Negative Externalities of Production

Much of the time, private and social costs do not diverge from one another, but at times social costs may be either greater or less than private costs. When marginal social costs of production are greater than that of the private cost function, we see the occurrence of a negative externality of production.

Productive processes that result in pollution are a textbook example of production that creates negative externalities. Such externalities are a result of firms externalising their costs onto a third party in order to reduce their own total cost.

As a result of externalising such costs we see that members of society will be negatively affected by such behaviour of the firm. In this case, we see that an increased cost of production on society creates a social cost curve that depicts a greater cost than the private cost curve. In an equilibrium state we see that markets creating negative externalities of production will overproduce that good. As a result, the socially optimal production level would be lower than that observed.

Positive Externalities of Production

When marginal social costs of production are less than that of the private cost function, we see the occurrence of a positive externality of production. Production of public goods are a textbook example of production that create positive externalities. An example of such a public good, which creates a divergence in social and private costs, includes the production of education.

It is often seen that education is a positive for any whole society, as well as a positive for those directly involved in the market. We see that such production creates a social cost curve that is less than that of the private curve. In an equilibrium state we see that markets creating positive externalities of production will under produce that good. As a result, the socially optimal production level would be greater than that observed.

Social Costs

Of great importance in the theory of marginal cost is the distinction between the marginal private and social costs. the marginal private cost shows the cost associated to the firm in question. it is the marginal private cost that is used by business decision makers in their profit maximization goals, and by individuals in their purchasing and consumption choices. marginal social cost is similar to private cost in that it includes the cost functions of private enterprise but also that of society as a whole, including parties that have no direct association with the private costs of production. It incorporates all negative and positive externalities, of both production and consumption. hence, when deciding whether or how much to buy, buyers take account of the cost to society of their actions if private and social marginal cost coincide. the equality of price with social marginal cost, by aligning the interest of the buyer with the interest of the community as a whole is a necessary condition for economically efficient resource allocation.

ENERGY EFFICIENCY AND LIFE-CYCLE COST ANALYSIS

Life-cycle cost (LCC) analysis is the most rational, objective method for selecting the optimum HVAC system for a laboratory facility. Through LCC analysis, all factors that influence total system cost can be identified and quantified. Subjective factors such as fuel cost adjustments, component reliability, and maintenance costs are also included. LCC analysis can be used to assess the economic consequences of any decision by comparing two or more alternatives.

Annual Cost Comparison

Review of the annual cost of space conditioning for a laboratory or cleanroom shows the high impact of energy costs. A Class 10,000 cleanroom system costs five to 10 times as much to operate annually as the conditioning system for the facility's office spaces; a Class 100 laboratory cleanroom system will cost 50 times as much.

In either case, however, the contributions to total cost are:

- Capital costs, *i.e.* interest plus depreciation, contributing 15 to 25 per cent;
- Energy costs, contributing 65 to 75 per cent; and
- Maintenance costs, contributing 10 per cent.

A life-cycle cost analysis does not need to be extremely complex to yield reasonably accurate figures for first and operational costs. A modified LCC, similar to a simple payback, does not account for inflation or cost of money; this modified LCC can give an order-of-magnitude appraisal to help determine whether or not to add an EEM to a system.

If LCC computations are easily understood, the analysis is more likely to be used by design teams and accepted by researchers/owners. One approach to simplifying life-cycle cost analysis is to convert facility operating costs to an equivalent annual expense per fume hood.

This number can serve as a common denominator for comparing the composite performances of various system designs and for examining the sensitivity of each design alteration. The energy engineer should concentrate on determining realistic values for the most sensitive design factors before selecting the HVAC system type.

LCC Factors

LCC factors that influence a laboratory's HVAC system design can be broken into three categories: design factors, economic factors, and performance factors. Sometimes other factors must be considered; for example, a functional-use factor may be developed based on efficiency studies of personnel in the operations of different laboratory systems or components.

Because laboratory personnel LCCs are very high, the more functional a design or system is, the more LCC savings are possible. An example is the workspace flexibility and reduced costs of space planning that can be afforded by a raised floor system.

JUST-IN-TIME

Just-in-time (JIT) is an inventory strategy that strives to improve a business's return on investment by reducing in-process inventory and associated carrying costs.

To meet JIT objectives, the process relies on signals or Kanban between different points in the process, which tell production when to make the next part. Kanban are usually 'tickets' but can be simple visual signals, such as the presence or absence of a part on a shelf. Implemented correctly, JIT can improve a manufacturing organization's return on investment, quality, and efficiency. Quick notice that stock depletion requires personnel to order new stock is critical to the inventory reduction at the center of JIT. This saves warehouse space and costs.

However, the complete mechanism for making this work is often misunderstood. For instance, its effective application cannot be independent of other key components of a lean manufacturing system or it can "...end up with the opposite of the desired result.". In recent years manufacturers have continued to try to hone forecasting methods, however some research demonstrates that basing JIT on the presumption of stability is inherently flawed.

ACTIVITY-BASED MANAGEMENT

Activity-based management (ABM) is a method of identifying and evaluating activities that a business performs using activity-based costing to carry out a value chain analysis or a re-engineering initiative to improve strategic and operational decisions in an organization. Activity-based costing establishes relationships between overhead costs and activities so that overhead costs can be more precisely allocated to products, services, or customer segments. Activity-based management focuses on managing activities to reduce costs and improve customer value. Kaplan and Cooper. Cost and effect: Using integrated cost systems to drive profitability and performance. (Boston: Harvard Business School Press.)

Divide ABM into operational and strategic:

- Operational ABM is about "doing things right", using ABC information to improve efficiency. Those activities which add value to the product can be identified and improved. Activities that don't add value are the ones that need to be reduced to cut costs without reducing product value.
- Strategic ABM is about "doing the right things", using ABC information to decide which products to develop and which activities to use. This can also be used for customer profitability analysis, identifying which customers are the most profitable and focusing on them more.

A risk with ABM is that some activities have an implicit value, not necessarily reflected in a financial value added to any product. For instance a particularly pleasant workplace can help attract and retain the best staff, but may not be identified as adding value in operational ABM. A customer that represents a loss based on committed activities, but that opens up leads in a new market, may be identified as a low value customer by a strategic ABM process. Managers should interpret these values and use ABM as a "common, yet neutral, ground ... this provides the basis for negotiation". ABM can give middle managers an understanding of costs to other teams to help them make decisions that benefit the whole organisation, not just their activities' bottom line.

COST-VOLUME-PROFIT ANALYSIS

Cost-volume-profit (CVP) analysis expands the use of information provided by breakeven analysis. A critical part of CVP analysis is the point where total revenues equal total costs (both fixed and variable costs). At this breakeven point (BEP), a company will experience no income or loss. This BEP can be an initial examination that precedes more detailed CVP analyses. Cost-volume-profit analysis employs the same basic assumptions as in breakeven analysis. The assumptions underlying CVP analysis are:

- All units produced are sold.
- Changes in activity are the only factors that affect costs.
- Costs can be classified accurately as either fixed or variable.
- The behaviour of both costs and revenues in linear throughout the relevant range of activity.
- When a company sells more than one type of product, the sales mix will remain constant.

INTERNAL RATE OF RETURN

The Internal Rate of Return (IRR) is the discount rate that generates a zero net present value for a series of future cash flows. This essentially means that IRR is the rate of return that makes the sum of present value of future cash flows and the final market value of a project equal its current market value. Internal Rate of Return provides a simple 'hurdle rate', whereby any project should be avoided if the cost of capital exceeds this rate. Usually a financial calculator has to be used to calculate this IRR, though it can also be mathematically calculated using the following formula:

$$CF_o + \frac{CF_1}{(1+r)^1} + \frac{CF_2}{(1+r)^2} + \frac{CF_3}{(1+r)^3} + \frac{CF_n}{(1+r)_n} + \frac{CF_n}{(1+r)^n} = 0$$

CF is the Cash Flow generated in the specific period. IRR, denoted by 'r' is to be calculated by employing trial and error method. Internal Rate of Return is the flip side of Net Present Value (NPV), where NPV is the discounted value of a stream of cash flows, generated from an investment. IRR thus computes the break-even rate of return showing the discount rate, below which an investment results in a positive NPV. A simple decision-making criteria can be stated to accept a project if its Internal Rate of Return exceeds the cost of capital and rejected if this IRR is less than the cost of capital. However, it should be kept in mind that the use of IRR may result in a number of complexities such as a project with multiple IRRs or no IRR. Moreover, IRR neglects the size of the project and assumes that cash flows are reinvested at a constant rate.

The Modified Internal Rate of Return (MIRR) is an other financial measure used to determine the attractiveness of an investment. In IRR calculations, positive cash flows are assumed to be 'paid' instantly to the investor who can use them immediately to reinvest on a new project. But in reality, the positive cash flows are not paid instantly to the investors, but rather kept by the 'project management entity' until the end of the project. The Modified Internal Rate of Return assumes that the positive cash flows are immediately re-invested until the end of the project. To make these calculations, it is common practice to use the weighted average cost of capital as interest rate on the positive cash flows.

5

Variance Analysis of Standard Costing

VARIANCE ANALYSIS

A variance is the difference between an actual result and an expected result. The process by which the total difference between standard and actual results is analysed is known as variance analysis. When actual results are better than the expected results, we have a favourable variance (F). If, on the other hand, actual results are worse than expected results, we have an adverse (A).

I will use this example throughout this Exercise:

Standard cost of Product A	$
Materials (5kgs x $10 per kg)	50
Labour (4hrs x $5 per hr)	20
Variable o/hds (4 hrs x $2 per hr)	8
Fixed o/hds (4 hrs x $6 per hr)	24
	102

Budgeted results		ACTUAL Results	
Production:	1,200 units	Production:	1,000 units
Sales:	1,000 units	Sales:	900 units
Selling price:	$150 per unit	Materials:	4,850 kgs, $46,075
		Labour:	4,200 hrs, $21,210
		Variable o/hds:	$9,450
		Fixed o/hds:	$25,000
		Selling price:	$140 per unit

VARIABLE COST VARIANCES

DIRECT MATERIAL VARIANCES

The direct material total variance is the difference between what the output actually cost and what it should have cost, in terms of material. From the example the material total variance is given by:

	$
1,000 units should have cost (x $50)	50,000
But did cost	46,075
Direct material total variance	**3, 925 (F)**

It can be divided into two sub-variances:

- Direct material price variance,

- Direct material Usage variance,
- Direct labour total variance,
- Direct labour rate variance,
- Direct labour effciency variance.

The Direct Material Price Variance

This is the difference between what the actual quantity of material used did cost and what it should have cost.

	$
4,850 kgs should have cost (x $10)	48,500
But did cost	46,075
Direct material price variance	**2,425 (F)**

The Direct Material Usage Variance

This is the difference between how much material should have been used for the number of units actually produced and how much material was used, valued at standard cost.

1,000 units should have used (x 5 kgs)	5,000 kgs
But did use	4,850 kgs
Variance in kgs	150 kgs (F)
Valued at standard cost per kg	x $10
Direct material usage variance in $	**$1,500 (F)**

The direct material price variance is calculated on material purchases in the period if closing stocks of raw materials are valued at standard cost or material used if closing stocks of raw materials are valued at actual cost (FIFO).

Direct Labour Total Variance

The direct labour total variance is the difference between what the output should have cost and what it did cost, in terms of labour.

	$
1,000 units should have cost (x $20)	20,000
But did cost	21,210
Direct material price variance	**1,210 (A)**

Direct Labour Rate Variance

This is the difference between what the actual number of hours worked should have cost and what it did cost.

4200hrs should have cost (4200hrs x $5)	$21000
But did cost	$21210
Direct labour rate variance	**$210(A)**

The Direct Labour Efficiency Variance

The is the difference between how many hours should have been worked for the number of units actually produced and how many hours were worked, valued at the standard rate per hour.

	$
1,000 units should have taken (x 4 hrs)	4,000 hrs
But did take	4,200 hrs
Variance in hrs	200 hrs
Valued at standard rate per hour	x $5
Direct labour efficiency variance	**$1,000 (A)**

When idle time occurs the efficiency variance is based on hours actually worked (not hours paid for) and an idle time variance (hours of idle time x standard rate per hour) is calculated.

VARIABLE PRODUCTION OVERHEAD TOTAL VARIANCES

The variable production overhead total variance is the difference between what the output should have cost and what it did cost, in terms of variable production overhead.

	$
1,000 units should have cost (x $8)	8,000
But did cost	9,450
Variable production o/hd expenditure variance	**1,450 (A)**

The Variable Production Overhead Expenditure Variance

This is the difference between what the variable production overhead did cost and what it should have cost

	$
4,200 hrs should have cost (x $2)	8,400
But did cost	9,450
Variable production o/hd expenditure variance	**1,050 (A)**

The Variable Production Overhead Efficiency Variance

This is the same as the direct labour efficiency variance in hours, valued at the variable production overhead rate per hour.

Labour ef ficiency variance in hours	200 hrs (A)
Valued @ standard rate per hour	x $2
Variable production o/hd efficiency variance	**$400 (A)**

FIXED PRODUCTION OVERHEAD VARIANCES

The total fixed production variance is an attempt to explain the under–or over–absorbed fixed production overhead.

$$\text{Remember that Overhead Absorption Rate} = \frac{\text{Budgeted Fixed Production Overhead}}{\text{Budgeted Level of Activity}}$$

If either the numerator or the denominator or both are incorrect then as suggested, have under- or over-absorbed production overhead:

- If actual expenditure ± budgeted expenditure (numerator incorrect) ≈ expenditure variance
- If actual production/hours of activity ≈ budgeted production/hours of activity (denominator incorrect) ≈ volume variance.
- The workforce may have been working at a more or less efficient rate than standard to produce a given output ≈ volume efficiency variance (similar to the variable production overhead efficiency variance).
- Regardless of the level of efficiency, the total number of hours worked could have been more or less than was originally budgeted (employees may have worked a lot of overtime or there may have been a strike and so actual hours worked were less than budgeted) » volume capacity variance.

THE FIXED PRODUCTION OVERHEAD VARIANCES

FIXED PRODUCTION OVERHEAD VARIANCE

This is the difference between fixed production overhead incurred and fixed production overhead absorbed (= the under–or over–absorbed fixed production overhead)

	$
Overhead incurred	25,000
Overhead absorbed (1,000 units x $24)	24,000
Overhead variance	**1,000 (A)**

Fixed Production Overhead Expenditure Variance

This is the difference between the budgeted fixed production overhead expenditure and actual fixed production overhead expenditure

	$
Budgeted overhead (1,200 x $24)	28,800
Actual overhead	25,000
Expenditure variance	**3,800 (F)**

Fixed Production Overhead Volume Variance

This is the difference between actual and budgeted production volume multiplied by the standard absorption rate per unit.

	$
Actual production at std rate (1,000 x $24)	24,000
Budgeted production at std rate (1,200 x $24)	28,800
	4,800 (A)

Fixed Production Overhead Volume Efficiency Variance

This is the difference between the number of hours that actual production should have taken, and the number of hours actually worked (usually the labour efficiency variance), multiplied by the standard absorption rate per hour.

Labour efficiency variance in hours	200 hrs (A)
Valued @ standard rate per hour	x $6
Volume efficiency variance	**$1,200 (A)**

Fixed Production Overhead Volume Capacity Variance

This is the difference between budgeted hours of work and the actual hours worked, multiplied by the standard absorption rate per hour.

Budgeted hours (1,200 x 4)	4,800 hrs
Actual hours	4,200 hrs
Variance in hrs	600 hrs (A)
x standard rate per hour	x $6
	$3,600 (A)

Key

The fixed overhead volume capacity variance is unlike the other variances in that an excess of actual hours over budgeted hours results in a favourable variance and not an adverse variance as it does when considering labour efficiency, variable overhead efficiency and fixed overhead volume efficiency.

Working more hours than budgeted produces an over absorption of fixed overheads, which is a favourable variance.

SELLING PRICE VARIANCE

The selling price variance is a measure of the effect on expected profit of a different selling price to standard selling price. It is calculated as the difference between what the sales revenue should have been for the actual quantity sold, and what it was.

	$
Revenue from 900 units should have been (x $150)	135,000
But was (x $140)	126,000
Selling price variance	**9,000 (A)**

Sales Volume Variance

The sales volume variance is the difference between the actual units sold and the budgeted quantity, valued at the standard profit per unit. In other words it measures the increase or decrease in standard profit as a result of the sales volume being higher or lower than budgeted.

Budgeted sales volume	1,000 units
Actual sales volume	900 units
Variance in units	100 units (A)
x standard margin per unit (x $ (150 - 102))	x $48
Sales volume variance	**$4,800 (A)**

Key

Don't forget to value the sales volume variance at standard contribution marginal costing is in use.

Operating Statement

The most common presentation of the reconciliation between budgeted and actual profit is as follows.

			$
Budgeted profit before sales and admin costs			X
Sales variances–price volume			X
Actual sales minus standard cost of sales			X
	(F)	(A)	
Cost variances	$	$	
Material price	X		
Material usage etc	X		
Labour rate		X	
Labour Efficency		X	
Overhead Expenditure	X		
Overhead Volume		X	
Sales and administration costs			
Actual profit			X

Variances in a standard marginal costing system:

- No fixed overhead volume variance
- Sales volume variances are valued at standard contribution margin (not standard profit margin)

REASONS FOR VARIANCES

Material Price

- (F)–unforseen discounts received, greater care taken in purchasing, change in material standard
- (A)–price increase, careless purchasing, change in material standard.

Material Usage

- (F)–material used of higher quality than standard, more effective use made of material
- (A)– defective material, excessive waste, theft, stricter quality control

Labour Rate

- (F)–use of workers at rate of pay lower than standard
- (A)–wage rate increase

Idle time

- Machine breakdown, non-availability of material, illness

Labour Efficiency

- (F)–output produced more quickly than expected because of work motivation, better quality of equipment or materials
- (A)–lost time in excess of standard allowed, output lower than standard set because of deliberate restriction, lack of training, sub-standard material used.

Overhead Expenditure

- (F)–savings in cost incurred, more economical use of services.
- (A)–increase in cost of services used, excessive use of services, change in type of services used

Overhead Volume

- (F)–production greater than budgeted
- (A)–production less than budgeted

INTERDEPENDENCE BETWEEN VARIANCES

The cause of one (adverse) variance may be wholly or partly explained by the cause of another (favourable) variance:

- Material price or material usage and labour efficiency
- Labour rate and material usage
- Sales price and sales volume

THE SIGNIFICANCE OF VARIANCES

The decision as to whether or not a variance is so significant that it should be investigated should take a number of factors into account:

- The type of standard being used
- Interdependence between variances
- Controllability
- Materiality

MATERIALS MIX AND YIELD VARIANCES

The materials usage variance can be subdivided into a materials mix variance and a materials yield variance if the proportion of materials in a mix is changeable and controllable. The mix variance indicates the effect on costs of changing the mix of material inputs. The yield variance indicates the effect on costs of material inputs yielding more or less than expected. Standard input to produce 1 unit of product X:

	$
Material A(20 kgs x $10)	200
Material B(30 kgs x $5)	150
	350

In period 3, 13 units of product X were produced from 250 kgs of material A and 350 kgs of material B.

Solution: Individual prices per kg as variance valuation cases

Mix Variance	**Kgs**
Standard mix of actual use: A: 2/5 x (250+350)	240
B: 3/5 x (250+350)	360
	600

	A	B
Mix should have been	240 kgs	360 kgs
But was	250 kgs	350 kgs
Mix variance in kgs	10 kgs (A)	10 kgs (F)
x standard cost per kg	x $10	x $5
Mix variance in $	$100 (A)	$50 (F)
	50 (A)	

Total mix variance in quantity is always zero.

Yield Variance

	A	**B**
13 units of product X should have used	260 kgs	390 kgs
but actual input in standard mix was	240 kgs	360 kgs
Yield variance in kgs	20 kgs (F)	30 kgs (F)
x standard cost per kg	x $10	x $5
	$200 (F)	$150 (F)
	$350 (F)	

Solution: budgeted weighted average price per unit of input as variance valuation base. Therefore, Budgeted weighted average price =$350/50 = $7 per kg.

- Mix variance

	A	B
13 units of product X should have used	260 kgs	390 kgs
but did use	250 kgs	350 kgs
Usage variance in kgs	10 kgs (F)	40 kgs (F)
x individual price per kg–budgeted	$ (10 - 7)	$ (5 - 7)
weighted average price per kg	x $3	x ($2)
	$30 (F)	$80 (A)
	$50 (A)	

- Yield variance

	A	B
Usage variance in kgs	10 kg (F)	40 kg (F)
x budgeted weighted average	x $7	x $7
Price per kg	$70 (F)	$ 280 (F)
	$350 (F)	

SALES MIX AND QUANTITY VARIANCES

The sales volume variance can be subdivided into a mix variance if the proportions of products sold are controllable.

Sales Mix Variance

This variance indicates the effect on profit of changing the mix of actual sales from the standard mix. It can be calculated in one of two ways:

- The difference between the actual total quantity sold in the standard mix and the actual quantities sold, valued at the standard margin per unit.
- The difference between actual sales and budgeted sales, valued at (standard profit per unit - budgeted weighted average profit per unit)

Sales Quantity Variance

This variance indicates the effect on profit of selling a different total quantity from the budgeted total quantity. It can be calculated in one of two ways:

- The difference between actual sales volume in the standard mix and budgeted sales valued at the standard margin per unit.
- The difference between actual sales volume and budgeted sales valued at the budgeted weighted average profit per unit.

STANDARD COSTING

You know that management accounting is managing a business through accounting information. In this process, management accounting is facilitating managerial control. It can also be applied to your own daily/monthly expenses, if necessary. These measures should be applied correctly so that performance takes place according to plans. Planning is the first tool for making the control effective.

The vital aspect of managerial control is cost control. Hence, it is very important to plan and control costs. Standard costing is a technique which helps you to control costs and business operations. It aims at eliminating wastes and increasing efficiency in performance through setting up standards or formulating cost plans.

MEANING OF STANDARD

When you want to measure some thing, you must take some parameter or yardstick for measuring. We can call this as standard. What are your daily expenses? An average of $50! If you have been spending this much for so many days, then this is your daily standard expense. The word standard means a benchmark or yardstick.

The standard cost is a predetermined cost which determines in advance what each product or service should cost under given circumstances. In the words of Backer and Jacobsen, "Standard cost is the amount the firm thinks a product or the operation of the process for a period of time should cost, based upon certain assumed conditions of efficiency, economic conditions and other factors."

DEFINITION

The CIMA, London has defined standard cost as "a predetermined cost which is calculated from managements standards of efficient operations and the relevant necessary expenditure." They are the predetermined costs on technical estimate of material labour and overhead for a selected period of time and for a prescribed set of working conditions. In other words, a standard cost is a planned cost for a unit of product or service rendered.

The technique of using standard costs for the purposes of cost control is known as standard costing. It is a system of cost accounting which is designed to find out how much should be the cost of a product under the existing conditions. The actual cost can be ascertained only when production is undertaken. The predetermined cost is compared to the actual cost and a variance between the two enables the management to take necessary corrective measures.

ADVANTAGES

Standard costing is a management control technique for every activity. It is not only useful for cost control purposes but is also helpful in production planning and policy formulation. It allows management by exception.

In the light of various objectives of this system, some of the advantages of this tool are given below:

- *Cost control:* Every costing system aims at cost control and cost reduction. The standards are being constantly analyzed and an effort is made to improve efficiency. Whenever a variance occurs, the reasons are studied and immediate corrective measures are undertaken. The action taken in spotting weak points enables cost control system.
- *Efficiency measurement*: The comparison of actual costs with standard costs enables the management to evaluate performance of various cost centers. In the absence of standard costing system, actual costs of different period may be compared to measure efficiency. It is not proper to compare costs of different period because circumstance of both the periods may be different. Still, a decision about base period can be made with which actual performance can be compared.
- *Eliminating inefficiencies*: The setting of standards for different elements of cost requires a detailed study of different aspects. The standards are set differently for manufacturing, administrative and selling expenses. Improved methods are used for setting these standards. The determination of manufacturing expenses will require time and motion study for labour and effective material control devices for materials. Similar studies will be needed for finding other expenses. All these studies will make it possible to eliminate inefficiencies at different steps.
- *Finding of variance:* The performance variances are determined by comparing actual costs with standard costs. Management is able to spot out the place of inefficiencies. It can fix responsibility for deviation in performance. It is possible to take corrective measures at the earliest. A regular check on various expenditures is also ensured by standard cost system.
- *Management by exception*: The targets of different individuals are fixed if the performance is according to predetermined standards. In this case, there is nothing to worry. The attention of the management is drawn only when actual performance is less than the budgeted performance. Management by exception means that everybody is given a target to be achieved and management need not supervise each and everything. The responsibilities are fixed and every body tries to achieve his/her targets.
- *Right decisions*: It enables and provides useful information to the management in taking important decisions. For example, the problem created by inflating, rising prices. It can also be used to provide incentive plans for employees etc.

LIMITATIONS OF STANDARD COSTING

- It cannot be used in those organizations where non-standard products are produced. If the production is undertaken according to the customer specifications, then each job will involve different amount of expenditures.
- The fixing of responsibility is not an easy task. The variances are to be classified into controllable and uncontrollable variances. Standard costing is applicable only for controllable variances.
- The process of setting standard is a difficult task, as it requires technical skills. The time and motion study is required to be undertaken for this purpose. These studies require a lot of time and money.
- There are no inset circumstances to be considered for fixing standards. The conditions under which standards are fixed do not remain static. With the change in circumstances, if the standards are not revised the same become impracticable.

For instance, if the industry changed the technology then the system will not be suitable. In that case, as suggested, have to change or revise the standards. A frequent revision of standards will become costly.

SETTING STANDARDS

Normally, setting up standards is based on the past experience. The total standard cost includes direct materials, direct labour and overheads. Normally, all these are fixed to some extent. The standards should be set up in a systematic way so that they are used as a tool for cost control. Various Elements which Influence the Setting of Standards

SETTING STANDARDS FOR DIRECT MATERIALS

There are several basic principles which ought to be appreciated in setting standards for direct materials. Generally, when you want to purchase some material what are the factors you consider. If material is used for a product, it is known as direct material. On the other hand, if the material cost cannot be assigned to the manufacturing of the product, it will be called indirect material.

Therefore, it involves two things:

1. Price of the material
2. Quality of material

When you want to purchase material, the quality and size should be determined. The standard quality to be maintained should be decided. The quantity is determined by the production department. This department makes use of historical records, and an allowance for changing conditions will also be given for setting standards. A number of test runs may be undertaken on different days and under different situations, and an average of these results should be used for setting material quantity standards.

The second step in determining direct material cost will be a decision about the standard price. Material's cost will be decided in consultation with the purchase department. The cost of purchasing and store keeping of materials should also be taken into consideration. The procedure for purchase of materials, minimum and maximum levels for various materials, discount policy and means of transport are the other factors which have bearing on the materials cost price.

It includes the following:

- Carrying cost
- Cost of materials
- Ordering cost

The purpose should be to increase efficiency in procuring and store keeping of materials. The type of standard used—ideal standard or expected standard—also affects the choice of standard price.

SETTING DIRECT LABOUR COST

If you want to engage a labour force for manufacturing a product or a service for which you need to pay some amount, this is called wages. If the labour is engaged directly to produce the product, this is known as direct labour. The second largest amount of cost is of labour. The benefit derived from the workers can be assigned to a particular product or a process. If the wages paid to workers cannot be directly assigned to a particular product, these will be known as indirect wages. The time required for producing a product would be ascertained and labour should be properly graded. Different grades of workers will be paid different rates of wages. The times spent by different grades of workers for manufacturing a product should also be studied for deciding upon direct labour cost.

The setting of standard for direct labour will be done basically on the following:

- Labour rate per hour
- Standard labour time for producing

Standard labour time indicates the time taken by different categories of labour force which are as under:

- Semi–skilled labour
- Skilled labour
- Unskilled labour

For setting a standard time for labour force, we normally take in to account previous experience, past performance records, test run result, work-study etc. The labour rate standard refers to the expected wage rates to be paid for different categories of workers. Past wage rates and demand and supply principle may not be a safe guide for determining standard labour rates. The anticipation of expected changes in labour rates will be an essential factor. In case there is an agreement with workers for payment of wages in the coming period, these rates should be used. If a premium or bonus scheme is in operation, then anticipated extra payments should also be included. Where a piece rate system is used, standard cost will be fixed per piece. The object of fixed standard labour time and labour rate is to device maximum efficiency in the use of labour.

COSTING MATERIALS ESTABLISHED

PAYMENTS AND DISCOUNTS

Discounts and allowances are reductions to a basic price of goods or services. The can occur anywhere in the distribution channel, modifying either the manufacturer's list price, the retail price, or the list price.

There are many purposes for discounting, including; to increase short-term sales, to move out-of-date stock, to reward valuable customers, to encourage distribution channel members to perform a function, or to otherwise reward behaviours that benefit the discount issuer. Some discounts and allowances are forms of sales promotion.

Types

Dealing with payment:

- *Prompt payment discount*: Trade Discount:Deduction in price given by the wholesaler/manufacturer to the retailer at the list price or catalogue price. Cash Discount:Reduction in price given by the creditor to the debitor is known as cash discount. This discount is intended to speed payment and thereby provide liquidity to the firm. They are sometimes used as a promotional device.
- *Preferred payment method discount*: Some retailers offer discounts to customers paying with cash, to avoid paying fees on credit card transactions.
- *Partial payment discount*: Similar to the Trade discount, this is used when the seller wishes to improve cash flow or liquidity, but finds that the buyer typically is unable to meet the desired discount deadline. A partial discount for whatever payment the buyer makes helps the seller's cash flow partially.
- *Sliding scale*: A discount offered based on one's ability to pay. More common with non-profit organizations than with for-profit retail.
- *Forward dating*: This is where the purchaser doesn't pay for the goods until well after they arrive. The date on the invoice is moved forward - example: purchase goods in November for sale during the December holiday season, but the payment date on the invoice is January 7.
- *Seasonal discount*: These are price reductions given when an order is placed in a slack period. On a shorter time scale, a happy hour

may fall in this category. Generally, this discount is referred to as "X-Dating" or "Ex-Dating".

Discounts and allowances dealing with trade:

- *Bargaining*: Bargaining is where the seller and the buyer negotiate a price, which the buyer hopes is lower than the marked price.
- *Trade discount*: These are payments to distribution channel members for performing some function. Examples of these functions are warehousing and shelf stocking. Trade discounts are often combined to include a series of functions, for example 20/12/5 could indicate a 20 per cent discount for warehousing the product, an additional 12 per cent discount for shipping the product, and an additional 5 per cent discount for keeping the shelves stocked. Trade discounts are most frequent in industries where retailers hold the majority of the power in the distribution channel.
- *Trade-in discount*: This can be a way of reducing the price. By offering more for a trade-in than it is actually worth, the net effect is to reduce the effective price earned by the seller. The advantage of this is it encourages replacement sales without altering the list price or the perceived value.
- *Trade rate discount*: A discount offered by a seller to a buyer in a related industry. For example, a pharmacist might offer a discount for over-the-counter drugs to physicians who are purchasing them for dispensing to the physicians' own patients.

Discounts and Allowances Dealing with Quantity

These are price reductions given for large purchases. The rationale behind them is to obtain economies of scale and pass some of these savings on to the customer. In some industries, buyer groups and co-ops have formed to take advantage of these discounts.

Generally there are three types:

- *Cumulative quantity discount*: These are price reductions based on the quantity purchased over a set period of time. The expectation is that they will impose an implied switching cost and thereby bond the purchaser to the seller.
- *Non-cumulative quantity discount*: These are price reductions based on the quantity of a single order. The expectation is that they will encourage larger orders, thus reducing billing, order filling, shipping, and sales personal expenses.
- *Dependence of price on quantity*: An extreme form of quantity discount is when, within a quantity range, the price does not depend on quantity: if one wants less than the minimum amount one has to be

pay for the minimum amount anyway. if one wants an amount between two of the fixed amounts on offer, one has to pay for the higher amount. These also apply in the case of a service with "quantity" referring to time. For example, an entrance ticket for a zoo is usually for a day; if one stays shorter, the price is the same. It is a kind of pass for unlimited use of a service during a day, where one can distinguish whether or not, when leaving and returning, one has to pay again. Similarly a pass can be for another period. In the case of long periods, it is obvious that one can leave and return without paying again. If one has to buy more than one wants, we can distinguish between the surplus just not being used, or the surplus being a nuisance, *e.g.* because of having to carry a large container.

Discounts and Allowances Dealing with Customer Characteristics

The following discounts have to do with specific characteristics of the customer:

- *Disability discount*: A discount offered to customers with a disability. Depending on the type of business or setting, what is considered a disability may vary.
- *Educational discount*: These are price reductions given to members of educational institutions, usually students but possibly also to educators and to other institution staff. The rationale is to build brand awareness early in a buyer's life, and/or to build product familiarity early so that when a student graduates, he/she is more likely to buy the same product for work at its normal price. Educational discounts are traditionally given by merchants directly, or via a student discount programme such as NUS and Studentdiscounts.co.uk in the United Kingdom or Edhance in the United States.
- *Employee discount*: A discount offered internally to the employees of a company that sell goods and/or services. This is used to entice more people interested in the goods and/or services of the company to work for the company to receive the discount, and then for the hired employees to put their wages right back into the company by purchasing the goods and/or services. Other perceived benefits of this discount: reaching out to potential employees that could be knowledgeable in the goods and/or services the company offers by offering a discount on what they like. reduce employee theft by making the hired employees feel they are already getting the items at a great price. keep current employees from leaving if they cannot also leave the discount they are receiving behind. In 2005, the American automakers marketed an employee discount for all promotional campaign in order to entice buyers, which saw some success.

- *Military discount*: A discount offered to customers who are and/or were enlisted in military services. The rationale may be that the servicemember is assumed to be on a limited budget, or it may be a way for the retailer to show support for members of the military.
- *Senior discount*: "senior discount" redirects here. For the band. A discount offered to customers who are above a certain age, typically 50, 55, or 60; the exact age varies with the business or setting. The rationale for a senior discount is that the customer is assumed to be retired, and/or have a limited income, and/or living on a budget.
- *Toddler discount*: A discount offered to children younger than a certain age, very common with regard to admission fees to entertainments and attractions. Another form of this discount is a "kids eat free" type of promotion. Often there is a requirement that the child must be accompanied by an adult paying full price.
- *Special prices offered to friends of the seller*: A discounted price offered to friends of the salesperson, an attitude which is parodied in the stereotype of a salesman saying "It costs such-and such, but for you..." In Australia and New Zealand, discounts to friends are known as "mates' rates." In French this discount is known as prix d'ami.
- *Special prices offered to local residents*: Common in tourist destinations, this discount is intended to promote local patronage. In Hawai'i, for example, many tourist attractions, hotels, and restaurants charge a deeply discounted price to someone who shows a Hawai'i drivers license or other proof that they live in Hawai'i; this is known as a "Kama'aina discount," after the Hawaiian word for an old-timer or native.

Coupons and Rebates

A discount, either of a certain specified amount or a percentage to the holder of a voucher, usually with certain terms. Commonly, such as being valid only if a certain quantity is bought or only if the customer is a senior.

Coupons can be distributed in places like newspapers, brochures, and the internet. A refund of part of sometimes the full price of the product following purchase, though some rebates are offered at the time of purchase.

Other discounts and allowances:

- *Promotional allowances*: These are price reductions given to the buyer for performing some promotional activity. These include an allowance for creating and maintaining an in-store display or a co-op advertising allowance.
- *Brokerage allowance*: From the point of view of the manufacturer, any brokerage fee paid is similar to a promotional allowance. It is usually based on a percentage of the sales generated by the broker.

DISCOUNTING

Discounting is a financial mechanism in which a debtor obtains the right to delay payments to a creditor, for a defined period of time, in exchange for a charge or fee. Essentially, the party that owes money in the present purchases the right to delay the payment until some future date.

The discount, or charge, is simply the difference between the original amount owed in the present and the amount that has to be paid in the future to settle the debt.

The discount is usually associated with a discount rate, which is also called the discount yield.

The discount yield is simply the proportional share of the initial amount owed that must be paid to delay payment for 1 year.

It is also the rate at which the amount owed must rise to delay payment for 1 year. Since a person can earn a return on money invested over some period of time, most economic and financial models assume the "Discount Yield" is the same as the Rate of Return the person could receive by investing this money elsewhere over the given period of time covered by the delay in payment.

The Concept is associated with the Opportunity Cost of not having use of the money for the period of time covered by the delay in payment.

The relationship between the "Discount Yield" and the Rate of Return on other financial assets is usually discussed in such economic and financial theories involving the inter-relation between various Market Prices, and the achievement of Pareto Optimality through the operations in the Capitalistic Price Mechanism, as well as in the discussion of the "Efficient Market Hypothesis".

The person delaying the payment of the current Liability is essentially compensating the person to whom he/she owes money for the lost revenue that could be earned from an investment during the time period covered by the delay in payment.

It is the relevant "Discount Yield" that determines the "Discount", and not the other way around. As indicated, the Rate of Return is usually calculated in accordance to an annual return on investment.

Since an investor earns a return on the original principle amount of the investment as well as on any prior period Investment income, investment earnings are "compounded" as time advances.

Therefore, considering the fact that the "Discount" must match the benefits obtained from a similar Investment Asset, the "Discount Yield" must be used within the same compounding mechanism to negotiate an increase in the size of the "Discount" whenever the time period the payment is delayed or extended.

The "Discount Rate" is the rate at which the "Discount" must grow as the delay in payment is extended. This fact is directly tied into the "Time Value of Money" and its calculations. The "Time Value of Money" indicates there is a difference between the "Future Value" of a payment and the "Present Value" of the same payment.

The Rate of Return on investment should be the dominant factor in evaluating the market's assessment of the difference between the "Future Value" and the "Present Value" of a payment; and it is the Market's assessment that counts the most.

Therefore, the "Discount Yield", which is predetermined by a related Return on Investment that is found in the financial markets, is what is used within the "Time Value of Money" calculations to determine the "Discount" required to delay payment of a financial liability for a given period of time.

Essential Calculation

If we consider the value of the original payment presently due to be \$P, and the debtor wants to delay the payment for t years, then an r% Market Rate of Return on a similar Investment Assets means the "Future Value" of \$P is $\$P * (1 + r\,\%)^t$, and the "Discount" would be calculated as:

$$\text{Discount} = \$P * (1 + r\,\%)^t - \$P$$

where

r% is also the "Discount Yield".

If \$F is a payment that will be made t years in the future, then the "Present Value" of this Payment, also called the "Discounted Value" of the payment, is

$$\$P = \$F / (1 + r\,\%)^t$$

Discount Rate

The discount rate which is used in financial calculations is usually chosen to be equal to the Cost of Capital. The Cost of Capital, in a financial market equilibrium, will be the same as the Market Rate of Return on the financial asset mixture the firm uses to finance capital investment. Some adjustment may be made to the discount rate to take account of risks associated with uncertain cash flows, with other developments. The discount rates typically applied to different types of companies show significant differences:

- *Early Startups*: 40–60 per cent
- *Late Startups*: 30–50 per cent
- *Mature Companies*: 10–25 per cent
- *Startups seeking money*: 50–100 per cent

Reason for high discount rates for startups:

- Limited number of investors willing to invest.
- Over optimistic forecasts by enthusiastic founders.
- Reduced marketability of ownerships because stocks are not traded publicly.
- Startups face high risks.

One method that looks into a correct discount rate is the capital asset pricing model. This model takes in account three variables that make up the discount rate:

- *Risk Free Rate*: The percentage of return generated by investing in risk free securities such as government bonds.
- *Beta*: The measurement of how a company's stock price reacts to a change in the market. A beta higher than 1 means that a change in share price is exaggerated compared to the rest of shares in the same market. A beta less than 1 means that the share is stable and not very responsive to changes in the market. Less than 0 means that a share is moving in the opposite of the market change.
- *Equity Market Risk Premium*: The return on investment that investors require above the risk free rate.

Discount Factor

The discount factor, P(T), is the factor by which a future cash flow must be multiplied in order to obtain the present value. For a fixed discount rate, r, discretely compounded over time, T,

$$P(T) = \frac{1}{(1+r)^{T}}$$

For a fixed continuously compounded discount rate, we have

$$P(T) = e^{-rT}$$

CARRIAGE INWARDS ON RAW MATERIALS

It represents the expenditure incurred in bringing raw materials to the factory from outside and include sea, land and air freight, insurance, duties, dock charges, etc. There is a difference of opinion as to treatment of carriage inwards. Accounting theory suggests that such charges are proper additions to the costs of materials purchased, since these costs are incurred in bringing the materials to the factory. But what is sound in theory is not always practicable, and deviations from theory are common. Where such costs are immaterial or it is difficult to trace or even allocate such charges to specific items of materials, then these charges should be treated as an indirect manufacturing cost which should be apportioned to product indirectly.

MATERIAL HANDLING CHARGES

Material handling includes the unloading of your exhibit materials, storing for up to 30 days in advance at the warehouse address, delivering to the booth, the handling of empty containers to and from storage and removing of material from the booth for reloading onto outbound carriers when the show closes.

It should not be confused with the cost to transport your exhibit materials to and from the convention or event. You have two options for shipping your advance freight–either to the warehouse or directly to show site.

How do I estimate my Material Handling charges:

- Charges will be based on the weight of your shipment. Each shipment received is considered separately. The shipment weight will be rounded up to the next 100 pounds. Each 100 pounds is considered one "cwt". There is a 200 pound minimum charge fore ach shipment weighing less than 200 pounds. All shipments are subject to reweigh.
- On the Material Handling Order Form, select whether the freight will arrive at the warehouse or be sent directly to show site.
- Next, select the category that best describes your shipment:

The categories of Freight:

- *Crated*: Material that is skidded or is in any type of shipping container that can be unloaded at the dock with no handling required.
- *Special Handling*: Material delivered by the carrier in such a manner that it requires additional handling, such as ground unloading, stacked and constricted space unloading, designated piece unloading, loads mixed with pad-wrapped material, loads failing to maintain shipping integrity, carpet and/or pad-only shipments, and shipments that require additional time, equipment or labour to unload. Federal Express and UPS are included in this category due to their delivery procedures.
- *Uncrated*: Material that is shipped loose or pad-wrapped and/or unskidded machinery without proper lifting bars or hooks.
- Add overtime charges for inbound if material is delivered to the booth during the overtime period stated in Quick Facts on Freeman OnLine. This includes warehouse and show-site shipments.
- Add overtime charges for outbound if material is loaded onto the outbound carrier during the overtime period stated in Quick Facts on Freeman OnLine.
- Add the late delivery charge listed on the Order Form if the shipment is accepted at the warehouse or at show site after the deadline date listed in Quick Facts on Freeman OnLine.
- The above services, whether used completely or in part, are offered as a package and the charges will be based on the total inbound weight of the shipment. Shipments received without receipts or freight bills, such as UPS and Federal Express, will be delivered to the booth without guarantee of piece count or condition.

How do I ship to the Warehouse:

- As suggested, accept freight beginning 30 days prior to show move-in.

- To check on your freight arrival, call Exhibitor Services at the location listed on your Quick Facts form. This form may be found in your Exhibitor Services Manual or on Freeman OnLine.
- To ensure timely arrival of your materials at show site, freight should arrive by the deadline date listed on Quick Facts. Your freight will still be received after the deadline date, but additional charges will be incurred.
- The warehouse will receive shipments Monday through Friday except on holidays. Refer to Quick Facts for warehouse hours. No appointment is necessary.
- The warehouse will accept crates, cartons, skids, trunks/cases and carpets. Loose or pad-wrapped material must be sent directly to show site.
- All shipments must have a bill of lading or delivery slip indicating the number of pieces, type of merchandise and weight.
- Certified weight tickets must accompany all shipments.
- Warehouse freight will be delivered to the booth prior to exhibitor setup.
- Please call the number located on Quick Facts if you want to ship oversized material that requires special equipment to the warehouse.

What about prepaid or collect shipping charges:

- Collect shipments will be returned to the delivery carrier.
- To ensure that your freight does not arrive collect, mark your bill of lading "Prepaid".
- "Prepaid" designates that the transportation charges will be paid by the exhibitor or third party.

How should I label my freight:

- The label should contain your exhibiting company name, the booth number and the name of the event.
- The specific shipping address for either the warehouse or show site is located on Quick Facts.

What happens to my empty containers during the show:

- Pick up "Empty Labels" at the Freeman Exhibitor Service Center. Place a label on each container. Labeled containers will be picked up periodically and stored in non-accessible storage during the show.
- At the close of the show, the empty containers will be returned to the booth in random order. Depending on the size of the show, this process may take several hours.

How do I protect my materials after they are delivered to the show or before they are picked up after the show:

- Consistent with trade show industry practices, there may be a lapse of time between the delivery of your shipment to your booth and your arrival. The same is true for the outbound phase of the show–

the time between your departure and the actual pick-up of your materials. During these times, your materials will be left unattended. We recommend that you arrange for a representative to stay with your materials or that you hire security services to safeguard your materials.

How do I ship my materials after the close of the show:

- Each shipment must have a completed Material Handling Agreement in order to ship materials from the show. All pieces must be labeled individually.
- To save time, complete and submit the Outbound Shipping Form in advance or you may contact the Freeman Exhibitor Service Center at show site for your shipping documents. The Material Handling Agreement and labels will be processed and available before the show closes.
- After materials are packed, labeled and ready to be shipped, the completed Material Handling Agreement must be turned in at the Freeman Exhibitor Service Center.
- Call your designated carrier with pick-up information. Please refer to Quick Facts for specific dates and times. In the event your selected carrier fails to show on final move-out day, your shipment will either be rerouted to the Freeman carrier of choice or delivered back to the warehouse at the exhibitor's expense.
- For your convenience, show-recommended carriers will be on site to handle outbound transportation.

Where do I get a forklift:

- Forklift orders to install or dismantle your booth after materials are delivered may be ordered in advance or at show site. We recommend that your order in advance to avoid additional charges at show site. Refer to the Order Form for available equipment.
- Advance and show-site orders for equipment and labour will be dispatched once a company representative signs the labour order at the Freeman Exhibitor Services Center.
- Start time is guaranteed only when equipment is requested for the start of the working day.

Do I need insurance:

- Be sure your materials are insured from the time they leave your firm until they are returned after the show. It is suggested that exhibitors arrange all-risk coverage. This can be done by riders to your existing policies.

SETTING STANDARDS OF OVERHEADS

The next important element comes under overheads. The very purpose of setting standard for overheads is to minimize the total cost. Standard overhead rates are computed by dividing overhead expenses by direct labour hours or units produced. The standard overhead cost is obtained by multiplying standard overhead rate by the labour hours spent or number of units produced. The determination of overhead rate involves three things:

- Determination of overheads
- Determination of labour hours or units manufactured
- Calculating overheads rate by dividing A by B

The overheads are classified into fixed overheads, variable overheads and semi-variable overheads. The fixed overheads remain the same irrespective of level of production, while variable overheads change in the proportion of production. The expenses increase or decrease with the increase or decrease in output.

Semi-variable overheads are neither fixed nor variable. These overheads increase with the increase in production but the rate of increase will be less than the rate of increase in production. The division of overheads into fixed, variable and semi-variable categories will help in determining overheads.

DETERMINATION OF STANDARD COSTS

How should the ideal standards for better controlling be determined?

Determination of Cost Center

J. Betty, *"A cost center is a department or part of a department or an item of equipment or machinery or a person or a group of persons in respect of which costs are accumulated, and one where control can be exercised."* Cost centers are necessary for determining the costs. If the whole factory is engaged in manufacturing a product, the factory will be a cost center. In fact, a cost center describes the product while cost is accumulated. Cost centers enable the determination of costs and fixation of responsibility. A cost center relating to a person is called personnel cost center, and a cost center relating to products and equipments is called impersonal cost center.

Current Standards

A current standard is a standard which is established for use over a short period of time and is related to current condition. It reflects the performance that should be attained during the current period. The period for current standard is normally one year. It is presumed that conditions of production will remain unchanged. In case there is any change in price or manufacturing condition, the standards are also revised. Current standard may be ideal standard and expected standard.

Ideal Standard

This is the standard which represents a high level of efficiency. Ideal standard is fixed on the assumption that favourable conditions will prevail and management will be at its best. The price paid for materials will be lowest and wastes etc. will be minimum possible. The labour time for making the production will be minimum and rates of wages will also be low.

The overheads expenses are also set with maximum efficiency in mind. All the conditions, both internal and external, should be favourable and only then ideal standard will be achieved. Ideal standard is fixed on the assumption of those conditions which may rarely exist. This standard is not practicable and may not be achieved.

Though this standard may not be achieved, even then an effort is made. The deviation between targets and actual performance is ignorable. In practice, ideal standard has an adverse effect on the employees. They do not try to reach the standard because the standards are not considered realistic.

Basic Standards

A basic standard may be defined as a standard which is established for use for an indefinite period which may a long period. Basic standard is established for a long period and is not adjusted to the preset conations. The same standard remains in force for a long period.

These standards are revised only on the changes in specification of material and technology productions. It is indeed just like a number against which subsequent process changes can be measured. Basic standard enables the measurement of changes in costs. For example, if the basic cost for material is ₹ 20 per unit and the current price is ₹25 per unit, it will show an increase of 25 per cent in the cost of materials. The changes in manufacturing costs can be measured by taking basic standard, as a base standard cannot serve as a tool for cost control purpose because the standard is not revised for a long time. The deviation between standard cost and actual cost cannot be used as a yardstick for measuring efficiency.

Normal Standards

As per terminology, normal standard has been defined as a standard which, it is anticipated, can be attained over a future period of time, preferably long enough to cover one trade cycle.

This standard is based on the conditions which will cover a future period of five years, concerning one trade cycle. If a normal cycle of ups and downs in sales and production is 10 years, then standard will be set on average sales and production which will cover all the years.

The standard attempts to cover variance in the production from one time to another time. An average is taken from the periods of recession and depression.

The normal standard concept is theoretical and cannot be used for cost control purpose. Normal standard can be properly applied for absorption of overhead cost over a long period of time.

Organization for Standard Costing

The success of standard costing system will depend upon the setting up of proper standards. For the purpose of setting standards, a person or a committee should be given this job. In a big concern, a standard costing committee is formed for this purpose.

The committee includes production manager, purchase manager, sales manager, personnel manager, chief engineer and cost accountant. The cost accountant acts as a co-coordinator of this committee.

Accounting System

Classification of accounts is necessary to meet the required purpose, *i.e.* function, asset or revenue item. Codes can be used to have a speedy collection of accounts. A standard is a pre-determined measure of material, labour and overheads. It may be expressed in quality and its monetary measurements in standard costs.

REVISION OF STANDARDS

For effective use of this technique, sometimes we need to revise the standards which follow for better control. Even standards are also subjected to change like the production method, environment, raw material, and technology. Standards may need to be changed to accommodate changes in the organization or its environment.

When there is a sudden change in economic circumstances, technology or production methods, the standard cost will no longer be accurate. Standards that are out of date will not act as effective feed forward or feedback control tools. They will not help us to predict the inputs required nor help us to evaluate the efficiency of a particular department. If standards are continually not being achieved and large deviations or variances from the standard are reported, they should be carefully reviewed. Also, changes in the physical productive capacity of the organization or in material prices and wage rates may indicate that standards need to be revised. In practice, changing standards frequently is an expensive operation and can cause confusion.

For this reason, standard cost revisions are usually made only once a year. At times of rapid price inflation, many managers have felt that the high level of inflation forced them to change price and wage rate standards continually. This, however, leads to reduction in value of the standard as a yardstick. At the other extreme is the adoption of basic standard which will remain unchanged for many years. They provide a constant base for comparison, but this is hardly satisfactory when there is technological change in working procedures and conditions.

6

Cost Accounting and Management Accounting

The term "management accounting", as defined by the NAA in SMA Statement No. 1A, is used in its broadest sense and better relates to the contents of this book.

The NAA defines management accounting as the process of:

- Identification The recognition and evaluation of business transactions and other economic events for appropriate accounting action.
- Measurement The quantification, including estimates, of business transactions or other economic events that have occurred or may occur.
- Accumulation The disciplined and consistent approach to recording and classifying appropriate business transactions and other economic events.
- Analysis The determination of the reasons for, and the relationships of, the reported activity with other economic events and circumstances.
- Preparation and Interpretation The meaningful coordination of accounting and/or planning data to satisfy a need for information presented in a logical format, and, if appropriate, including the conclusions drawn from those data.
- Communication The reporting of pertinent information to management and others for internal and external uses.

Management accounting is used by management to:

- Plan To gain an understanding of expected business transactions and other economic events and their impact on the organization.
- Evaluate To judge the implications of various past and/or future events.
- Control To ensure the integrity of financial information concerning an organization's activities or its resources.
- Assure accountability To implement the system of reporting that is closely aligned to organizational responsibilities and that contributes to the effective measurement of management performance.

ADVANTAGES OF COST ACCOUNTING

CLASSIFICATION AND SUBDIVISION OF COSTS

In the contrast to a single profit or loss figure supplied by general accounting, the cost accounting classifies costs and income by every conceivable subdivision of the business enterprise.

In a good costing system data regarding costs by departments, processes, functions, products, orders, jobs, contracts and services can easily computed. This detailed cost information for managerial control is one of the most important contributions of cost accounting.

ADEQUACY OR INADEQUACY OF SELLING PRICES

Unit cost of production, administration and safe made possible by cost accounting aids management in deciding the adequacy or inadequacy of selling prices *i.e.* neither too high detracting business, nor too low resulting in losses to the concern.

In period of depressions, slumps, or in case of competition management forced to lower prices even below cost of production and sale. In such circumstances, cost accounting will help management in deciding the proper reduction.

DISCLOSURE OF PROFITABLE PRODUCTS

Cost Accounting will disclose activities, departments, products and territories, which bring profit and those that result in losses. Management to determine what products because of profit margin the sales department because of their greater profit margin should emphasize will use this information.

What products arte unprofitable or less profitable and might be eliminated or lesser sales pressure be given to them.

What activities or territories are not producing sufficient profit and should be either further improved or eliminated and what methods of production and distribution are most profitable for the firm. This will increase the overall profit of the concern.

CONTROL OF MATERIAL AND SUPPLIES

In a good costing system materials and supplies must be accounted for in terms of departments, jobs, units of production or service.

This will eliminate altogether or reduce to the minimum misappropriations, embezzlements, deterioration, obsolescence, and losses from defective, spoiled, scrap and out of date materials and supplies.

MAINTENANCE OF PROPER INVESTMENT IN INVENTORIES

A costing system will help in the maintenance of various inventory items of materials and supplies in line with production and sale requirements. If these quantities are too small, production may stop or sales may be lost. On the other hand, if quantities of such materials and supplies are in excess of the production and sales requirements, too much working capital may unnecessarily tie up in inventories. The detailed quantity information furnished by the cost accountant at all times will go a long way in reducing or eliminating this possibility.

CORRECT VALUATION OF INVENTORIES

Cost Accounting plays a basic role in the correct valuation of inventories of finished goods, work in process, materials and supplies. The book inventory method (as opposed to physical inventory method) made possible by cost accounting system will involve the operation of the various inventory control accounts in such a manner that the balances of these accounts well be inventory valuations required for periodic financial statements.

This enables the preparation of monthly financial statements without the trouble and expense of taking monthly physical inventories. Further, the value of inventories shown by the book inventory will be more accurate than inventory values shown by the physical inventory method. If no cost system is in use and inventory values computed by physical inventory method, then the value of these inventories must either bean estimate of cost or be determined at market values. But in a cost accounting system accurate procedures and techniques are available by which inventory values can be computed in a relatively more exact fashion.

The requirements of management, stockh olders, creditors, employees and other groups interested in the financial statements of the firm naturally attach more emphasis on this objective of cost accounting. In most cases, this objective of cost accounting dominates the formal cost records and routines.

WHETHER TO MANUFACTURE OR PURCHASE FROM OUTSIDERS

Cost records furnish information regarding the cost of manufacturing of different finished parts, which assist management in making a decision whether to purchase these parts from outside manufacturers or manufacture them in the factory.

CONTROL OF LABOUR COST

Orders, jobs, contracts, departments, processes, or services record cost of labour. In many manufacturing enterprises, daily time reports are prepared showing the number of hours and minutes spent and the wage rate for each worker per job or operation. This enables management to compare the current cost of labour per job or operation with some previously incurred or determined cost thus measuring the efficiency or inefficiency of the labour force and assigning the work to employees best suited for it.

USE OF COMPANY-WIDE WAGE INCENTIVE PLANS

When labour cost is accounted for by jobs and operations, it is possible to use effectively wage incentive plans or bonus schemes for the remuneration of labour force. Carefully planned and administered incentive schemes are an effective means of enforcing superior performance and cost reduction.

Workers are more co-operative, responsive and productive when some form of incentive offered to them for surpassing stipulated standards of perfection and performance.

Cost of accounting has developed incentive plans, which are applicable not only to factory workers but also to clerks, salespersons, and other executives for standard performance.

CONTROLLABLE AND UNCONTROLLABLE COST

Cost accounting exhibits at each stage of production and sale the controllable and uncontrollable items in the manufacturing, selling and administrative cost thus enabling management to concentrate attention on those costs, which can reduced of, eliminated. There is very little the management can do to reduce such uncontrollable items as idle time of machines and labour, wastage in the use of materials, supplies and power can controlled much more effectively.

USE OF STANDARDS FOR MEASURING EFFICIENCY

A complete cost accounting system, generally, has a well-developed plan of standards to measure the efficiency of the organization in the use of materials, incurrence of labour and other manufacturing cost. Cora does this appraisal paring the work of factory workers, office and sales personnel and other executive with what should have done in manufacturing and selling a given quantity of units in a given period.

REDUCTION OF LOSSES DUE TO SEASONAL CONDITIONS

Cost accounting provides data for making a complete analysis of losses due to idle plant and equipment or due to the use of plant and equipment beyond normal capacity, irregular employment of labour, wastes in the use of materials. It indicates cost variations between active and inactive periods and seasonal conditions in the business or industry. Seasonal fluctuations in business activity affect profoundly the earnings of the concern. In many industries, seasonal variations are responsible for higher costs and lower profits.

BUDGETING

In a good cost accounting system, preparation of various budgets periods in advance of actual production and sale of goods is necessary. These budgets include budgeted statement of profits, budgeted cost of plant improvements, budgeted cost of production, budgeted cash receipts and payments, and so forth. These budgets show the plans of the management for future periods and they reflect the expected results of these plans. They are of great help in getting the sales manager, the works manager, and the treasurer into agreement as to a plan that can sold, manufactured and financed. In fact, the use of budgets has made costing a preventive device for the rectification of inefficiencies before they creep into the business operations or as they occur from day to day. In other words, budgeting, inculcates the habit of thinking and calculations before taking decisions.

RELIABLE CHECK ON GENERALACCOUNTING

Finally, an efficient and proper system of cost accounting is a most reliable and independent check on the accuracy of the financial accounts. This check made effective through reconciliation of the balance of profit or loss shown by the costing profit and loss account and the balance of profit of profit or loss revealed by the general accounting profit and loss account.

MANAGEMENT ACCOUNTING

Management accounting or managerial accounting is concerned with the provisions and use of accounting information to managers within organizations, to provide them with the basis to make informed business decisions that will allow them to be better equipped in their management and control functions.

In contrast to financial accountancy information, management accounting information is:

- Designed and intended for use by managers within the organization, instead of being intended for use by shareholders, creditors, and public regulators;
- Usually confidential and used by management, instead of publicly reported;
- Forward-looking, instead of historical;
  computed by reference to the needs of managers, often using management information systems, instead of by reference to general financial accounting standards.

According to the Chartered Institute of Management Accountants (CIMA), Management Accounting is"the process of identification, measurement, accumulation, analysis, preparation, interpretation and communication of information used by management to plan, evaluate and control within an entity and to assure appropriate use of and accountability for its resources. Management accounting also comprises the preparation of financial reports for non-management groups such as shareholders, creditors, regulatory agencies and tax authorities" (CIMA Official Terminology).

The American Institute of Certified Public Acco-untants(AICPA) states that management accounting as practice extends to the following three areas:

- Strategic Management-Advancing the role of the management accountant as a strategic partner in the organization.
- Performance Management-Developing the practice of business decision-making and managing the performance of the organization.
- Risk Management-Contributing to frameworks and practices for identifying, measuring, managing and reporting risks to the achievement of the objectives of the organization.

The Institute of Certified Management Acco-untants (ICMA), states"A management accountant applies his or her professional knowledge and skill in the preparation and presentation of financial and other decision oriented information in such a way as to assist management in the formulation of policies and in the planning and control of the operation of the undertaking." Management Accountants therefore are seen as the"value-creators" amongst the accountants. They are much more interested in forward looking and taking decisions that will affect the future of the organization, than in the historical recording and compliance (scorekeeping) aspects of the profession. Management accounting knowledge and experience can therefore be obtained from varied fields and functions within an organization, such as information management, treasury, efficiency auditing, marketing, valuation, pricing, logistics, etc.

TRADITIONAL VS. INNOVATIVE PRACTICES

In the late 1980s, accounting practitioners and educators were heavily criticized on the grounds that management accounting practices (and, even more so, the curriculum taught to accounting students) had changed little over the preceding 60 years, despite radical changes in the business environment. Professional accounting institutes, perhaps fearing that management accountants would increasingly be seen as superfluous in business organizations, subsequently devoted considerable resources to the development of a more innovative skills set for management accountants.

The distinction between'traditional' and'innovative' accounting practices can be showed by reference to cost control techniques. Cost accounting is a central method in management accounting, and traditionally, management accountants' principal technique was variance analysis, which is a systematic approach to the comparison of the actual and budgeted costs of the raw materials and labour used during a production period. While some form of variance analysis is still used by most manufacturing firms, it nowadays tends to be used in conjunction with innovative techniques such as life cycle cost analysis and activity-based costing, which are designed with specific aspects of the modern business environment in mind. Life-cycle costing recognizes that managers' ability to influence the cost of manufacturing a product is at its greatest when the product is still at the design stage of its product life-cycle (*i.e.*, before the design has been finalized and production commenced), since small changes to the product design may lead to significant savings in the cost of manufacturing the products. Activity-based costing (ABC) recognizes that, in modern factories, most manufacturing costs are determined by the amount of'activities' (*e.g.*, the number of production runs per month, and the amount of production equipment idle time) and that the key to effective cost control is therefore optimizing the efficiency of these activities. Activity-based accounting is also known as Cause and Effect accounting.

Both lifecycle costing and activity-based costing recognize that, in the typical modern factory, the avoidance of disruptive events (such as machine breakdowns and quality control failures) is of far greater importance than (for example) reducing the costs of raw materials. Activity-based costing also deemphasizes direct labour as a cost driver and concentrates instead on activities that drive costs, such as the provision of a service or the production of a product component.

ROLE WITHIN A CORPORATION

Consistent with other roles in today's corporation, management accountants have a dual reporting relationship. As a strategic partner and provider of decision based financial and operational information, management accountants are responsible for managing the business team and at the same time having to report relationships and responsibilities to the corporation's finance organization.

The activities management accountants provide inclusive of forecasting and planning, performing variance analysis, reviewing and monitoring costs inherent in the business are ones that have dual accountability to both finance and the business team. Examples of tasks where accountability may be more meaningful to the business management team vs. the corporate finance department are the development of new product costing, operations research, business driver metrics, sales management scorecarding, and client profitability analysis.

Conversely, the preparation of certain financial reports, reconciliations of the financial data to source systems, risk and regulatory reporting will be more useful to the corporate finance team as they are charged with aggregating certain financial information from all segments of the corporation. One widely held view of the progression of the accounting and finance career path is that financial accounting is a stepping stone to management accounting. Consistent with the notion of value creation, management accountants help drive the success of the business while strict financial accounting is more of a compliance and historical endeavor.

In corporations that derive much of their profits from the information economy, such as banks, publishing houses, telecommunications companies and defence contractors, IT costs are a significant source of uncontrollable spending, which in size is often the greatest corporate cost after total compensation costs and property related costs. A function of management accounting in such organizations is to work closely with the IT department to provide IT Cost Transparency.

An Alternative View

A very rarely expressed alternative view of management accounting is that it is neither a neutral or benign influence in organizations, rather a mechanism for management control through surveillance. This view locates management accounting specifically in the context of management control theory.

Stated differently, Management Accounting information is the mechanism which can be used by managers as a vehicle for the overview of the whole internal structure of the organization to facilitate their control functions within an organization.

SPECIFIC CONCEPTS

Grenzplankostenrechnung (GPK)

Grenzplankostenrechnung is a German costing methodology, developed in the late 1940s and 1950s, designed to provide a consistent and accurate application of how managerial costs are calculated and assigned to a product or service.

The term Grenzplankostenrechnung, often referred to as GPK, has best been translated as either Marginal Planned Cost Accounting or Flexible Analytic Cost Planning and Accounting.

The origins of GPK are credited to Hans Georg Plaut, an automotive engineer and Wolfgang Kilger, an academic, working towards the mutual goal of identifying and delivering a sustained methodology designed to correct and enhance cost accounting information.

Lean Accounting (Accounting for Lean Enterprise)

In the mid to late 1990s several books were written about accounting in the lean enterprise (companies implementing elements of the Toyota Production System). The term lean accounting was coined during that period. These books contest that traditional accounting methods are better suited for mass production and do not support or measure good business practices in just in time manufacturing and services. The movement reached a tipping point during the 2005 Lean Accounting Summit in Dearborn, MI. 320 individuals attended and discussed the merits of a new approach to accounting in the lean enterprise. 520 individuals attended the 2nd annual conference in 2006.

Resource Consumption Accounting (RCA)

Resource Consumption Accounting (RCA) is formally defined as a dynamic, fully integrated, principle-based, and comprehensive management accounting approach that provides managers with decision support information for enterprise optimization. RCA emerged as a management accounting approach around 2000 and was subsequently developed at CAM-I the Consortium for Advanced Manufacturing–International, in a Cost Management Part RCA interest group in December 2001.

Throughput Accounting

The most significant recent direction in managerial accounting is throughput accounting; which recognizes the interdependencies of modern production processes. For any given product, customer or supplier, it is a tool to measure the contribution per unit of constrained resource.

Transfer Pricing

Management accounting is an applied discipline used in various industries. The specific functions and principles followed can vary based on the industry. Management accounting principles in banking are specialized but do have some common fundamental concepts used whether the industry is manufacturing based or service oriented. For example, transfer pricing is a concept used in manufacturing but is also applied in banking.

It is a fundamental principle used in assigning value and revenue attribution to the various business units. Essentially, transfer pricing in banking is the method of assigning the interest rate risk of the bank to the various funding sources and uses of the enterprise.

Thus, the bank's corporate treasury department will assign funding charges to the business units for their use of the bank's resources when they make loans to clients. The treasury department will also assign funding credit to business units who bring in deposits (resources) to the bank. Although the funds transfer pricing process is primarily applicable to the loans and deposits of the various banking units, this proactive is applied to all assets and liabilities of the business segment.

Once transfer pricing is applied and any other management accounting entries or adjustments are posted to the ledger (which are usually memo accounts and are not included in the legal entity results), the business units are able to produce segment financial results which are used by both internal and external users to evaluate performance.

RESOURCES AND CONTINUOUS LEARNING

There are a variety of ways to keep current and continue to build one's knowledge base in the field of management accounting. Certified Management Accountants (CMAs) are required to achieve continuing education hours every year, similar to a Certified Public Accountant. A company may also have research and training materials available for use in a corporate owned library. This is more common in "Fortune 500" companies who have the resources to fund this type of training medium.

MANAGEMENT ACCOUNTING TASKS/SERVICES PROVIDED

The primary tasks/services performed by management accountants. The degree of complexity relative to these activities are dependent on the experience level and abilities of any one individual.

- Rate and Volume Analysis
- Business Metrics Development
- Price Modeling
- Product Profitability
- Geographic vs. Industry or Client Segment Reporting
- Sales Management Scorecards
- Cost Analysis
- Cost Benefit Analysis
- Cost-Volume-Profit Analysis
- Life cycle cost analysis
- Client Profitability Analysis
- IT Cost Transparency
- Capital Budgeting
- Buy vs. Lease Analysis
- Strategic Planning
- Strategic Management Advise
- Internal Financial Presentation and Communication
- Sales and Financial Forecasting
- Annual Budgeting
- Cost Allocation

WHAT IS MANAGEMENT ACCOUNTING

Management accounting is the internal business building role of accounting and finance professionals who work inside organizations.

These professionals are involved in designing and evaluating business processes, budgeting and forecasting, implementing and monitoring internal controls, and analyzing, synthesizing, and aggregating information—to help drive economic value.

The role of management accounting differs from that of public accounting, since management accountants work at the "beginning" of the value chain, supporting decision making, planning and control, while audit and tax functions involve checking the work after the fact. Management accountants are valued business partners, directly supporting an organization's strategic goals. With a renewed emphasis on good internal controls and sound financial reporting, the role of the management accountant is more important than ever. It obviously takes more people to "do" the work than it does to "check" the work. In fact, of the five million finance function professionals in the U.S., more than 90 per cent work inside organizations as management accountants and finance professionals.

Some common job titles for management accountants in organizations of all sizes and structure include:

- Staff Accountant
- Cost Accountant
- Senior Accountant
- Corporate or Division Planner
- Financial Analyst
- Budget Analyst
- Internal Auditor
- Finance Manager
- Controller
- Vice President, Finance
- Treasurer
- Chief Financial Officer (CFO)
- Chief Executive Officer (CEO)

ROLE OF MANAGEMENT ACCOUNTING

- Analysing overall business and operational data.
- Assisting in decision-making process at all cadres of management.
- Breaking down of cost/expenditure into functions and processes to facilitate cost control at each operational level.
- Contributing to Total Quality Management (TQM).
- Deploying informatic tools for an efficient management information system.
- Developing standards for all operating areas and evaluating actuals with the standards.
- Ensuring optimum utilisation of available resources.
- Identifying areas of wastages, leakages and inefficiencies or invisible losses.
- Suggesting alternatives to improve productivity.

FINANCIAL AND MANAGERIAL ACCOUNTING

Financial accounting reports are prepared for external parties such as shareholders and creditors, whereas managerial accounting reports are prepared for managers inside the organization.

This contrast in orientation results in a number of major differences between financial and managerial accounting, even though they often rely on the same under-lying financial data. Comparison of Financial and Managerial Accounting

Identify the major differences and similarities between financial and managerial accounting.

As shown in Exhibit 1-3, financial and managerial accounting differ not only in their user orientation but also in their emphasis on the past and the future, in the type of data provided to users, and in several other ways. These differences are discussed in the following paragraphs.

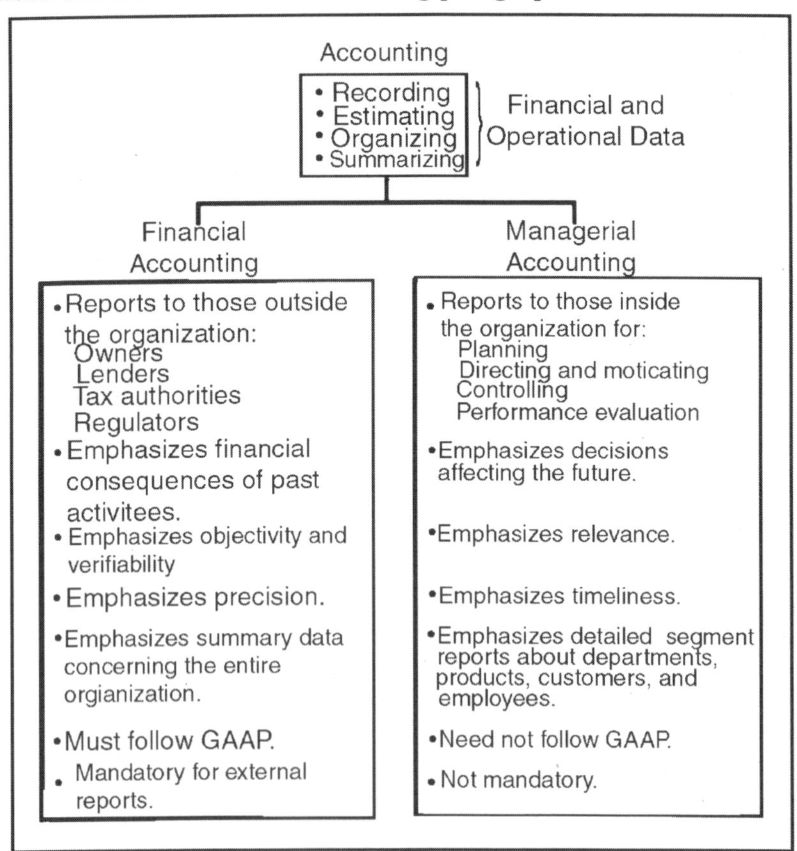

Emphasis on the Future

Since *planning* is such an important part of the manager's job, managerial accounting has a strong future orientation. In contrast, financial accounting primarily summarizes past financial transactions. These summaries may be useful in planning, but only to a point.

The future is not simply a reflection of what has happened in the past. Changes are constantly taking place in economic conditions, customer needs and desires, competitive conditions, and so on.

All of these changes demand that the manager's planning be based in large part on estimates of what will happen rather than on summaries of what has already happened.

Relevance of Data

Financial accounting data should be objective and verifiable. However, for internal uses managers want information that is relevant even if it is not completely objective or verifiable.

By relevant, we mean *appropriate for the problem at hand.* For example, it is difficult to verify estimated sales volumes for a proposed new store at Good Vibrations, but this is exactly the type of information that is most useful to managers. Managerial accounting should be flexible enough to provide whatever data are relevant for a particular decision.

Less Emphasis on Precision

Making sure that dollar amounts are accurate down to the last dollar or penny takes time and effort. While that kind of accuracy is required for external reports, most managers would rather have a good estimate immediately than wait for a more precise answer later.

For this reason, managerial accountants often place less emphasis on precision than financial accountants do. For example, in a decision involving hundreds of millions of dollars, estimates that are rounded off to the nearest million dollars are probably good enough.

In addition to placing less emphasis on precision than financial accounting, managerial accounting places much more weight on non-monetary data. For example, data about customer satisfaction may be routinely used in managerial accounting reports.

Segments of an Organization

Financial accounting is primarily concerned with report-ing for the company as a whole. By contrast, managerial accounting focuses much more on the parts, or segments , of a company.

These segments may be product lines, sales territories, divisions, departments, or any other categorization that management finds useful. Financial accounting does require some breakdowns of revenues and costs by major segments in external reports, but this is a secondary emphasis. In managerial accounting, segment reporting is the primary emphasis.

Generally Accepted Accounting Principles (GAAP)

Financial accounting statements prepared for external users must comply with generally accepted accounting principles (GAAP). External users must have some assurance that the reports have been prepared in accordance with a common set of ground rules. These common ground rules enhance comparability and help reduce fraud and misrepresentation, but they do not necessarily lead to the type of reports that would be most useful in internal decision making.

For example, if management at Good Vibrations is considering selling land to finance a new store, they need to know the current market value of the land.

However, GAAP requires that the land be stated at its original, historical cost on financial reports. The more relevant data for the decision—the current market value—is ignored under GAAP.

Managerial accounting is not bound by GAAP. Managers set their own rules concerning the content and form of internal reports.

The only constraint is that the expected benefits from using the information should outweigh the costs of collecting, analyzing, and summarizing the data.

Nevertheless, as we shall see in subsequent chapters, it is undeniably true that financial reporting requirements have heavily influenced management accounting practice.

Managerial Accounting—Not Mandatory

Financial accounting is mandatory; that is, it must be done. Various outside parties such as the Securities and Exchange Commission (SEC) and the tax authorities require periodic financial statements. Managerial accounting, on the other hand, is not mandatory.

A company is completely free to do as much or as little as it wishes. No regulatory bodies or other outside agencies specify what is to be done, or, for that matter, whether anything is to be done at all.

Since managerial accounting is completely optional, the important question is always, "Is the information useful?" rather than, "Is the information required?"

ROLE OF FINANCIAL AND MANAGEMENT ACCOUNTING

Learning Objectives

- Outline to participants on the major differences between financial and management accounting
- Explaining to the participants on the role manag-ement accountant in an organization.
- Briefing the participants on the useful qualities of management information.

Important Terms

- Financial accounting
- Management accounting
- Data
- Information

Management accounting is the process of identification, measurement, accumulation, analysis, preparation, interpreta-tion and communication of information used by management to plan, evaluate and control within an entity and to assure appropriate use of and accountability for its resources.

Management accounting also comprises the preparation of financial reports for non- management groups such as shareholders, creditors, regulatory agencies and tax authorities.The core activities of management accounting include:

- Participation in the planning process at both strategic and operational levels. This involves the establish-ment of policies and the formulation of plans and budgets which will subsequently be expressed in the financial terms.
- The initiation of and the provision of guidance for management decisions. This involves the generation, analysis, presentation and interpretation of appropriate information.
- Contributing to the monitoring and control performance through the provision of reports on organisational performance, including comparisons of actual with planned or budgeted performance, and their analysis and interpretation.

  Financial accounting is the periodic reporting of accounting as required by statue for shareholders, government agencies and other parties external to the business. As such, various conventions and rules are necessary to ensure consistency between the sets of accounts.

FEATURE OF MANAGEMENT ACCOUNTING

- It should be relevant for its purpose.
- It should be complete for its purpose.
- It should be sufficiently accurate for its purpose.
- It should be clear to the manager using it.
- The manager using it should have confidence in it.
- It should be communicated to the appropriate manager.
- Its volume should be manageable.
- It should be timely.
- It should be communicated through appropriate channel of communication.
- It should be provided at a cost which is less than the value of the benefits it provides.

Role of Management Accountant

Assistance in Planning

The management accountant assists planning by providing information. This information may be about pricing, capital expenditure projects, product costs or competition. In the short-term planning process of budgeting, the management accountant provides information on past costs and revenues which may be used as guidance. The management accountant is also involved in the budgeting process itself.

Assistance in Controlling

The management accountant supplies performance reports which compare actual performance with the planned performance and which therefore highlight those activities which are not conforming to plan.

Assistance in Organizing

By ensuring that the accounting system is tailored to the organisational structure, the management accountant reinforces the objectives of the organisational framework.

Assistance in Motivating

Budgets prepared by the prepared by the management accountant serve to motivate managers and subordinates to attempt to achieve the organisation's objectives.

Formalized targets are more likely to motivate than vague comments. Performance reports produced by the management accountant for the control process also motivate by communicating performance information in relation to the targets which have been set.

Assistance in Decision Making

The management accountant is a vital cog in the organisation's decision making process. He or she collects and analyses data, and presents information to managers to help in the decision making.

FINANCIAL, COST AND MANAGEMENT ACCOUNTING

Having discussed the differences and similarities between the financial, cost and management accounting systems, as suggested, now show the difference with the help of an example:

The statement reveals that the business has made comparatively higher profit than previous year through increased sales, lower material cost, controlled factory expenses, better inventory management, etc., but it does not reflect how the profit was earned, or what was the profitability of each of the products.

Table. In Financial Accounts (in ₹.'000).

	Current year	Previous year
Income:		
Sales	1600	1200
Other income	15	9
(A)	**1615**	**1209**
Expenditure:		
Opening stock of finished goods and work in progress	200	184
Add: Purchases/consumption of raw materials	880	760
	1080	**944**
Less: Closing stock of finished goods and work in progress	144	200
Cost of goods consumed/sold	936	744
Manufacturing expenses	124	115
Selling expenses	40	26
Salaries wages andother employee benefits	175	124
Interest on loan	9	8
Depreciation	21	19
Amortisation of preliminary expenses	10	8
Total (B)	**1315**	**1044**
Profit before tax (A-B)	**300**	**165**

IN COST ACCOUNTS

Cost accounting records reveal the following results:

Table. Productwise Profit Statement (₹ '000).

Cost elements	Product X	Product Y	Product Z	Total
Direct material	400	276	260	936
Direct wages	50	40	30	120
Direct expense	10	4	6	20
Prime cost	460	320	236	1076
Applied overheads: Factory, admn., selling and distrn.	93	73	54	220
Cost of sales	553	393	350	1296
Profit/(Loss)	147	207	(50)	304
Sales	700	600	300	1600

The profit statement leads to further analysis of product costs to find out what went wrong with product Z? Should it be discontinued? If so, what would be the effect on profit? Obviously, the answers cannot be obtained straightaway from the statement.

In fact so that ail expenses can be classified under product costs, which are variable with the increase or reduction of unit-product and period costs which are fixed overhead expenses and remain unaffected with change in volume during the period. This technique of marginal cost system is applied and the profit statement reveals the following position:

Cost Elements	Product X	Product Y	Product Z	Total
	₹ '000	₹ '000	₹ '000	₹ '000
Sales (A)	700	600	300	1600
Less: Direct cost of sales:				
Material	400	276	260	936
Labour	50	40	30	120
Expenses	30	14	8	52
Total (B)	**480**	**330**	**298**	**1108**
Contribution(A – B.)	**220**	**270**	**2**	**492**
Less: Fixed over-heads				188
Profit				**304**

The statement indicates the relative profitability of the three products and also establishes the fact that the product Z just recovers its direct cost of sales. Investigation shall immediately start to find out whether:

- Material cost is too high, or
- There is generation of excessive scrap and defective, or
- The selling price is too low.

When such questions are raised, the dividing line between cost accounting and management accounting vanishes. With a view to increase overall efficiency and profit improvement, the management accountant will have to collect various data for analysing other norms to judge efficient use of resources.

For example, he may find out that there is more stress on product Y than product X while establishing costly materials used in the products fearing drop in sales.

A value engineering exercise on the usage of materials for Product X may reveal the scope for further substitution without impairing quality. A 15 per cent drop in material cost *i.e.* 15 per cent of ₹ 400, will increase the profit by ₹ 60 *i.e.* by 8.6 per cent.

Now, this exercise can be done by the cost accountant or management accountant with the assistance of marketing, industrial engineering, production, purchasing and materials management departments. Can you, therefore, make any line of demarcation between cost and management accounting today?

INTERORGANIZATIONAL COST MANAGEMENT (IOCM)

A fundamental concept of supply chain management is that organizations must look beyond their own boundaries to consider relationships with their suppliers and customers along the value chain. For most of the 20th century, the norm for inter-organizational behaviour has been that of autonomous firms engaging in arm's length transactions with other firms. This internal focus by firms has made it difficult for organizations to take advantage of cost management synergies that may be obtained through the cooperation and collaboration of business partners. These synergies require additional coordination mechanisms to extend cost management programmes beyond organizational boundaries, with the overall objective of finding lower cost solutions than would be possible if the firm and its customers and suppliers attempted to reduce costs independently.

These synergies may be obtained through vertical integration; but now many organizations engage in IOCM instead. These organizations can be described as hybrid organizations who achieve the cost management synergy benefits of vertical integration while maintaining the efficiency of arms-length transactions. From this view, the strategic employment of IOCM can be viewed as a hybrid between strategic intra-firm cost management focus and strategic inter-firm cost management focus as presented by Shank.

STRATEGIC COST MANAGEMENT

The origin of IOCM can be traced to the work of Porter (1985) and Shank (1989). Porter (1985) identified strategic cost analysis as a means of better managing the linkages with buyers and suppliers in a value chain in order to reduce costs and enhance differentiation. Shank builds upon Porter's value chain concept and defines the term strategic cost management as "the managerial use of cost information explicitly directed at one or more of the four stages of the strategic management cycle."

The four stages of the strategic management cycle as defined by Shank are:

1. Formulating strategies
2. Communicating those strategies throughout the firm
3. Developing and carrying out tactics to implement the strategies
4. Developing and implementing controls to monitor the strategy implementation

Based on the strategic management cycle, Shank defines strategic cost management in terms of three underlying themes from the strategic management literature

- Value chain analysis;
- Strategic position analysis; and
- Cost driver analysis.

Shank, each of the three themes represents "a stream of research and analysis in which cost information is cast in a much different light than viewed in traditional management accounting." In general, IOCM blends of inter-organizational value chain analysis and intra-organizational cost driver analysis by focusing on the management of costs related to activities that impact the focal firm as well as its business partners.

Even before this combination was described as IOCM, researchers as well as practitioners have recognized the value of merging these ideas. LaLonde and Pohlen were critical of ABC's internal focus because they recognized the potential advantages provided by ABC within a supply chain. Traditionally, the only use of ABC in terms of being extra-organizationally focused is in determining how supply chain partners affect the firm's cost and profitability -- an internally-focused orientation.

Organizations have ignored an orientation that looks outside of the firm to determine where in the supply chain activities can best be performed in terms of cost, time, or quality. Dekker and Van Goor also recognize the importance of cooperative relationships within the supply chain and through a case study in the pharmaceutical industry, they demonstrate how ABC can be used to support decisions about relocating and changing logistics activities in order to optimize across the entire supply chain.

The implication of this study is that organizations can benefit by engaging in cost analysis throughout the entire supply chain. In general, organizational boundaries are blurring and strategic exploitation of linkages within the firm's value chain and between value chains of business partners are important to an organization's performance.

INTERORGANIZATIONAL COST MANAGEMENT PRACTICES

From its origins with Porter and Shank, IOCM has emerged in the management accounting field as a general-purpose term referring to a portfolio of specific strategic management accounting practices that are specifically targeted at optimizing and integrating cost management systems in order to jointly reduce costs between partners.

Cooper and Slagmulder, IOCM practices facilitate the coordination of cost reduction in 2 ways:

- Helps identify ways to make the interface between the firms more efficient and
- Helps the firm and its buyers and suppliers find additional ways to reduce the costs of products.

Among the accounting practices commonly discussed in IOCM literature are:

- Interorganizational Target Costing
- Interorganizational Kaizen costing
- Open Book Accounting
- Information Sharing

INTERORGANIZATIONAL TARGET COSTING

Target costing focuses on managing the product development and design processes of a firm. Target costing is defined by Cooper as a "structured approach for determining the cost at which a proposed product with specified functionality and quality must be produced to generate the desired level of profitability at the product's anticipated selling price." Specifically, Cooper identifies 3 steps associated with target costing:

- Estimate the selling price at which a proposed product will sell, utilizing market research techniques
- Determine the new product's target profit margin
- Determine the product's target cost by subtracting the target profit from the target selling price.

Next, organizations apply value engineering techniques to determine how they can effectively design a product that can be manufactured at the target cost. During the value engineering process, an analysis is performed to assess ways of increasing functionality without increasing costs, as well as reducing costs without reducing functionality.

The literature regarding target costing suggests that target costing itself is an internal cost management technique in that it does not actively involve the partner firm in the focal firm's cost management programme. Instead, it is the focal firm's cost management system that contains the design information that is applicable to meeting the target price of a product. It is this design information that can be used by the partner firm to identify where cost reductions may be possible. Therefore, the key extension of target costing that brings it into the realm of IOCM is the active involvement by both the focal firm's and the partner firm's design teams in the joint identification, management, and resolution of cost issues.

Cooper and Slagmulder identify three specific IOCM techniques resulting from target costing processes that progressively involve more collaboration between the focal firm and the partner firm.

The first IOCM technique is the functionality-price-quality tradeoffs, which Cooper and Slagmulder identify as useful for resolving minor cost overrun problems and requiring limited interaction between the design teams of the focal and partner firms. The second technique is an interorganizational cost investigation, which is used when FPQ tradeoff analysis is not able to achieve the desired level of cost reductions.

The third IOCM technique related to target costing processes is concurrent cost management, which requires significant interaction and collaboration between design teams and can lead to fundamental changes in both firms' product and processes. Cooper and Slagmulder provide a complete discussion of these three techniques via case analysis, demonstrating how these IOCM techniques have been used in three Japanese supply chains to cooperatively identify mutually beneficial low-cost solutions.

INTERORGANIZATIONAL KAIZEN COSTING

Originating from successful cost management practices in Japanese firms, kaizen costing is a system of incremental and continuous cost reduction improvements of the product manufacturing process. Kaizen costing is similar to target costing in that both processes focus on cost reduction activities. However, target costing focuses on the design and development phases of a product, whereas kaizen costing is used to reduce costs in the manufacturing and delivery phases. Kaizen costing has interorganizational implications in that firms can use kaizen costing to identify and set cost-reduction objectives for suppliers. Cooper and Slagmulder identify the real benefit of interorganizational kaizen costing as being "when the firms in the supply chain cooperate to find new low-cost solutions that they cannot identify in isolation." Guilding go as far as to classify kaizen costing as a strategic management accounting practice when it focuses on an external, market-oriented approach "that is forward-looking and closely aligned to a quest for competitive advantage."

OPEN BOOK ACCOUNTING

Open book accounting refers to the practice of partners within a supply chain opening up their internal accounting information to each other in order to support their collaboration on cost management.

Open book accounting increases the transparency of cost information between partner firms, as evidenced by Lamming:

1. Cost transparency means the sharing of costing information between customer and supplier including data which would traditionally be kept secret by each party, for use in negotiations. The purpose of this is to make it possible for customer and supplier to work together to reduce costs.

By increasing information transparency between partners, open book accounting can improve the effectiveness of other IOCM techniques (*i.e.* by enabling more in-depth and strategic target costing and kaizen costing).

Mouritsen identify open book accounting as an effective inteorganizational management control to "create new possibilities for management intervention." These new possibilities extend the reach of a firm's management beyond the boundaries of their own firm and outward towards the control of a partner firm's activities. Mouritsen demonstrate these new possibilities through a case analysis where they document the benefits of one firm's experience with open book accounting. In the case study, open book accounting not only improved efficiencies in the firm's production system, but also impacted its strategic direction by transforming the firm's core competencies and competitive strategy via the insights gained from access to the supplier's production processes.

INFORMATION SHARING

Ramos points out that managerial accounting systems should include a more comprehensive set of organizational and external data, thus facilitating and perhaps even standardizing the information sharing processes in order to support supply chain activities.

Supply chain management emphasizes the benefits that can be achieved by all parties along the chain through cooperation and information sharing. The operations management literature has explored the role of including customer requirements in the new product development process, as well as including supplier integration in the new product development process. In the accounting literature, Coad and Cullen state that information sharing is critical for partners to jointly learn new skills and identify new opportunities.

This is exemplified by Cooper and Slagmulder who explore the processes that enable firms to collaborate effectively, specifically investigating the role of guest engineers in joint development projects and identifying guest engineers as an example of an IOCM practice that facilitates information sharing. Several specific forms of information sharing have been identified as salient in supply chain integration, including the sharing of real-time information about material flow and the sharing of real-time documents that can be used to create collaborative forecasts and plans and the sharing of information related to order entry, shipping, and billing through business process automation.

Furthermore, Malhotra identify the breadth of information exchange as having an impact on leveraging interorganizational partnerships and specifically identify information related to market demand and forecasts, demand shifts and changes in customer preferences, and the sharing of future plans such as long-term production plans and capital investments.

From the managerial accounting literature, we have identified several practices/ techniques associated with interorganizational cost management in a supply chain context. Additionally, we used studies from the operations management field to more fully explore the role of information sharing in managing costs throughout the supply chain. Our synthesis of the primary practices and techniques associated with interorganizational cost management.

7

Marginal Costing

MARGINAL COSTING—DEFINITION

Marginal costing distinguishes between fixed costs and variable costs as convention ally classified. The marginal cost of a product —" is its variable cost". This is normally taken to be; direct labour, direct material, direct expenses and the variable part of overheads.

Marginal costing is formally defined as: 'the accounting system in which variable costs are charged to cost units and the fixed costs of the period are written-off in full against the aggregate contribution. Its special value is in decision making'. (Terminology.) The term 'contribution' mentioned in the formal definition is the term given to the difference between Sales and Marginal cost. Thus

Marginal Cost =Variable Cost Direct Labour Direct Material + Directexpense + Variable Overheads

CONTRIBUTION SALES - MARGINAL COST

The term marginal cost sometimes refers to the marginal cost per unit and sometimes to the total marginal costs of a department or batch or operation. The meaning is usually clear from the context.

Note: Alternative names for marginal costing are the contribution approach and direct costing In this session, as suggested, study marginal costing as a technique quite distinct from absorption costing.

CHARACTERISTICS OF MARGINAL COSTING

Marginal costing is also termed as variable costing, a technique of costing which includes only variable manufacturing costs, in the form of direct materials, direct labour, and variable manufacturing overheads while determining the cost per unit of a product. Where as Absorption costing, is a costing technique that includes all manufacturing costs, in the form of direct materials, direct labour, and both variable and fixed manufacturing overheads, while determining the cost per unit of a product. It is also referred to as the full- cost technique. In the costing of product/service, a marginal costing technique considers the behavioural characteristics of costs (segregations of costs into fixed and variable elements), because per unit variable cost is fixed and total costs are variable in nature, where as total fixed costs are fixed and per unit fixed cost is variable in nature and furthermore variable costs are controllable in nature, while total fixed costs are un-controllable in nature.

Marginal costing is useful for short-term planning, control and decision-making, particularly in a business where multi-products are produced. In marginal costing technique, the contribution is calculated after deducting variable costs from sales value with reference to each product or service, in order to calculate the total contribution from all products/services which are made towards the total fixed costs incurred by the business.

As the fixed costs are treated as period costs, are deducted from total contribution to arrive at net profit. In the context of costing of a product/service, an absorption costing considers a share of all costs incurred by a business to each of its products/services.

In absorption costing technique; costs are classified according to their functions. The gross profit is calculated after deducting production costs from sales and from gross profit, costs incurred in relation to other business functions are deducted to arrive at the net profit.

Absorption costing gives better information for pricing products as it includes both variable and fixed costs. Marginal costing may lead to lower prices being offered if the firm is operating below capacity. Customers may still expect these lower prices as demand/capacity increases.

Profit Statements

The net profit shown by marginal costing and absorption costing techniques may not be the same due to the different treatment of fixed manufacturing overheads.

Marginal costing technique treats fixed manufacturing overheads as period costs, where as in absorption costing technique these are absorbed into the cost of goods produced and are only charged against profit in the period in which those goods are sold. In absorption costing income statement, adjustment pertaining to under or over-absorption of overheads is also made to arrive at the profit.

TERMS

Product and Period Costs

- *Product costs*: The costs of manufacturing the products;
- *Period costs*: These are the costs other than product costs that are charged to, debited to, or written off to the income statement each period.

Example

Data for a Quarter for a Manufacturing Company.

Level of Activity	**60%**	**100%**
Sales and Production(Units)	36,000	60,000
	₹. ('000)	**₹. ('000)**
Sales	432	720
Production costs: (Variable and fixed)	366	510
Sales, distribution and administration costs (Variable and fixed)	126	150

The normal level of activity for the current year is 60,000 units, and fixed costs are incurred evenly throughout the year. There were no stocks of the product at the start of the quarter, in which 16,500 units were made and 13,500 units were sold. Actual fixed costs were the same as budgeted. Then, various calculations regarding Absorption vs. Marginal costing can be worked out as under:

	Production Costs (Rs.)	**Sales etc costs (Rs.)**
Total costs of 60,000 units (fixed plus variable)	5,10,000	1,50,000
Total costs of 36,000 units (fixed plus variable)	3,66,000	1,26,000
Difference = variable costs of 24,000 units	1,44,000	24,000
Variable costs per unit	Rs.6	Re.1
	Production Costs (Rs.)	Sales etc. Costs (Rs.)
Total costs of 60,000 units	5,10,000	1,50,00 0
Variable costs of 60,000 units	3,60,000	60,000
Fixed costs	1,50,000	90,000

The rate of absorption of fixed production overheads will therefore be:

$$₹.1,50,000 \div 60,000 = ₹.\ 2.50 \text{ per unit.}$$

- The fixed production overhead absorbed by the products would be 16,500 units produced × ₹. 2.50 = ₹. 41,250
- Budgeted annual fixed production overhead = ₹.1,50,000

	Rs.
Actual quarterly fixed production overhead = budgeted quarterly fixed production overhead (1,50,000 ÷ 4)	37,500
Production overhead absorbed into production [see (i) above]	41,250
Over -absorption of fixed production overhead	3,750

- Profit statement for the quarter, using Absorption Costing

	Rs.	Rs.	Rs.
Sales (13,500× Rs.12)			1,62,000
Costs of production (no opening stocks)			
Value of stocks produced (16,500 × Rs. 8.50)		1,40,250	
Less value of closing stock			
(3,000 units × full production cost of Rs. 8.50)		(25,500)	
		1,14,750	
Sales etc costs			
Variable (13,500 × Re. 1)	13,500		
Fixed (1/4 of Rs. 90,000)	22,500		
		36,000	
Total cost of sales		1,50,750	
Less over-absorbed production overhead		3,750	
			1,47,000
Profit			15,000

– Profit statement for the quarter using Marginal Costing

	Rs.	Rs.
Sales (13,500×Rs.12)		1,62,000
Variable costs of production (16,500 × Rs. 6)	99,000	
Less value of closing stocks (3,000 × Rs. 6)	18,000	
Variable production cost of sales	81,000	
Variable sales etc. costs (13,500 × Re.1)	13,500	
Total variable cost of sales (13,500 × Rs. 7)		94,500
Contribution (13,500 × Rs. 5)		67,500
Fixed Costs: Production	37,500	
Sales etc.	22,500	
		60,000
Profit		7,500

ABSORPTION AND MARGINAL COSTING SYSTEMS

A popular topic for examination at Foundation Level has been the preparation of profit statements in both absorption and marginal costing formats, and the reconciliation of the profits reported by the two systems.

Example: A company sells a single product at a price of £14 per unit. Variable manufacturing costs of the product are £6.40 per unit. Fixed manufacturing overheads, which are absorbed into the cost of production at a unit rate (based on normal activity of 20,000 units per period), are £92,000 per period.

Any over-absorbed or under-absorbed fixed manufacturing overhead balances are transferred to the profit and loss account at the end of each period, in order to establish the manufacturing profit. Sales and production (in units) for two periods are as follows:

	Period 1	Period 2
Sales	15,000	21,600
Production	18,000	21,000

Required:

- Prepare a trading statement to identify the manufacturing profit for Period 2 using the existing absorption costing method.
- Determine the manufacturing profit that would be reported in Period 2 if marginal costing was used.
- Explain, with supporting calculations, why the manufacturing profit in.

ABSORPTION COSTING PRINCIPLES

In product/service costing, an absorption costing system allocates or apportions a share of all costs incurred by a business to each of its products/services. In this way, it can be established whether, in the long run, each product/service makes a profit. This can only be a guide. Arbitrary assumptions have to be made about the apportionment of many of the costs which, given that some costs will tend to remain fixed during a period, will also be dependent on the level of activity. An absorption costing system traditionally classifies costs by function. Sales less production costs (of sales) measures the gross profit (manufacturing profit) earned. Gross profit less costs incurred in other business functions establishes the net profit (operating profit) earned. Using an absorption costing system, the profit reported for a manufacturing business for a period will be influenced by the level of production as well as by the level of sales. This is because of the absorption of fixed manufacturing overheads into the value of work-in-progress and finished goods stocks. If stocks remain at the end of an accounting period, then the fixed manufacturing overhead costs included within the stock valuation will be transferred to the following period.

ABSORPTION COSTING PROFIT STATEMENT

The first stage in the preparation of absorption costing profit statements is the measurement of the gross profit (manufacturing profit) earned. This requires the calculation of unit production costs, including the establishment of absorption rates for manufacturing overheads. Referring to the example being used for illustration in this article (see earlier), variable manufacturing costs per units are given in the question (at £6.40 per unit). Fixed manufacturing overheads of £92,000 per period are to be absorbed at a unit rate (based on normal production activity of 20,000 units per period). The fixed manufacturing overhead absorption rate is therefore £4.60 per unit (£92,000 ÷ 20,000 units) giving a total manufacturing cost of £11.00 per unit (£6.40 + £4.60).

The use of normal activity as the basis for overhead absorption is similar to the use of budgeted activity. It is to be expected that actual activity (and indeed actual expenditure also) will be different to normal/budget thus giving rise to overhead over or under absorption. It is important that this is highlighted in profit statements. The use of normal (or budgeted) activity and expenditure to establish the absorption rate not only helps to focus attention on overhead recovery but also has the effect of 'normalising' per unit product/service costs.

Referring again to the example, fixed manufacturing overheads will be over-absorbed in Period 2 because the actual production of 21,000 units exceeds the normal activity, the basis used to establish the absorption rate, by 1,000 units. The extent of the over-absorption (the balance remaining in the fixed manufacturing overhead account) is, therefore, £4,600 (1,000 units at £4.60 per unit). This amount will be transferred to the profit and loss account in order to establish the manufacturing profit. It will have a positive effect (*i.e.*, it will be added to profit) because more manufacturing overhead has been absorbed into stock in the period than has been incurred (see the entries in the fixed manufacturing overhead account demonstrated later in examples).

The Examiner's Report for the June 2000 Paper 3 noted that the over-absorption of fixed manufacturing overhead caused problems for many candidates. It was frequently not identified. Where it was calculated, it was at times described as 'under-absorbed' or was at least treated as such in terms of its impact on the manufacturing profit. Other candidates wrongly calculated the over/under- absorption based upon the difference between sales and production quantities, rather than upon the difference between actual production and normal production. Preparation of the remainder of the trading statement (to identify the manufacturing profit for Period 2 using absorption costing) should be straightforward (see Example 2). The manufacturing cost of sales (the transfer out of the finished goods stock account) is simply the 21,600 units sold in the period (which at a selling price of £14.00 per unit yields total sales for the period of £302,400) multiplied by the unit manufacturing cost of £11.00.

Example:

Period 2 Trading Statement:	£000	
Sales	302.4	(21,600 units at £14.00 per unit)
Manufacturing cost of goods sold	237.6	(21,600 units at £11.00 per unit)
Manufacturing profit (before adjustment)	64.8	(21,600 units at £3.00 per unit)
Fixed manufacturing overhead over-absorbed	4.6	(1,000 units at £4.60 per unit)
Manufacturing profit (after adjustment)	69.4	

The Examiner's Report noted that there were many examples (in the examination scripts marked) of candidates matching the cost of the goods produced in the period (not the manufacturing cost of the goods sold) with sales.

Many examination candidates also got into difficulty because they attempted to introduce stock into the profit statement. There is generally no requirement to do this (unless opening and closing stocks are valued at a different rate per unit) but such an approach should (but often did not) lead to the same profit result.

In this example, no details of stock are provided in the question, but it could be assumed, for example, that 3,000 units were in stock at the end of Period I (production of 18,000 units less sales of 15,000 units). Finished goods stock at the end of Period 2 would then be 2,400 units due to the excess of sales over production of 600 units in that period.

Example:

A trading statement including stock would be.		
Period 2 Trading Statement	£000	
Sales	302.4	
Manufacturing cost of goods sold:		
Opening stock of finished goods	33.0	(3,000 units at £11.00 per unit)
Cost of goods produced	231.0	(21,000 units at £11.00 per unit)
Closing stock of finished goods	(26.4)	(2,400 units at £11.00 per unit)
	237.6	
Manufacturing profit (before adjustment)	64.8	
Fixed manufacturing overhead over-absorbed	4.6	

In the adapted question used for illustration is no information provided about costs incurred in other business functions (selling, administration, distribution) and thus it is not possible to complete the profit statement. If information on other costs was available, the costs incurred in the period would simply be deducted from the adjusted manufacturing profit to arrive at net profit.

THEORY OF MARGINAL COSTING

The theory of marginal costing as set out in "A report on Marginal Costing" published by CIMA, London is as follows: In relation to a given volume of output, additional output can normally be obtained at less than proportionate cost because within limits, the aggregate of certain items of cost will tend to remain fixed and only the aggregate of the remainder will tend to rise proportionately with an increase in output. Conversely, a decrease in the volume of output will normally be accompanied by less than proportionate fall in the aggregate cost. The theory of marginal costing may, therefore, by understood in the following two steps:

- If the volume of output increases, the cost per unit in normal circumstances reduces. Conversely, if an output reduces, the cost per unit increases. If a factory produces 1000 units at a total cost of $3,000 and if by increasing the output by one unit the cost goes up to $3,002, the marginal cost of additional output will be $.2.
- If an increase in output is more than one, the total increase in cost divided by the total increase in output will give the average marginal

cost per unit. If, for example, the output is increased to 1020 units from 1000 units and the total cost to produce these units is \$1,045, the average marginal cost per unit is \$2.25. It can be described as follows:

$$\frac{\text{Additional cost}}{\text{Additional units}} = \frac{\$45}{20} = \$2.25$$

The ascertainment of marginal cost is based on the classification and segregation of cost into fixed and variable cost. In order to understand the marginal costing technique, it is essential to understand the meaning of marginal cost. Marginal cost means the cost of the marginal or last unit produced. It is also defined as the cost of one more or one less unit produced besides existing level of production. In this connection, a unit may mean a single commodity, a dozen, a gross or any other measure of goods. For example, if a manufacturing firm produces X unit at a cost of \$ 300 and X+1 units at a cost of \$ 320, the cost of an additional unit will be \$ 20 which is marginal cost. Similarly if the production of X–1 units comes down to \$ 280, the cost of marginal unit will be \$ 20 (300–280).

The marginal cost varies directly with the volume of production and marginal cost per unit remains the same. It consists of prime cost, *i.e.* cost of direct materials, direct labour and all variable overheads. It does not contain any element of fixed cost which is kept separate under marginal cost technique. Marginal costing may be defined as the technique of presenting cost data wherein variable costs and fixed costs are shown separately for managerial decision-making. It should be clearly understood that marginal costing is not a method of costing like process costing or job costing. Rather it is simply a method or technique of the analysis of cost information for the guidance of management which tries to find out an effect on profit due to changes in the volume of output. There are different phrases being used for this technique of costing.

In UK, marginal costing is a popular phrase whereas in US, it is known as direct costing and is used in place of marginal costing. Variable costing is another name of marginal costing. Marginal costing technique has given birth to a very useful concept of contribution where contribution is given by: Sales revenue less variable cost (marginal cost) Contribution may be defined as the profit before the recovery of fixed costs. Thus, contribution goes towards the recovery of fixed cost and profit, and is equal to fixed cost plus profit (C = F + P). In case a firm neither makes profit nor suffers loss, contribution will be just equal to fixed cost (C = F). this is known as break even point. The concept of contribution is very useful in marginal costing. It has a fixed relation with sales. The proportion of contribution to sales is known as P/V ratio which remains the same under given conditions of production and sales.

ADVANTAGES AND DISADVANTAGE OF MARGINAL COSTING TECHNIQUE

ADVANTAGES

- Marginal costing is simple to understand.
- By not charging fixed overhead to cost of production, the effect of varying charges per unit is avoided.
- It prevents the illogical carry forward in stock valuation of some proportion of current year's fixed overhead.
- The effects of alternative sales or production policies can be more readily available and assessed, and decisions taken would yield the maximum return to business.
- It eliminates large balances left in overhead control accounts which indicate the difficulty of ascertaining an accurate overhead recovery rate.
- Practical cost control is greatly facilitated. By avoiding arbitrary allocation of fixed overhead, efforts can be concentrated on maintaining a uniform and consistent marginal cost. It is useful to various levels of management.
- It helps in short-term profit planning by breakeven and profitability analysis, both in terms of quantity and graphs. Comparative profitability and performance between two or more products and divisions can easily be assessed and brought to the notice of management for decision making.

DISADVANTAGES

- The separation of costs into fixed and variable is difficult and sometimes gives misleading results.
- Normal costing systems also apply overhead under normal operating volume and this shows that no advantage is gained by marginal costing.
- Under marginal costing, stocks and work in progress are understated. The exclusion of fixed costs from inventories affect profit and true and fair view of financial affairs of an organization may not be clearly transparent.
- Volume variance in standard costing also discloses the effect of fluctuating output on fixed overhead. Marginal cost data becomes unrealistic in case of highly fluctuating levels of production, *e.g.*, in case of seasonal factories.
- Application of fixed overhead depends on estimates and not on the actuals and as such there may be under or over absorption of the same.

- Control affected by means of budgetary control is also accepted by many. In order to know the net profit, we should not be satisfied with contribution and hence, fixed overhead is also a valuable item. A system which ignores fixed costs is less effective since a major portion of fixed cost is not taken care of under marginal costing.
- In practice, sales price, fixed cost and variable cost per unit may vary. Thus, the assumptions underlying the theory of marginal costing sometimes becomes unrealistic. For long term profit planning, absorption costing is the only answer.

PRESENTATION OF COST DATA UNDER MARGINAL COSTING AND ABSORPTION COSTING

Table. Marginal Costing Pro-forma.

	£	£
Sales Revenue		xxxxx
Less Marginal Cost of Sales		
Opening Stock (Valued @ marginal cost)	xxxx	
Add Production Cost (Valued @ marginal cost)	xxxx	
Total Production Cost	xxxx	
Less Closing Stock (Valued @ marginal cost)	(xxx)	
Marginal Cost of Production	xxxx	
Add Selling, Admin and Distribution Cost	xxxx	
Marginal Cost of Sales		(xxxx)
Contribution		xxxxx
Less Fixed Cost		(xxxx)
Marginal Costing Profit		xxxxx

Table. Absorption Costing Pro-forma.

	£	£
Sales Revenue		xxxxx
Less Absorption Cost of Sales		
Opening Stock (Valued @ absorption cost)	xxxx	
Add Production Cost (Valued @ absorption cost)	xxxx	
Total Production Cost	xxxx	
Less Closing Stock (Valued @ absorption cost)	(xxx)	
Absorption Cost of Production	xxxx	
Add Selling, Admin and Distribution Cost	xxxx	
Absorption Cost of Sales		(xxxx)
Un-Adjusted Profit		xxxxx
Fixed Production O/H absorbed	xxxx	
Fixed Production O/H incurred	(xxxx)	
(Under)/Over Absorption		xxxxx
Adjusted Profit		xxxxx

Marginal costing is not a method of costing but a technique of presentation of sales and cost data with a view to guide management in decision-making. The traditional technique popularly known as total cost or absorption costing technique does not make any difference between variable and fixed cost in the calculation of profits.

But marginal cost statement very clearly indicates this difference in arriving at the net operational results of a firm.

Following presentation of two Performa shows the difference between the presentation of information according to absorption and marginal costing techniques:

RECONCILIATION STATEMENT FOR MARGINAL COSTING AND ABSORPTION COSTING PROFIT

	$
Marginal Costing Profit	xx
ADD(Closing stock – opening Stock) x OAR	xx
= Absorption Costing Profit	xx

Where OAR(overhead absorption rate) =Budgeted fixed production overheadBudgeted levels of activities

THE PRINCIPLES OF MARGINAL COSTING

The principles of marginal costing are as follows:

- For any given period of time, fixed costs will be the same, for any volume of sales and production (provided that the level of activity is within the 'relevant range'). Therefore, by selling an extra item of product or service the following will happen.
  - Revenue will increase by the sales value of the item sold.
  - Costs will increase by the variable cost per unit.
  - Profit will increase by the amount of contribution earned from the extra item.
- Similarly, if the volume of sales falls by one item, the profit will fall by the amount of contribution earned from the item.
- Profit measurement should therefore be based on an analysis of total contribution. Since fixed costs relate to a period of time, and do not change with increases or decreases in sales volume, it is misleading to charge units of sale with a share of fixed costs.
- When a unit of product is made, the extra costs incurred in its manufacture are the variable production costs. Fixed costs are unaffected, and no extra fixed costs are incurred when output is increased.

MARGINAL COSTING PRINCIPLES

In product/service costing, a marginal costing system emphasises the behavioural, rather than the functional, characteristics of costs.

The focus is on separating costs into variable elements (where the cost per unit remains the same with total cost varying in proportion to activity) and fixed elements (where the total cost remains the same in each period regardless of the level of activity).

Whilst this is not easily achieved with accuracy, and is an oversimplification of reality, marginal costing information can be very useful for short-term planning, control and decision-making, especially in a multi-product business. In a marginal costing system, sales less variable costs (regardless of function) measures the contribution that individual products/services make towards the total fixed costs incurred by the business.

The fixed costs (regardless of function) are treated as period costs and, as such, are simply deducted from contribution in the period incurred to arrive at net profit.

MARGINAL COSTING PROFIT STATEMENT

Referring back to Example 1, as there is no information regarding non-manufacturing costs, it may be assumed that sales less variable manufacturing costs measures contribution. NB.

If any variable costs are incurred in non-manufacturing functions then they would also be deducted from sales in the measurement of contribution. The trading statement for Period 2, assuming that a marginal costing system was in place instead.

Example:

Period 2 Trading Statement:	£000	
Sales	302.40	
Variable cost of goods sold	138.24	(21,600 units at £6.40 per unit)
Contribution	164.16	(21,600 units at £7.60 per unit)
Fixed manufacturing overhead	92.00	
Manufacturing profit	72.16	

Costing approach is more straightforward. The Examiner's Report noted that candidates generally had rather more success with the marginal costing statement in part (b) than with the absorption costing statement in part (a), although some confusion between the two was demonstrated.

In practice, the marginal costing profit statement would be completed by the further deduction of fixed costs incurred in other functions.

PROFIT RECONCILIATION

The net profit reported by absorption and marginal costing systems may not be the same owing to the differing treatment of fixed manufacturing overheads.

As has been demonstrated above, whilst marginal costing systems treat fixed manufacturing overheads as period costs (*i.e.* a charge against profit in the period incurred), in absorption costing systems they are absorbed into the cost of goods produced and are only charged against profit in the period in which those goods are sold.

As a result, if quantities produced and sold in a period are not the same (*i.e.*, if the levels of work-in-progress or finished goods stock change) a different profit will be reported by the two systems.

The differing profits can be reconciled, and the difference explained, by an analysis of the product of the stock change and the fixed manufacturing overhead absorption rate. Thus, in answer to part (c) of Example 1:

Period 2 finished goods stock reduction 600 unitsx fixed manufacturing overhead absorption rate, £4.60 per unit = £2,760 difference in profit *i.e.*, the difference between the absorption costing manufacturing profit of £69,400 and the marginal costing manufacturing profit of £72,160.

Absorption costing has a lower profit because more goods are being taken out of stock (including a charge for fixed manufacturing overhead) than are going into stock. This is demonstrated by the entries in the respective cost accounting systems.

Example: In the absorption costing system.

Table. Fixed Manufacturing Overhead Account.

Incurred	**£92,000**	**Absorbed into Finished Goods**	**£96,600** —
Over-absorbed – to P&L A/c (1,000 units at £4.60/unit)	£4,600	(21,000 units at £4.60/unit)	
	£96,600	£96,600	

Table. Finished Goods Stock Account.

Fixed mfg o'hd absorbed (21,600 units at £4.60/unit)	£96,600	Cost of sales (fixed mfg o'hd only)	£99,360

Table. The Total Fixed Manufacturing Overhead Charged Against Profit in the Period.

Overhead in cost of sales	£99,360
Less over-absorption	£4,600
	£94,760

Table. In the Marginal Costing System.

	Fixed Manufacturing	Overhead Account
Incurred	£92,000	P&L A/c-period cost £92,000

Absorption costing £94,760 less marginal costing £92,000 =£2,760 more fixed manufacturing overheads and less profit in absorption costing. The difference in profit between absorption and marginal costing systems is nothing to do with overhead over/under absorption, a popular misconception amongst examination candidates.

Despite an over-absorption of £4,600, which is a positive adjustment to the absorption costing profit, the profit was nevertheless less than the marginal costing profit. *To emphasise again*: The difference in reported profit demonstrated above, which can only be a timing difference, is due to changes in the level of finished goods stock which in an absorption costing system moves overhead, and therefore profit, from one period to another.

As a general rule: If production quantity > sales quantity then absorption costing profit > marginal costing profit. If production quantity < sales quantity then absorption costing profit <marginal costing profit. Many candidates, when answering examination questions on this topic, do appreciate that the different treatment of fixed manufacturing overhead is the reason for profit differences but they are rarely able to reconcile the profits.

FEATURES OF MARGINAL COSTING

The main features of marginal costing are as follows:

- *Cost Classification*: The marginal costing technique makes a sharp distinction between variable costs and fixed costs. It is the variable cost on the basis of which production and sales policies are designed by a firm following the marginal costing technique.
- *Stock/Inventory Valuation*: Under marginal costing, inventory/stock for profit measurement is valued at marginal cost. It is in sharp contrast to the total unit cost under absorption costing method.
- *Marginal Contribution*: Marginal costing technique makes use of marginal contribution for marking various decisions. Marginal contribution is the difference between sales and marginal cost. It forms the basis for judging the profitability of different products or departments.

MARGINAL COSTING VERSUS ABSORPTION COSTING

After knowing the two techniques of marginal costing and absorption costing, we have seen that the net profits are not the same because of the following reasons.

OVER AND UNDER ABSORBED OVERHEADS

In absorption costing, fixed overheads can never be absorbed exactly because of difficulty in forecasting costs and volume of output. If these balances of under or over absorbed/recovery are not written off to costing profit and loss account, the actual amount incurred is not shown in it.

In marginal costing, however, the actual fixed overhead incurred is wholly charged against contribution and hence, there will be some difference in net profits.

DIFFERENCE IN STOCK VALUATION

In marginal costing, work in progress and finished stocks are valued at marginal cost, but in absorption costing, they are valued at total production cost. Hence, profit will differ as different amounts of fixed overheads are considered in two accounts.

The profit difference due to difference in stock valuation is summarized as follows:

- When there is no opening and closing stocks, there will be no difference in profit.
- When opening and closing stocks are same, there will be no difference in profit, provided the fixed cost element in opening and closing stocks are of the same amount.
- When closing stock is more than opening stock, the profit under absorption costing will be higher as comparatively a greater portion of fixed cost is included in closing stock and carried over to next period.
- When closing stock is less than opening stock, the profit under absorption costing will be less as comparatively a higher amount of fixed cost contained in opening stock is debited during the current period.

The features which distinguish marginal costing from absorption costing are as follows:

- In absorption costing, items of stock are costed to include a 'fair share' of fixed production overhead, whereas in marginal costing, stocks are valued at variable production cost only. The value of closing stock will be higher in absorption costing than in marginal costing.
- As a consequence of carrying forward an element of fixed production overheads in closing stock values, the cost of sales used to determine profit in absorption costing will:
  - Include some fixed production overhead costs incurred in a previous period but carried forward into opening stock values of the current period;

- Exclude some fixed production overhead costs incurred in the current period by including them in closing stock values.

In contrast marginal costing charges the actual fixed costs of a period in full into the profit and loss account of the period. (Marginal costing is therefore sometimes known as period costing.)

- In absorption costing, 'actual' fully absorbed unit costs are reduced by producing in greater quantities, whereas in marginal costing, unit variable costs are unaffected by the volume of production (that is, provided that variable costs per unit remain unaltered at the changed level of production activity). Profit per unit in any period can be affected by the actual volume of production in absorption costing; this is not the case in marginal costing.
- In marginal costing, the identification of variable costs and of contribution enables management to use cost information more easily for decision-making purposes (such as in budget decision making). It is easy to decide by how much contribution (and therefore profit) will be affected by changes in sales volume. (Profit would be unaffected by changes in production volume).

In absorption costing, however, the effect on profit in a period of changes in both:

- Production volume; and
- Sales volume; is not easily seen, because behaviour is not analysed and incremental costs are not used in the calculation of actual profit.

LIMITATIONS OF ABSORPTION COSTING

The following are the criticisms against absorption costing:

- You might have observed that in absorption costing, a portion of fixed cost is carried over to the subsequent accounting period as part of closing stock. This is an unsound practice because costs pertaining to a period should not be allowed to be vitiated by the inclusion of costs pertaining to the previous period and vice versa.
- Further, absorption costing is dependent on the levels of output which may vary from period to period, and consequently cost per unit changes due to the existence of fixed overhead. Unless fixed overhead rate is based on normal capacity, such changed costs are not helpful for the purposes of comparison and control.

The cost to produce an extra unit is variable production cost. It is realistic to the value of closing stock items as this is a directly attributable cost. The size of total contribution varies directly with sales volume at a constant rate per unit.

For the decision-making purpose of management, better information about expected profit is obtained from the use of variable costs and contribution approach in the accounting system.

MARGINAL COSTS, CONTRIBUTION AND PROFIT

A marginal cost is another term for a variable cost. The term 'marginal cost' is usually applied to the variable cost of a unit of product or service, whereas the term 'variable cost' is more commonly applied to resource costs, such as the cost of materials and labour hours. Marginal costing is a form of management accounting based on the distinction between:

- The marginal costs of making selling goods or services, and
- Fixed costs, which should be the same for a given period of time, regardless of the level of activity in the period.

Suppose that a firm makes and sells a single product that has a marginal cost of £5 per unit and that sells for £9 per unit. For every additional unit of the product that is made and sold, the firm will incur an extra cost of £5 and receive income of £9. The net gain will be £4 per additional unit. This net gain per unit, the difference between the sales price per unit and the marginal cost per unit, is called contribution. Contribution is a term meaning 'making a contribution towards covering fixed costs and making a profit'. Before a firm can make a profit in any period, it must first of all cover its fixed costs. Breakeven is where total sales revenue for a period just covers fixed costs, leaving neither profit nor loss. For every unit sold in excess of the breakeven point, profit will increase by the amount of the contribution per unit. C-V-P analysis is broadly known as cost-volume-profit analysis. Specifically speaking, we all are concerned with in-depth analysis and application of CVP in practical world of industry management.

COST-VOLUME-PROFIT (C-V-P) RELATIONSHIP

We have observed that in marginal costing, marginal cost varies directly with the volume of production or output. On the other hand, fixed cost remains unaltered regardless of the volume of output within the scale of production already fixed by management. In case if cost behaviour is related to sales income, it shows cost-volume-profit relationship. In net effect, if volume is changed, variable cost varies as per the change in volume. In this case, selling price remains fixed, fixed remains fixed and then there is a change in profit. Being a manager, you constantly strive to relate these elements in order to achieve the maximum profit.

Apart from profit projection, the concept of Cost-Volume-Profit (CVP) is relevant to virtually all decision-making areas, particularly in the short run. The relationship among cost, revenue and profit at different levels may be expressed in graphs such as breakeven charts, profit volume graphs, or in various statement forms. Profit depends on a large number of factors, most important of which are the cost of manufacturing and the volume of sales. Both these factors are interdependent. Volume of sales depends upon the volume of production and market forces which in turn is related to costs. Management has no control over market. In order to achieve certain level of profitability, it has to exercise control and management of costs, mainly variable cost. This is because fixed cost is a non-controllable cost. But then, cost is based on the following factors:

- Internal efficiency and the productivity of the factors of production
- Methods of production and technology
- Product mix
- Size of batches
- Size of plant
- Volume of production

Thus, one can say that cost-volume-profit analysis furnishes the complete picture of the profit structure. This enables management to distinguish among the effect of sales, fluctuations in volume and the results of changes in price of product/services. In other words, CVP is a management accounting tool that expresses relationship among sale volume, cost and profit. CVP can be used in the form of a graph or an equation. Cost-volume- profit analysis can answer a number of analytical questions. Some of the questions are as follows:

- What is the breakeven revenue of an organization?
- How much revenue does an organization need to achieve a budgeted profit?
- What level of price change affects the achievement of budgeted profit?
- What is the effect of cost changes on the profitability of an operation?

Cost-volume-profit analysis can also answer many other "what if" type of questions. Cost-volume-profit analysis is one of the important techniques of cost and management accounting. Although it is a simple yet a powerful tool for planning of profits and therefore, of commercial operations. It provides an answer to "what if" theme by telling the volume required to produce. Following are the three approaches to a CVP analysis:

- Cost and revenue equations
- Contribution margin
- Profit graph

OBJECTIVES OF COST-VOLUME-PROFIT ANALYSIS

- In order to forecast profits accurately, it is essential to ascertain the relationship between cost and profit on one hand and volume on the other.
- Cost-volume-profit analysis is helpful in setting up flexible budget which indicates cost at various levels of activities.
- Cost-volume-profit analysis assist in evaluating performance for the purpose of control.

- Such analysis may assist management in formulating pricing policies by projecting the effect of different price structures on cost and profit.

ASSUMPTIONS AND TERMINOLOGY

Following are the assumptions on which the theory of CVP is based:

- The changes in the level of various revenue and costs arise only because of the changes in the number of product (or service) units produced and sold, *e.g.*, the number of television sets produced and sold by Sigma Corporation. The number of output (units) to be sold is the only revenue and cost driver. Just as a cost driver is any factor that affects costs, a revenue driver is any factor that affects revenue.
- Total costs can be divided into a fixed component and a component that is variable with respect to the level of output.
  Variable costs include the following:
  - Direct materials
  - Direct labour
  - Direct chargeable expenses

  Variable overheads include the following:
  - Variable part of factory overheads
  - Administration overheads
  - Selling and distribution overheads
- There is linear relationship between revenue and cost.
- When put in a graph, the behaviour of total revenue and cost is linear (straight line), *i.e.* $Y = mx + C$ holds good which is the equation of a straight line.
- The unit selling price, unit variable costs and fixed costs are constant.
- The theory of CVP is based upon the production of a single product. However, of late, management accountants are functioning to give a theoretical and a practical approach to multi-product CVP analysis.
- The analysis either covers a single product or assumes that the sales mix sold in case of multiple products will remain constant as the level of total units sold changes.
- All revenue and cost can be added and compared without taking into account the time value of money.
- The theory of CVP is based on the technology that remains constant.
- The theory of price elasticity is not taken into consideration.

Many companies, and divisions and sub-divisions of companies in industries such as airlines, automobiles, chemicals, plastics and semiconductors have found the simple CVP relationships to be helpful in the following areas:

- Strategic and long-range planning decisions
- Decisions about product features and pricing

In real world, simple assumptions described above may not hold good. The theory of CVP can be tailored for individual industries depending upon the nature and peculiarities of the same. For example, predicting total revenue and total cost may require multiple revenue drivers and multiple cost drivers.

Some of the multiple revenue drivers are as follows:

- Number of output units
- Number of customer visits made for sales
- Number of advertisements placed

Some of the multiple cost drivers are as follows:

- Number of units produced
- Number of batches in which units are produced

Managers and management accountants, however, should always assess whether the simplified CVP relationships generate sufficiently accurate information for predictions of how total revenue and total cost would behave. However, one may come across different complex situations to which the theory of CVP would rightly be applicable in order to help managers to take appropriate decisions under different situations.

LIMITATIONS OF COST-VOLUME PROFIT ANALYSIS

The CVP analysis is generally made under certain limitations and with certain assumed conditions, some of which may not occur in practice.

Following are the main limitations and assumptions in the cost-volume-profit analysis:

- It is assumed that the production facilities anticipated for the purpose of cost-volume-profit analysis do not undergo any change. Such analysis gives misleading results if expansion or reduction of capacity takes place.
- In case where a variety of products with varying margins of profit are manufactured, it is difficult to forecast with reasonable accuracy the volume of sales mix which would optimize the profit.
- The analysis will be correct only if input price and selling price remain fairly constant which in reality is difficulty to find. Thus, if a cost reduction programme is undertaken or selling price is changed, the relationship between cost and profit will not be accurately depicted.
- In cost-volume-profit analysis, it is assumed that variable costs are perfectly and completely variable at all levels of activity and fixed cost remains constant throughout the range of volume being considered. However, such situations may not arise in practical situations.
- It is assumed that the changes in opening and closing inventories are not significant, though sometimes they may be significant.
- Inventories are valued at variable cost and fixed cost is treated as period cost. Therefore, closing stock carried over to the next financial

year does not contain any component of fixed cost. Inventory should be valued at full cost in reality.

SENSITIVITY ANALYSIS OR WHAT IF ANALYSIS AND UNCERTAINTY

Sensitivity analysis is relatively a new term in management accounting. It is a "what if" technique that managers use to examine how a result will change if the original predicted data are not achieved or if an underlying assumption changes. In the context of CVP analysis, sensitivity analysis answers the following questions:

- What will be the operating income if units sold decrease by 15 per cent from original prediction?
- What will be the operating income if variable cost per unit increases by 20 per cent?

The sensitivity of operating income to various possible outcomes broadens the perspective of management regarding what might actually occur before making cost commitments.

A spreadsheet can be used to conduct CVP-based sensitivity analysis in a systematic and efficient way. With the help of a spreadsheet, this analysis can be easily conducted to examine the effect and interaction of changes in selling prices, variable cost per unit, fixed costs and target operating incomes.

EXAMPLE

Following is the spreadsheet of ABC Ltd.

Statement Showing CVP Analysis for Dolphy Software Ltd.

Revenue required at $. 200 Selling Price per unit to earn Operating Income of,					
Fixed cost	**Variable cost per unit**	**0**	**1,000**	**1,500**	**2,000**
2,000	100	4,000	6,000	7,000	8,000
	120	5,000	7,500	8,750	10,000
	140	6,667	10,000	11,667	13,333
2,500	100	5,000	7,000	8,000	9,000
	120	6,250	8,750	10,000	11,250
	140	8,333	11,667	13,333	15,000
3,000	100	6,000	8,000	9,000	10,000
	120	7,500	10,000	11,250	12,500
	140	10,000	13,333	15,000	16,667

One can immediately see the revenue that needs to be generated to reach a particular operating income level, given alternative levels of fixed costs and variable costs per unit. For example, revenue of $. 6,000 (30 units @ $. 200

each) is required to earn an operating income of $. 1,000 if fixed cost is $. 2,000 and variable cost per unit is $. 100. You can also use exhibit 3-4 to assess what revenue the company needs to breakeven (earn operating income of Re. 0) if, for example, one of the following changes takes place:

- The booth rental at the ABC convention raises to $. 3,000 (thus increasing fixed cost to $. 3,000)
- The software suppliers raise their price to $. 140 per unit (thus increasing variable costs to $. 140)

An aspect of sensitivity analysis is the margin of safety which is the amount of budgeted revenue over and above breakeven revenue. The margin of safety is sales quantity minus breakeven quantity. It is expressed in units. The margin of safety answers the"what if" questions, *e.g.*, if budgeted revenue are above breakeven and start dropping, how far can they fall below budget before the breakeven point is reached? Such a fall could be due to competitor's better product, poorly executed marketing programmes and so on.

Assume you have fixed cost of $. 2,000, selling price of $. 200 and variable cost per unit of $. 120. For 40 units sold, the budgeted point from this set of assumptions is 25 units ($. 2,000 ÷ $. 80) or $. 5,000 ($. 200 x 25). Hence, the margin of safety is $. 3,000 ($. 8,000 – 5,000) or 15 (40 –25) units. Sensitivity analysis is an approach to recognizing uncertainty, *i.e.* the possibility that an actual amount will deviate from an expected amount.

MARGINAL COST EQUATIONS AND BREAKEVEN ANALYSIS

From the marginal cost statements, one might have observed the following:

Sales – Marginal cost = Contribution

Fixed cost + Profit = Contribution

By combining these two equations, we get the fundamental marginal cost equation as follows:

Sales - Marginal cost = Fixed cost + Profit

This fundamental marginal cost equation plays a vital role in profit projection and has a wider application in managerial decision-making problems.

The sales and marginal costs vary directly with the number of units sold or produced. So, the difference between sales and marginal cost, *i.e.*

contribution, will bear a relation to sales and the ratio of contribution to sales remains constant at all levels. This is profit volume or P/V ratio.

Thus,

$$\text{P/V Ratio (or C/S Ratio)} = \frac{\text{Contribution (c)}}{\text{Sales (s)}}$$

It is expressed in terms of percentage, *i.e.* P/V ratio is equal to (C/S) × 100.

Or, Contribution = Sales × P/V ratio

Or, Sales = Contribution / P/V ratio

CONTRIBUTION

Contribution is the difference between sales and marginal or variable costs. It contributes towards fixed cost and profit. The concept of contribution helps in deciding breakeven point, profitability of products, departments etc. to perform the following activities:

- Selecting product mix or sales mix for profit maximization
- Fixing selling prices under different circumstances such as trade depression, export sales, price discrimination etc.

PROFIT VOLUME RATIO (P/V RATIO), ITS IMPROVEMENT AND APPLICATION

The ratio of contribution to sales is P/V ratio or C/S ratio. It is the contribution per rupee of sales and since the fixed cost remains constant in short term period, P/V ratio will also measure the rate of change of profit due to change in volume of sales. The P/V ratio may be expressed as follows:

P / V ratio = Sales – Marginal cost of sales = Contribution in contribution = Change in profit
Sales Changes in sales Change in sale

A fundamental property of marginal costing system is that P/V ratio remains constant at different levels of activity. A change in fixed cost does not affect P/V ratio. The concept of P/V ratio helps in determining the following:

- Breakeven point
- Profit at any volume of sales
- Sales volume required to earn a desired quantum of profit
- Profitability of products
- Processes or departments

The contribution can be increased by increasing the sales price or by reduction of variable costs. Thus, P/V ratio can be improved by the following:

- Increasing selling price
- Reducing marginal costs by effectively utilizing men, machines, materials and other services
- Selling more profitable products, thereby increasing the overall P/V ratio

BREAKEVEN POINT

Breakeven point is the volume of sales or production where there is neither profit nor loss. Thus, we can say that:

Contribution = Fixed cost

Now, breakeven point can be easily calculated with the help of fundamental marginal cost equation, P/V ratio or contribution per unit.

Using Marginal Costing Equation

S (sales) – V (variable cost) = F (fixed cost) + P (profit)

At BEP P = 0,

BEP S – V = F

By multiplying both the sides by S and rearranging them, one gets the following equation:

S BEP = F.S / S - V

Using P/V Ratio

$$\text{Sales S BEP} = \frac{\text{Contribution}}{\text{P / V ratio}} = \frac{\text{Fixed Cost}}{\text{P / V ratio}}$$

Thus, if sales is \$. 2,000, marginal cost \$. 1,200 and fixed cost \$. 400, then:

Breakeven point = 400 × 2000 = \$. 1000

2000 - 1200

Similarly, P/V ratio = 2000 – 1200 = 800 = 0.4 or 40 per cent

So, breakeven sales = \$. 400/.4 = \$. 1000

Using Contribution per Unit

Breakeven point =Fixed cost= 100 units
or \$. 1000 Contribution per unit

MARGIN OF SAFETY (MOS)

Every enterprise tries to know how much above they are from the breakeven point. This is technically called margin of safety. It is calculated as the difference between sales or production units at the selected activity and the breakeven sales or production. Margin of safety is the difference between the total sales (actual or projected) and the breakeven sales. It may be expressed in monetary terms (value) or as a number of units (volume).

It can be expressed as profit/P/V ratio. A large margin of safety indicates the soundness and financial strength of business. Margin of safety can be improved by lowering fixed and variable costs, increasing volume of sales or selling price and changing product mix, so as to improve contribution and overall P/V ratio.

Margin of safety = Sales at selected activity – Sales at BEP =Profit at selected activity.

P/V ratio: Margin of safety is also presented in ratio or percentage as follows:

$$\frac{\text{Margin of Safety(Sales)} \times 100\%}{\text{Sales at Selected Activity}}$$

The size of margin of safety is an extremely valuable guide to the strength of a business. If it is large, there can be substantial falling of sales and yet a profit can be made. On the other hand, if margin is small, any loss of sales may be a serious matter. If margin of safety is unsatisfactory, possible steps to rectify the causes of mismanagement of commercial activities as listed below can be undertaken.

- Increasing the selling price— It may be possible for a company to have higher margin of safety in order to strengthen the financial health of the business. It should be able to influence price, provided the demand is elastic. Otherwise, the same quantity will not be sold.
- Reducing fixed costs
- Reducing variable costs
- Substitution of existing product(s) by more profitable lines e. Increase in the volume of output
- Modernization of production facilities and the introduction of the most cost effective technology

Problem 1

A company earned a profit of $. 30,000 during the year 2000-01. Marginal cost and selling price of a product are $. 8 and $. 10 per unit respectively. Find out the margin of safety.

Solution

Margin of safety = Profit

P/V ratio

P/V ratio = Contribution × 100 / Sales

Problem 2

A company producing a single substance sells it at $. 10 each. The marginal cost of production is $. 6 each and fixed cost is $. 400 per annum. You are required to calculate the following:

- Profits for annual sales of 1 unit, 50 units, 100 units and 400 units
- P/V ratio
- Breakeven sales
- Sales to earn a profit of $. 500
- Profit at sales of $. 3,000
- New breakeven point if sales price is reduced by 10 per cent
- Margin of safety at sales of 400 units

Solution:

Marginal Cost Statement.

Particulars	Amount	Amount	Amount	Amount
Units produced	1	50	100	400
Sales (units * 10)	10	500	1000	4000
Variable cost	6	300	600	2400
Contribution (sales – VC)	4	200	400	1600
Fixed cost	400	400	400	400
Profit (Contribution – FC)	–396	–200	0	1200

- Profit Volume Ratio (PVR) = Contribution/Sales * 100 = 0.4 or 40 per cent.
- Breakeven sales ($.) = Fixed cost / PVR = 400/40 * 100 = $. 10,000.
- Sales at BEP = Contribution at BEP / PVR = 100 units.
- Sales at profit $. 500.
- Contribution at profit $. 500 = Fixed cost + Profit = $. 900.
- Sales = Contribution / PVR = 900 / .4 = $. 2,250 (or 225 units).
- Profit at sales $. 3,000.
- Contribution at sale $. 3,000 = Sales × P/V ratio = 3000 × 0.4 = $ 1,200.
- Profit = Contribution – Fixed cost = $. 1200 – $. 400 = $. 800.
- New P/V ratio = $. 9 – $. 6/$. 9 = 1/3.
- Sales at BEP = Fixed cost / PV ratio = $. 400 = $. 1,200 1/3.
- Margin of safety (at 400 units) = 4000-1000 / 9.
  4000*100 = 75 per cent.
  (Actual sales – BEP sales/Actual sales * 100).

BREAKEVEN ANALYSIS—GRAPHICAL PRESENTATION

Apart from marginal cost equations, it is found that breakeven chart and profit graphs are useful graphic presentations of this cost-volume-profit relationship. Breakeven chart is a device which shows the relationship between sales volume, marginal costs and fixed costs, and profit or loss at different levels of activity.

Such a chart also shows the effect of change of one factor on other factors and exhibits the rate of profit and margin of safety at different levels. A breakeven chart contains, inter alia, total sales line, total cost line and the point of intersection called breakeven point.

It is popularly called breakeven chart because it shows clearly breakeven point (a point where there is no profit or no loss). Profit graph is a development of simple breakeven chart and shows clearly profit at different volumes of sales.

CONSTRUCTION OF A BREAKEVEN CHART

The construction of a breakeven chart involves the drawing of fixed cost line, total cost line and sales line as follows:

- Select a scale for production on horizontal axis and a scale for costs and sales on vertical axis.
- Plot fixed cost on vertical axis and draw fixed cost line passing through this point parallel to horizontal axis.
- Plot variable costs for some activity levels starting from the fixed cost line and join these points. This will give total cost line. Alternatively, obtain total cost at different levels, plot the points starting from horizontal axis and draw total cost line.
- Plot the maximum or any other sales volume and draw sales line by joining zero and the point so obtained.

USES OF BREAKEVEN CHART

A breakeven chart can be used to show the effect of changes in any of the following profit factors:

- Volume of sales
- Variable expenses
- Fixed expenses
- Selling price

Problem

A company produces a single substance and sells it at $. 10 each. The marginal cost of production is $. 6 each and total fixed cost of the concern is $. 400 per annum. Construct a breakeven chart and show the following.

- Breakeven point
- Margin of safety at sale of $. 1,500
- Angle of incidence
- Increase in selling price if breakeven point is reduced to 80 units

Solution

A breakeven chart can be prepared by obtaining the information at these levels:

Output units	**40**	**80**	**120**	**200**
Sales	**$.**	**$.**	**$.**	**$.**
	400	800	1,200	2,000
Fixed cost	400	400	400	400
Variable cost	240	480	400	720
Total cost	640	880	1,120	1,600

Fixed cost line, total cost line and sales line are drawn one after another following the usual procedure described herein:

This chart clearly shows the breakeven point, margin of safety and angle of incidence.

- Breakeven point— Breakeven point is the point at which sales line and total cost line intersect. Here, B is breakeven point equivalent to sale of $. 1,000 or 100 units.
- Margin of safety— Margin of safety is the difference between sales or units of production and breakeven point. Thus, margin of safety at M is sales of ($. 1,500 - $. 1,000), *i.e.* $. 500 or 50 units.
- Angle of incidence— Angle of incidence is the angle formed by sales line and total cost line at breakeven point. A large angle of incidence shows a high rate of profit being made. It should be noted that the angle of incidence is universally denoted by data. Larger the angle, higher the profitability indicated by the angel of incidence.
- At 80 units, total cost (from the table) = $. 880. Hence, selling price for breakeven at 80 units = $. 880/80 = $. 11 per unit. Increase in selling price is Re. 1 or 10 per cent over the original selling price of $. 10 per unit.

8

Control Costing System

COST CONTROL

Cost control, also known as cost management or cost containment, is a broad set of cost accounting methods and management techniques with the common goal of improving business cost-efficiency by reducing costs, or at least restricting their rate of growth. Businesses use cost control methods to monitor, evaluate, and ultimately enhance the efficiency of specific areas, such as departments, divisions, or product lines, within their operations.

During the 1990s cost control initiatives received paramount attention from corporate America. Often taking the form of corporate restructuring, divestment of peripheral activities, mass layoffs, or outsourcing, cost control strategies were seen as necessary to preserve—or boost—corporate profits and to maintain—or gain—a competitive advantage. The objective was often to be the low-cost producer in a given industry, which would typically allow the company to take a greater profit per unit of sales than its competitors at a given price level.

Some cost control proponents believe that such strategic cost-cutting must be planned carefully, as not all cost reduction techniques yield the same benefits. In a notable late 1990s example, chief executive Albert J. Dunlap, nicknamed "Chainsaw Al" because of his penchant for deep cost cutting at the companies he headed, failed to restore the ailing small appliance maker Sunbeam Corporation to profitability despite his drastic cost reduction tactics. Dunlap laid off thousands of workers and sold off business units, but made little contribution to Sunbeam's competitive position or share price in his two years as CEO. Consequently, in 1998 Sunbeam's board fired Dunlap, having lost confidence in his "one-trick" approach to management.

APPLICATIONS OF COST CONTROL

A complex business requires frequent information about operations in order to plan for the future, to control present activities, and to evaluate the past performance of managers, employees, and related business segments. To be successful, management guides the activities of its people in the operations of the business according to pre-established goals and objectives.

Management's guidance takes two forms of control:

1. The management and supervision of behaviour, and
2. The evaluation of performance.

Behavioural management deals with the attitudes and actions of employees. While employee behaviour ultimately impacts on success, behavioural management involves certain issues and assumptions not applicable to accounting's control function. On the other hand, performance evaluation measures outcomes of employee's actions by comparing the actual results of business outcomes to predetermined standards of success. In this way management identifies the strengths it needs to maximize, and the weaknesses it seeks to rectify. This process of evaluation and remedy is called cost control.

Cost control is a continuous process that begins with the proposed annual budget.

The budget helps:

- To organize and coordinate production, and the selling, distribution, service, and administrative functions; and
- To take maximum advantage of available opportunities.

As the fiscal year progresses, management compares actual results with those projected in the budget and incorporates into the new plan the sessions learned from its evaluation of current operations.

Control refers to management's effort to influence the actions of individuals who are responsible for performing tasks, incurring costs, and generating revenues. Management is a two-phased process: planning refers to the way that management plans and wants people to perform, while control refers to the procedures employed to determine whether actual performance complies with these plans. Through the budget process and accounting control, management establishes overall company objectives, defines the centres of responsibility, determines specific objectives for each responsibility centre, and designs procedures and standards for reporting and evaluation.

A budget segments the business into its components or centres where the responsible party initiates and controls action. Responsibility centres represent applicable organizational units, functions, departments, and divisions. Generally a single individual heads the responsibility centre exercising substantial, if not complete, control over the activities of people or processes within the centre and controlling the results of their activity. Cost centres are accountable only for expenses, that is, they do not generate revenue. Examples include accounting departments, human resources departments, and similar areas of the business that provide internal services. Profit centres accept responsibility for both revenue and expenses. For example, a product line or an autonomous business unit might be considered profit centres. If the profit centre has its own assets, it may also be considered an investment centre, for which returns on investment can be determined. The use of responsibility centres allows management to design control reports to pinpoint accountability, thus aiding in profit planning.

A budget also sets standards to indicate the level of activity expected from each responsible person or decision unit, and the amount of resources that a responsible party should use in achieving that level of activity. A budget establishes the responsibility centre, delegates the concomitant responsibilities, and determines the decision points within an organization.

The planning process provides for two types of control mechanisms:

- *Feedforward*: providing a basis for control at the point of action; and
- *Feedback*: providing a basis for measuring the effectiveness of control after implementation.

Management's role is to feedforward a futuristic vision of where the company is going and how it is to get there, and to make clear decisions coordinating and directing employee activities.

Management also oversees the development of procedures to collect, record, and evaluate feedback. Therefore, effective management controls results from leading people by force of personality and through persuasion; providing and maintaining proper training, planning, and resources; and improving quality and results through evaluation and feedback.

CONTROL REPORTS

Control reports are informational reports that tell management about an entity's activities. Management requests control reports only for internal use, and, therefore, directs the accounting department to develop tailor-made reporting formats.

Accounting provides management with a format designed to detect variations that need investigating. In addition, management also refers to conventional reports such as the income statement and funds statement, and external reports on the general economy and the specific industry.

Control reports, then, need to provide an adequate amount of information so that management may determine the reasons for any cost variances from the original budget. A good control report highlights significant information by focusing management's attention on those items in which actual performance significantly differs from the standard.

Because key success factors shift in type and number, accounting revises control reports when necessary. Accounting also varies the control period covered by the control report to encompass a period in which management can take useful remedial action. In addition, accounting disseminates control reports in a timely fashion to give management adequate time to act before the issuance of the next report. Managers perform effectively when they attain the goals and objectives set by the budget. With respect to profits, managers succeed by the degree to which revenues continually exceed expenses. In applying the following simple formula, managers, especially those in operations, realise that they exercise more control over expenses than they do over revenue.

While they cannot predict the timing and volume of actual sales, they can determine the utilization rate of most of their resources, that is, they can influence the cost side. Hence, the evaluation of management's performance and its operations is cost control.

STANDARDS

For cost control purposes, a budget provides standard costs. As management constructs budgets, it lays out a road map to guide its efforts. It states a number of assumptions about the relationships and interaction among the economy, market dynamics, the abilities of its sales force, and its capacity to provide the proper quantity and quality of products demanded.

An examination of the details of the budget calculations and assumptions indicates that management expects the sales force to spend only so much in pursuit of the sales forecast. The details also reveal that management expects operations to produce the required amount of units within a certain cost range. Management bases its expectations and projections on the best historical and current information, as well as its best business judgement.

When calculating budget expenses, management's review of the historic and current data might strongly suggest that the production of 1,000 units of a certain luxury item will cost $100,000, or $100 per unit. In addition, management also determines that the sales force will expend about $80,000 to sell the 1,000 units. This is a sales expenditure of $80. With total expenditures of $180, management sets the selling price of $500 for this luxury item.

At the close of a month, management compares the actual results of that month to the standard costs to determine the degree and direction of any variance. The purpose for analyzing variances is to identify areas where costs need containment.

In the illustration, accounting indicates to management that the sales force sold 100 units for a gross revenue of $50,000. Accounting data also shows that the sales force spent $7,000 that month, and that production incurred $12,000 in expenses.

While revenue was on target, actual sales expense came in less than projected, with a per unit cost of $70. This is a favourable variance. Production expenses registered an unfavourable variance since actual expenditures exceeded the projected.

The company produced units at $120 per item, $20 more than projected. This variance of 20 per cent significantly differs from the standard costs of $100 and would call management to action if the variance exceeded acceptable levels.

THE ROLE OF ACCOUNTING

Accounting plays a key role in all planning and control. It does this in four key areas:

- Data collection,
- Data analysis,
- Budget control and administration,
- Consolidation and review.

Data Collection

Accurate and timely information is the foundation of any accounting system, and thus detailed cost data are essential to any cost control endeavor. Management must understand—in great detail—how funds have been spent in the past and how they are being spent currently. As a result, companies invest large sums into sophisticated and error-resistant accounting systems in order to gain a nuanced understanding of their finances.

Table. Comparison of Actual and Standard Costs.

	Projected		Actual		
	Total	**Per Unit**	**Units Sold**	**Month**	**Projected—Actual**
Units	1,000	1.00	100.00	100.00	0.00
Gross Revenues	$500,000	$500	$50,000	$50,000	$0
Expenses	$180,000	$180	$18,000	$19,000	-$1,000
Sales Expense	$80,000	$80	$8,000	$7,000	$1,000
Production Expense	$100,000	$100	$10,000	$12,000	-$2000.00
Total Variance = -2000					

Data Analysis

Accounting's specialty is in the control function, yet its analysis is indispensable to the planning process. Accounting adjusts and interprets the data to allow for changes in company specific, industry specific, and economy-wide conditions.

Budget and Control Administration

The accountants play a key role in designing and securing support for the procedural aspects of the planning process. In addition, they design and distribute forms for the collection and booking of detailed data on all aspects of the business.

Consolidation and Review

Although operating managers have the main responsibility of planning, accounting compiles and coordinates the elements. Accountants subject proposed budgets to feasibility and profitability analyses to determine conformity to accepted standards and practices.

STRATEGIC COST CONTROL

Management relies on such accounting data and analysis to choose from several cost control alternatives, or management may direct accounting to prepare reports specifically for evaluating such options. As the Chainsaw Al episode indicated, all costs may not be viable targets for cost-cutting measures. For instance, in mass layoffs, the company may lose a significant share of its human capital by releasing veteran employees who are experts in their fields, not to mention by creating a decline in morale among those who remain. Thus management must identify which costs have strategic significance and which do not.

To determine the strategic impact of cost-cutting, management has to weigh the net effects of the proposed change on all areas of the business. For example, reducing variable costs related directly to manufacturing a product, such as materials and transportation costs, could be the key to greater incremental profits. However, management must also consider whether saving money on production is jeopardizing other strategic interests like quality or time to market. If a cheaper material or transportation system negatively impacts other strategic variables, the nominal cost savings may not benefit the company in the bigger picture, *e.g.*, it may lose sales. In such scenarios, managers require the discipline not to place short-term savings over long-term interests.

One trend in cost control has been towards narrowing the focus of corporate responsibility centres, and thereby shifting some of the cost control function to day-to-day managers who have the most knowledge of and influence over how their areas spend money. This practice is intended to promote bottom-up cost control measures and encourage a widespread consensus over cost management strategies.

CONCEPT OF ACTIVITY-BASED-COSTING

Activity Based Costing is an accounting technique that allows an organization to determine the actual cost associated with each product and service produced by the organization without regard to the organizational structure. It is developed to provide more-accurate ways of assigning the costs of indirect and support resources to activities, bushiness processes, products, services, and customers.

ABC systems recognize that many organizational resources are required not for physical production of units of product but to provide a broad array of support activities that enable a variety of products and services to be produced for a diverse group of customers.

The goal of ABC is not to allocate common costs to products. The goal is to measure and then price out all the resources used for activities that support the production and delivery of products and services to customers. An organization performs activities to do its business. These activities define the kind of business you are in: a ship owner has an activity to unpack boats; an accounting firm prepares tax returns; a manufacturer produces products; a council delivers services; a university teaches students. All activities consume resources.

It is the consumption of these resources that adds to overhead costs. The basis of Activity Based Costing is: look at the activities required to produce the cost of the product or service. The activities consume resources and the cost of these can be calculated.

The amount of activity required for each product and service is determined, hence the real cost can be determined:

- The activity is the work that is done.
- The resource is what the activity uses to do the work *e.g.* people, equipment, and services. Resources cost money.
- The cost of the activity depends on the quantity of resources used to accomplish the activity.
- The cost driver for an activity is the factor that influences the amount of the resources that will be consumed by this activity.
- The activity driver measures how much of the activity is used by the cost object. Example: Product A is delivered once a month, whereas product B is delivered once a week. Products A and B require a different number of deliveries, hence the cost of the delivery activity should be assigned to each product on the basis of the number of deliveries each uses.
- The cost object is whatever it is you wish to cost. It could be a product, service, process, job or customer.

While traditional costing arbitrarily allocates overhead costs, ABC traces overhead costs by looking at the activities that each product and service calls upon. With ABC the products consume the activities. It is the activities that cost money. If there were no activities, no resources would be consumed. It is the activities that you do that define your business.

USE OF ACTIVITY-BASED-COSTING

Activity-Based-Costing is necessary for the following reasons:

- Identify opportunities to reduce costs and/or increase efficiency
- Obtain actionable information to negotiate price increases for unprofitable clients
- Quantify the cost of non-value added activities such as errors and reworks

- Stratify overhead costs so they can be managed more effectively
- Understand TRUE profitability of your customers, products, or services
- Understand why profitability may be mediocre despite good strategic fundamentals

HOW DOES ABC WORK?

The first stage in an initial ABC study is to develop a fundamental understanding of the Resources and Activities of an organization. The Resources are then mapped to the Activities, thereby quantifying the cost of performing each of these Activities. These costs are traced to Cost Objects providing tremendous insight into where an organization is making and losing money.

ABC MODEL

The objective of an ABC implementation is to relate all of the costs of doing business to products, services, or customers.

Developing the initial model consists of the following five steps:

- Define Cost Objects
- Determine Activities that are supported by Resources
- Develop Cost Drivers to link Activities to Cost Objects
- Develop Resource Drivers to link Resources to Activities
- Identify the Resources of an organization

Identify Resources

Resources represent the expenditures of an organization. Examples include production labour, sales and marketing labour, occupancy and utilities, equipment, and supplies. These are the same costs that are represented in a traditional accounting view; unlike traditional accounting, ABC links these costs to products, customers, or services.

Identify Activities

Activities represent the work performed in an organization.

ABC Activities for the sales department in a typical organization might include:

- Attending trade shows and other events
- Distributing samples
- Evaluating products and improving product knowledge
- Making customer service calls
- Making sales calls to existing customers
- Making sales calls to potential customers
- Training product representatives

Traditional accounting will often break the cost of the sales department into salaries, benefits, allocated rent, supplies, and so on. Unlike traditional accounting, which reports what the costs are, ABC accounts for these costs based on what activities caused them to occur.

By determining the actual activities that occur in various departments, such as accounting, customer service, and sales, it is then possible to more accurately relate these costs to customers, products, and services.

Identify Cost Objects

ABC provides profitability by one or more cost object, usually represented by products, customers, and/or services.

Cost Object profitability is utilized to identify money losing customers, to validate separate divisions or business units, or to measure the performance of individual projects, jobs, or contracts.

Defining the outputs to be viewed is an important step in a successful ABC implementation.

Determine Resource Drivers

Resource Drivers provide the link between the expenditures of an organization and the Activities performed within the organization. For example, the total salary of a customer service representative would likely be allocated to the Activities performed based on the amount of time spent performing the Activity. If 50 per cent of her time is spent performing the activity, taking orders for existing customers, 50 per cent of her salary would be allocated to this Activity.

Determine Cost Drivers

Determination of Cost Drivers completes the last stage of the model. Cost Drivers trace, or link, the cost of performing certain Activities to Cost Objects. For example, taking orders for existing customers may be linked to specific customers based on the number of orders taken, if each order takes approximately the same amount of time. If order taking time varies based on the customer, this cost may be linked based on another driver or multiple drivers.

INSTALLATION OF A COSTING SYSTEM

The costing system of an organization should be carefully planned in order to achieve its objectives.

DETERMINATION OF OBJECTIVES

The first and foremost stop is to clearly lay down the objectives of the costing system. If the objective is only to ascertain the cost, a simple system will be sufficient. However, if the objective is to get information for decision making, planning and control, a more elaborate system of costing is necessary.

STUDY OF THE NATURE OF BUSINESS

The nature of the business and other technical aspects like nature of the products, methods and stages of production cycle should be carefully analysed.

Such an analysis is necessary to decide the method of costing to be adopted. For example, contract costing is suitable for large construction projects. Operating costing is adopted by service industries like transport.

STUDY OF THE NATURE OF THE ORGANIZATION

The costing system should be designed to meet the requirements of the organization. Hence, it is necessary to study the nature, size and layout of the organization. The factors to be considered are:

- Size of the organization and the size of the departments.
- The physical layout of the organization.
- The different levels of management.
- The extent of decentralization of authority.
- The nature of authority relationships.

DECIDING THE STRUCTURE OF COST ACCOUNTS

A suitable costing system can be developed on the basis of the study of the nature of business and organization. The structure of cost accounts should be simple and in accordance with the natural production process.

DETERMINATION OF COST RATES

This step involves a thorough study of the following points for developing an integrated costing system:

- Classification of costs into direct and indirect cots.
- Grouping of indirect costs into production, administration, selling and distribution etc.
- Methods of pricing issues.
- Treatment of wastes of all types.
- Absorption of overheads.
- Calculation of overhead rates.

ORGANIZATION OF THE COST OFFICE

The cost office is responsible for the efficient operation of the costing system. The cost office, with adequate staff must be located a close as possible to the factory. The following are the major functions of the cots office:

- Stores accounts.
- Labour accounting

- Recording of cost data and
- Cost control.

Further, the role and duties and responsibilities of the cost accountant must be clearly defined. He must have the necessary authority to discharge his duties effectively.

INTRODUCING THE SYSTEM

After completion of the steps, the costing system may be formally introduced. Introduction of the system in an existing organization should be done gradually. Before introduction, the feature of the systems, its working and advantages must be explained to the concerned employees to secure their co-operation.

CHARACTERISTICS OF A GOOD COSTING SYSTEM

An ideal system of cost accounting must possess some characteristics which bring all the advantages; to the business, in order to be ideal and objective.

The main characteristics are:

- *Simplicity*: It must be simple, flexible and adaptable to the changing conditions. And it must be easily understandable to the personnel. The information provided must be in the proper order, in right time and to the right persons so as to be utilized fully.
- *Flexibility and Adaptability*: The costing system must be flexible to accommodate the changing conditions and circumstances. The expansion, contraction of changes must be adopted in the existing system with minimum change s.
- *Economy*: The costing system must suit the finance available. The expenditure must be less than the benefits derived from the system adopted.
- *Comparability*: The management must be able to make comparison of the facts and figures with the past figures, figures of other concerns, or other departments of the same concern.
- *Suitability to the Firms*: Before accepting a costing system, the nature, requirements, size, conditions of the business etc., must be carefully considered. The system must be capable of prompt and accurate reporting to different levels of management according to their requirements.
- *Minimum Changes to the Existing one*: When introducing a costing system, it may cause minimum disturbance to the existing set up of the business.
- *Uniformity of Forms*: Forms of different colours can be used to distinguish them. Forms must be uniform in size and quality. Form should contain instructions to fill, to use and for disposal.

- *Less Clerical Work*: Printed forms will involve less labour to fill in, as the workers may be a little educated. They may not like to spend much time in filling the forms.
- *Efficient Material Control and Wage System*: There must be a proper procedure for recording the time spent on different jobs, by workers for the payment of wages. A systematic method of wage system will help in the control of labour cost. Since the cost of material forms a great proportion to the total cost, there must be an efficient system of stores control.
- *A Sound Plan*: There must be proper and sound plans to collect, to allocate and to apportion overhead expenses on each job or each product in order to find out the cost accurately.
- *Reconciliation*: The systems of costing and financial accounting must be facilitated to reconcile in the easiest manner.
- *Overall Efficiency of Cost Accountant*: The work of the cost accountant under a good system of costing must be clearly defined as to his duties and responsibilities to the firm are very essential.

COSTING SYSTEM

Costing systems are components of a broader accounting system used by a given company or organization. The main function of the costing system is to keep a focused eye on expenditures made by the company. While the data that is collected and generated by the costing system is also integrated into the overall accounting system, the costing approach allows for easy extraction of the data for reports to upper management.

The information that typically is gathered by a costing system allows owners and managers to quickly identify the current status of two key factors that are relevant to the success of the company. Operational costs are often the foundation of the data collected by a costing system. Here, management is able to get a snapshot of all expenditures that are directly connected with the general operation of the organization, especially in terms of production costs.

A second important bloc of information that is retrieved with the use of a costing system is performance cost. Here, management is able to view any and all expenditures that are related to helping the company remain profitable, less the direct cost of operations. Expenses associated with marketing, public relations, and sales efforts are examples of the type of expenditures that are captured in the performance cost module.

A costing system is not intended to replace an accounting system. Instead, the systems actually work within the broad framework of general accounting systems to extract specific data for quick and easy analysis. By making use of a costing system, it is possible to quickly identify expenditures that were intended to benefit the company, but are failing to do so in a significant way.

This makes it possible for owners and managers to make the necessary adjustments to the company's working strategy and thus exercise a more responsible use of available resources. From this perspective.

It can be said that regular use of a costing system can help to minimize waste and also make it possible to direct available resources in more productive directions rather than continuing to spend money on items that are accomplishing little or nothing for the company.

THROUGHPUT COSTING

A costing methodology that focuses on capacity utilization is called "throughput costing". It assumes that there is always one bottleneck operation in a production process that governs the speed with which products or services can be completed. This operation becomes the defining issue in determining what products should be manufactured first, since this in turn results in differing levels of profitability.

WHY COST ACCOUNTING IS MOST CRUCIAL

Cost accounting is one of the most crucial aspects of the accounting profession, for it is the primary means by which the accounting department transmits company-related performance information to the management team. A properly organized cost accounting function can give valuable feedback regarding the impact of product pricing, cost trends, the performance of cost and profit centres, and production and personnel capacity, and can even contribute to some degree to the formulation of company strategy.

Despite this wide array of uses, many accountants rarely give due consideration to the multitude of uses to which cost accounting can be put. Instead, they only think of how cost accounting will feed information into the financial statements. This orientation comes from a strong tendency in business schools to train students in generally accepted accounting principles (GAAP) and how they are used to create financial statements.

THE PURPOSE OF COST ACCOUNTING INFORMATION

The purpose of cost accounting differs from that of many other topics discussed in financial accounting and its reporting. It is primarily concerned with helping the management team to understand the company's operations. This is in opposition to many other accounting topics, which are more concerned with the proper observance of very precise accounting rules and regulations, as laid down by various accounting oversight entities, to ensure that reported results meet certain standards. The cost accounting function works best without any oversight rules and regulations, because, in accordance with its stated purpose of assisting management, it tends to result in hybrid systems that are custom-designed to meet specific company needs. For example, a company may find that a major requirement is to determine the incremental cost that it incurs for each additional unit of production, so that it can make accurate decisions regarding the price of incremental units sold (possibly at prices very close to the direct cost). If it were to use accounting standards, it would be constrained to use only a costing system that allocated a portion of overhead costs to product costs—even though these are not incremental costs.

Accordingly, the cost accounting system used for this specific purpose will operate in contravention of GAAP, because following GAAP would yield results that do not assist management. Because there are many different management decisions for which the cost accounting profession can provide valuable information, it is quite common to have several costing systems in place, each of which may use different costing guidelines. The incremental costing system used for incremental pricing decisions may not be adequate for a different problem, which is creating profit centres that are used to judge the performance of individual managers. For this purpose, a second costing system must be devised that allocates costs from internal service centres to the various profit centres; in this instance, we are adding an allocation function to the incremental costing system that was already in place. Even more systems may be required for other applications, such as transfer pricing between company divisions and the costing of inventory for external financial reporting purposes (which does require attention to GAAP guidelines).

Consequently, cost accounting frequently results in a multitude of costing systems, which may only follow GAAP guidelines by accident. The cost accountant's primary concern is whether or not the information resulting from each system adequately meets the needs of the recipients. Any cost accounting system is comprised of three functional areas: the collection of raw data, the processing of this data in accordance with a costing methodology, and the reporting of the resulting information to management in the most understandable format.

The area that receives the most coverage is the processing function, for there are a number of different methodologies available, each of which applies to different situations. For example, job costing is used for situations where specifically identifiable goods are produced in batches, while direct costing is most applicable in situations in which management does not want to see any overhead allocation attached to the directly identifiable costs of a product.

BASIC THROUGHPUT COSTING MODEL

The basic calculation used for throughput accounting is shown below. This format is a simplified version of the layout used by Thomas Corbett of

Throughput Accounting, though all of the numbers contained within the example have been changed.

For example: the 19" colour television produces $81.10 of throughput, but requires 10 minutes of processing time in the bottleneck operation, resulting in throughput per minute of $8.11. The various electronic devices are sorted in the exhibit from top to bottom in order of largest throughput per minute. This ordering tells the user how much of the most profitable products can be produced before the total amount of available time in the bottleneck is used up. The calculation for bottleneck utilization is shown in the "Unit Demand/Actual Production" column.

In that column, the 19" colour television has a current demand for 1,000 units, which requires 10,000 minutes of bottleneck time.

This allocation of bottleneck time progresses downward through the various products until we come to the 50" High Definition TV at the bottom of the list, for which there is only enough bottleneck time left to manufacture 1,700 units.

By multiplying the dollars of throughput per minute times the number of minutes of production time, we arrive at the cumulative throughput dollars resulting from the manufacture (and presumed sale) of each product, which yields a total throughput of $405,360. We then add up all other expenses, totaling $375,000, and subtract them from the total throughput, which gives us a profit of $30,360. These calculations comprise the basic throughput accounting analysis model.

THROUGHPUT COSTING ANALYSIS BASED ON ADDITIONAL ALLOCATED COST

Now let's re-examine the model based on a re-juggling of the priority of orders. If the cost accounting manager were to examine each of the products based on the addition of allocated overhead and direct labour costs to the direct materials that were used as the foundation for the throughput dollar calculation, she may arrive at the conclusion that, when fully burdened, the 50" High Definition TV is actually the most profitable, while the 19" Colour Television is the least profitable.

The result is a significant loss, rather than the increase in profits that had been expected.

The trouble is that allocated overhead costs have no bearing on throughput, because allocated costs will not change in accordance with incremental production decisions, such as which product will be manufactured first.

Instead, the overhead cost pool will exist, irrespective of any modest changes in activity levels.

Consequently, it makes no sense to apply allocated costs to the production scheduling decision, when the only issue that matters is how much throughput per minute a product can generate.

THROUGHPUT COSTING ANALYSIS BASED ON ADDITIONAL INVESTMENT

Capital budgeting is an area in which throughput costing analysis can be applied with excellent results. The trouble with most corporate capital budgeting systems is that they do not take into consideration the fact that the only valid investment is one that will have a positive impact on the amount of throughput that can be pushed through a bottleneck operation. Any other investment will result in greater production capacity in other areas of the company that still cannot produce any additional quantities, since the bottleneck operation controls the total amount of completed production.

For example: the throughput model in the next exhibit shows the result of an investment of $28,500 in new equipment that is added later in the production process than the bottleneck operation. The result is an increase in the total investment, to $528,500, and absolutely no impact on profitability, which yields a reduced return on investment of 5.7 per cent.

A more profitable solution would have been to invest in anything that would increase the productivity of the bottleneck operation, which could be either a direct investment in that operation, or an investment in an upstream operation that would reduce the amount of processing required for a product by the bottleneck operation.

THROUGHPUT COSTING ANALYSIS WITH ONE LESS PRODUCT

As another example, the cost accounting staff has conducted a lengthy activity-based costing analysis, which has determined that a much larger amount of overhead cost must be allocated to the high definition television, which results in a loss on that product.

The result is a reduction in profits. The reason is that the cost accounting staff has made the incorrect assumption that, by eliminating a product, all of the associated overhead cost will be eliminated, too. Though a small amount of overhead might be eliminated when the production of a single product is stopped, the bulk of it will still be incurred.

Throughput accounting does a very good job of tightly focusing attention on the priority of production in situations where there is a choice of products that can be manufactured. It can also have an impact on a number of other decisions, such as whether to grant volume discounts, outsource manufacturing, stop the creation of a product, or invest in new capital items.

Given this wide range of activities, it should find a place in the mix of costing methodologies at many companies.

We now shift to a discussion of activity-based costing (ABC), whose emphasis is the complete reverse of throughput accounting—it focuses on the proper allocation of overhead.

METHODS OF COSTING SYSTEM

Manufacturing costing methods are accounting techniques that are used to help understand the value of inputs and outputs in a production process. By tracking and categorizing this information according to a rigorous accounting system, corporate management can determine with a high degree of accuracy the cost per unit of production and other key performance indicators.

Management needs this information in order to make informed decisions about production levels, pricing, competitive strategy, future investment, and a host of other concerns. Such information is primarily necessary for internal use, or managerial accounting.

OVERVIEW OF CURRENT METHODS

Process and Job-Order Costing

There are two conventional costing approaches used in manufacturing. The first, and more common, is process costing. Used in most mass-production settings, a process cost system analyses the net cost of a manufacturing process, say filling bottles with soda, over a specified period of time. The unit cost for filling bottles is simply the net costs incurred while filling all the bottles during the period divided by the number of bottles filled. Since most manufacturing processes involve more than one step, a similar calculation is made for each step to arrive at a unit cost average for the entire production system. By contrast, the second major costing method, job-order costing, is concerned with tracking all the costs on an individual product basis.

This is useful in settings where each unit of production is customised or where there are very few units produced, such as in building pianos, ships, or airplanes. Under job order costing, the exact costs incurred in the production of a particular unit are recorded and are not necessarily averaged with those of any other unit, since every unit may be different. Job-order costing is also widely used outside manufacturing. A single manufacturer may use both process and job-order costing for different parts of its operations.

Activity-based Costing

Activity-based costing(ABC) is a secondary and somewhat complementary (or better, supplementary) method to the two traditional costing techniques. Whereas traditional methods might classify costs in generic categories like direct materials, labour, and other overhead, ABC clusters all the costs associated with a single manufacturing task, regardless of whether they fall under the headings of labour or materials or something else. So in the bottling example activity-based costs might include operating the dispensing machines, performing quality checks, moving pallets of bottles, and so forth. Each of these activities may involve human labour, equipment costs, energy and expendable resources, and materials, but for analytic purposes the costs are all lumped together under a single activity concept. The advantage of this approach is that management can then observe which tasks cost the most versus which add the most value; this analysis may indicate that a disproportionate amount of money is being spent on low-value activities, signaling a need for process changes or for outsourcing to a vendor that can perform the tasks less expensively. Use of this method is sometimes referred to as activity-based cost management (ABCM) or simply activity-based management (ABM).

HISTORY OF COSTING METHODS

Double-entry bookkeeping, developed in Northern Italy in the 14th and 15th centuries, was the predecessor to modem accounting methods. Early modem methods were developed in the United States in the 1850s and 1860s by accountants in the railroad industry. These methods were just one of several innovations originating with the railroads that marked the transition from traditional to modem business enterprise. Most important were the developments of J. Edgar Thomson and his cohorts at the Pennsylvania Railroad. The work of these and other pioneering accountants in the railroad industry was the subject of widespread public discussion and numerous substances in the new financial journals of the day.

Emergence of Cost Accounting

Cost accounting was one of three interrelated types of accounting developed at the time, the others being financial and capital accounting. Financial accounting addressed issues relating to a firm's daily financial transactions, as well as overall profitability. For example, railroads began deriving operating ratios in the late 1850s, which for the first time related absolute quantities of profit and loss to business volume. Capital accounting addressed issues relating to the valuation of a firm's capital goods. This was particularly important in the railroad industry given the unprecedented quantities of capital involved and the problem of how to account for the repair and renewal of capital. Innovations in cost accounting followed those in financial and capital accounting. Cost accounting involved the determination and comparison of costs among a firm's divisions or operations. Thus the historical development of cost accounting accommodated the development of the multidivisional firm towards the end of the 19th century. There was necessarily a considerable amount of overlap among financial, capital, and cost accounting. For example, to accurately determine unit costs, it was necessary to relate overhead costs and capital depreciation to the volume of production. At the same time, unit costs were typically used to determine prices, which in turn affected financial accounts. The separation of these types of accounting followed their historical institutional separation. That is, until the innovations of E.I. Du Pont de Nemours and Co. in the 20th century, financial, capital, and cost accounting operations were carried out in relative autonomy within firms.

Cost accounting was first used by the Louisville and Nashville Railroad in the late 1860s. This enabled the company to determine such measures as comparative cost per ton-mile among its branches, and it was by these measures, rather than earnings or net income, that the company evaluated the performance of its managers. The accounting methods developed by the railroads were adopted by the first large manufacturing firms in the United States upon their formation in the last quarter of the 19th century.

Expanding Uses

The largest U.S. manufacturing firms in the 1870s were textile producers. Because these years were a period of hardship for the industry, textile producers began to devote more attention to the determination and control of costs. By 1886, Lyman Mills, one of the country's largest textile producers, began to determine unit costs for its various products, though it did not use this information to make pricing or investment decisions. The Standard Oil Trust, formed in 1882, also began to determine the comparative costs of their different refineries in the 1880s and on this basis opted to concentrate production in their largest units. However, the enterprise did not accurately account for overhead or capital depreciation in its determination of costs. The firm with the most detailed and sophisticated costing methods in the 1880s was the Carnegie Company, a steel producer. In this case, the connection between costing methods in the railroad and manufacturing industries was direct, as Andrew Carnegie patterned the organization of his firm after the Pennsylvania Railroad, where he had been an executive. Carnegie's costing method was referred to as the voucher system of accounting. In this system, each of the company's departments kept track of the quantity and price of materials and labour for each order. These data were aggregated into cost sheets that the company's accountants were able to produce on a daily basis. Though the Carnegie Company made extensive use of its cost sheets to determine prices, it focused on prime rather than overhead and depreciation costs.

In 20th-century Advances

In the early 1900s, firms came to systematically relate overhead costs to variations in the quantity of goods produced. Accountants began determining standard costs, based on a standard level of capacity utilization. The greater unit costs of running below standard capacity were defined as unabsorbed burden, whereas the lesser unit costs of running standard capacity were defined as over-absorbed burden. Such methods of accounting for overhead were widely discussed in trade journals at the time. It was not until later that modern methods of accounting for capital depreciation came into widespread use. Until then, manufacturing firms continued to use the renewal accounting methods borrowed from the railroads. That is, the repair and renewal of capital goods was charged to operating expenses and profits were determined as the difference between earnings and expenses. Firms did not determine changes in the value of capital resulting from depreciation, repair, and renewal, and thus profitability could not be determined as the ratio of profits to the value of capital.

Chemical producer Du Pont was among the first firms to integrate cost, capital, and financial accounting. This resulted in part from Du Pont's rejection of traditional renewal capital accounting in which profitability rates were typically determined in relation to sales or costs. Du Pont's accountants established careful records of changes in fixed capital, made up of plant and equipment, and working capital, made up of inventories, financial assets, and accounts receivable. By doing so, Du Pont was able to derive monthly reports on profitability as a return on capital invested. In his 1977 volume The Visible Hand, Chandler described the critical role of Du Pont manager Donaldson Brown in accounting for stock turnover and thus contemporary calculations of profitability. He wrote: "Brown ... related turnover to earnings as a percentage of sales (still the standard definition of profit in American industry). He did this by multiplying turnover by profit so defined, which gave a rate of return that reflected the intensity with which the enterprise's resources were being used."

THE BASICS OF COSTING METHODS

Fixed Costs

One of the key issues in conventional costing methods (*i.e.*, process costing and job-order costing) is distinguishing among types of costs. A basic distinction is made between fixed and variable costs. Fixed costs are those costs that are invariant with respect to changes in output and would accrue even if no output were produced. Such costs might include interest payments on the purchase of plant and equipment, rent, property taxes, and executive salaries. The notion of fixed costs is restricted within a certain time frame, since over the long run fixed costs can vary. For example, a manufacturer may decide to expand capacity in the face of increased demand for its product, requiring a higher level of expenditure on plant and equipment.

Variable Costs

Variable costs change proportionately to the level of output. For manufacturers, a key variable cost is the cost of materials. In terms of total costs at increasing output levels, fixed costs are constant and variable costs are increasing at a constant rate. In terms of unit costs at increasing output levels, fixed costs are declining, and variable costs constant. Manufacturers are vitally interested in unit costs with respect to changes in output levels, since this determines profit per unit of output at any given price level. The characteristics of fixed and variable costs indicates that as output increases, unit costs will decline, since there is constant variable cost and lesser fixed cost embodied in each unit. These costing methods thus suggest that it is in manufacturers' interest to run, within the limits of plant design, at high capacity levels.

Direct Costs

Costing methods distinguish between the direct and indirect costs of any costed object. Direct costs are those costs readily traceable to the costed object, whereas indirect costs are less-readily traceable. Direct costs typically include the major components of any manufactured good and the labour directly required to produce that good. Direct costs are often subdivided into direct material costs and direct labour costs. Direct costs are also referred to as prime costs.

Indirect Costs

Indirect costs include plant-wide costs such as those resulting from the use of energy and fixed capital, but indirect costs may also include the costs of minor components such as solder or glue. While all costs are conceivably traceable to a costed object, the determination of whether to do so depends on the cost-effectiveness with which this can be done. Indirect costs of all kinds are sometimes referred to as overhead, and in this sense prime costs can be distinguished from overhead costs.

ESTIMATING TOTAL COSTS

Several methods are used in manufacturing to estimate total cost equations, in which total costs are determined as a function of fixed costs per time period, variable costs per unit of output, and the level of output. These methods include account analysis, the engineering approach, the high-low approach, and linear regression analysis. In all these methods, the central issue is how total costs change in relation to changes in output.

Account Analysis

In account analysis, all costs are classified as either strictly fixed or variable. This has the advantage of ease of computation. However, some costs may be semivariable costs or step costs. Utility bills are typically semivariable in that they contain fixed and variable components. Step costs increase in discrete jumps as the level of output increases. In account analysis, such costs are typically categorized as either fixed or variable depending which element predominates. Thus, the accuracy of account analysis depends in large part on the proportion of costs that are not strictly fixed or variable. For many manufacturing firms, account analysis provides a sufficiently accurate estimation of total costs over a range of output levels.

Engineering Approach

The engineering approach infers costs from the specifications of a product. The approach works best for determining direct material costs and less well for direct labour costs and overhead costs. The advantage of the engineering approach is that it enables manufacturers to estimate what a product would cost without having previously produced that product, whereas the other methods are based on the costs of production that has already occurred.

High-low Approach

In the high-low approach, a firm must know its total costs for previous high and low levels of output. Graphing total costs against output, total costs over a range of output are estimated by fitting a straight line through total cost points at high and low levels of output. If changes in total costs can be accurately described as a linear function of output, then the slope of the line indicates changes in variable costs. The problem with the high-low approach is that the two data points may not, for whatever reasons, accurately represent the underlying total cost-output relationship. That is, if additional total cost-output points were plotted, they might lay significantly wide of the line connecting the two initial high-low points.

Linear Regression

Linear regression analysis addresses the shortcomings of the high low approach by fitting a line through all total cost-output points. The line is fitted to minimize the sum of squared differences between total cost-output points and the line itself, in standard linear regression fashion. The drawback of this approach is that it requires more data points than the other approaches.

STANDARD COSTS

The relation of total costs to output levels is combined in the idea of standard costs. Standard costs are estimates of unit costs at targeted output levels, including direct materials costs, direct labour costs, and indirect costs. Standard costs are used to prepare budgets for planned production and to assess production that has occurred. The estimation of standard costs requires the separate estimation of standards for direct materials, direct labour, and overhead.

Direct Materials

Direct material standards are the easiest to estimate. Costs are determined from the prices of all necessary material inputs into the product, plus sales tax, shipping, and other related costs. Unanticipated price changes complicate this otherwise straightforward process. Since standard costs are a measure of unit costs, it is also necessary to determine the quantity of materials per unit. This can be done using an engineering approach.

Direct Labour

Direct labour standards are somewhat more difficult to estimate. The determination of costs must account for wages, though if workers in a production process are earning different wages, it is necessary to estimate a weighted average of wage costs. The cost of benefits, employment related taxes, and overtime pay must also be accounted for. As with direct material standards, the quantity of direct labour required to produce a unit of output can be estimated with an engineering approach. Average set-up time and downtime must also be included in the estimation. Many union contracts codify labour time standards, which can make budgeting easier.

Overhead

Overhead standards are the most difficult to estimate, and they are typically accounted for in an approximate manner. The problem of accounting for overhead costs per unit of output—it is often difficult to trace indirect costs to a particular product. The problem is made more complicated if these costs are highly centralized within a plant and if multiple products are produced within a plant. Overhead standards are typically estimated by taking total overhead costs and relating them to a more readily-knowable measure, such as direct labour hours, direct labour costs, or machine hours used. Direct labour hours was traditionally the most widely-used measure for determining overhead standards, but the growth of automated plants resulted in a shift to machine hours used.

DETERMINING PROFITABILITY THROUGH CVP ANALYSIS

Cost equations are combined with revenue equations to determine profitability at different levels of output. This is referred to as cost-volume-profit(CVP) analysis. That is, net income equals total revenue minus total cost; total cost equals average variable cost times the quantity of output plus fixed cost; and total revenue equals price times the quantity of output sold. Combining cost and revenue equations reveals that net income equals price times quantity of output sold minus average variable cost times the quantity of output minus fixed costs. That is,

where,

P = Price,

Q = Quantity of output,

AVC = Average variable cost

FC = Fixed costs

This is referred to as the cost-volume-profit equation, and is one of the most widely-used of cost accounting tools.

CVP analysis allows a firm to determine a breakeven point, the level of output at which total revenue equals total cost. That total cost and total revenue functions will be equal at some non-zero level of output is assured by the fact that at zero units of output, total costs will be positive as a result of fixed costs and total revenues will be zero. This is based on the assumption that the unit price for which a product can be sold is greater than the unit cost, so that total revenue increases faster than total cost as output increases. In addition to estimating profitability across a range of output levels, firms use CVP analysis to determine whether projected sales are sufficiently beyond the breakeven point to warrant production.

Economic theory also concerns itself with changing costs as a function of changing output within a given plant. This is an analog to the slope of an accountant's cost function curve and is referred to as marginal cost. "Economic Concepts in Cost Accounting," Shillinglaw describes the relationship between mainstream economic theory and cost accounting as follows: "Cost accounting springs mainly from the needs of managers and others to make decisions affecting the allocation of economic resources. This might suggest that cost accounting is based directly on a fairly well-defined set of concepts drawn from economic theory. The truth is something else.... The uneasy and ambiguous relationship between cost accounting and economics is nowhere more apparent than in the application of the concept of short-run marginal cost." In mainstream economic theory, marginal costs are generally assumed to be decreasing at lower levels of output, more or less flat over medium levels, and increasing at an accelerating rate at higher levels. Cost accountants generally base their calculations on the assumption that costs change at a constant rate with respect to output.

FUTURE OF COST ACCOUNTING

Expansion And Integration Of Abc

Widespread corporate interest in activity-based costing (ABC), which started in the late 1980s and has continued through the late 1990s, has created dueling cost accounting systems for some companies. Managers want the analytic power of an ABC system, yet may also require some of the conventional abilities and rigour of a traditional system like process or job costing.

The failure to integrate these competing needs has caused some firms to abandon or at least reconsider ABC initiatives, which can be expensive and time-consuming to implement in a large operation. Some managers have viewed it as an either-or dilemma, and often ABC is eyed with some suspicion, as indeed early formulations of it were not effective substitutes for conventional costing methods. However, many successful ABC implementations use it as a supplement to, rather than a replacement for, standard methods. Advocates of ABC have begun to formulate ways in which ABC can be better integrated with conventional methods so that companies can enjoy the benefits of both. In 1999 the Institute of Management Accountants (IMA), the leading professional organization for managerial accountants, published renewed guidelines for companies wishing to implement ABC practices, following a series of previous statements on using ABC dating back to the early 1990s. The IMA's statements included a number of cautions against potential pitfalls in establishing an ABC system.

Target Costing

A related practice that has also enjoyed quite a bit of attention since the mid-1990s is target costing, which is a method of engineering a product and its manufacturing process from the start with a specific cost model in mind. This approach, which is essentially an elaboration of the engineering costing approach, attempts to create an optimally efficient process from the start—with a profitable yet marketable selling price in mind—rather than waiting until a product is already being manufactured and then setting prices and looking for cost savings.

Some implementations of target costing actually don't involve accountants as much as they invlolve product marketing managers, engineers, and others who are part of the actual design and production processes. IMA guidelines also exist for target costing systems.

ABSORPTION COSTING

Absorption costing means that all of the manufacturing costs are *absorbed* by the units produced. In other words, the cost of a finished unit in inventory will include direct materials, direct labour, and both variable and *fixed manufacturing overhead*. As a result, absorption costing is also referred to as full costing or the full absorption method. Absorption costing is often contrasted with variable costing or direct costing. Under variable or direct costing, the fixed manufacturing overhead costs are not allocated or assigned to (not absorbed by) the products manufactured. Variable costing is often useful for management's decision-making. However, absorption costing is required for external financial reporting and for income tax reporting.

BUDGET CONTROL SYSTEM

The State University of New York Fiscal and Accounting Procedures for Mandatory Student Activity Fee Programmes require the custodial and disbursing agent to establish and maintain budgetary accounts.

The basic structure for recording and monitoring revenues and expenditures is the Annual Operating Budget. As part of its accounting system, Sub-Board I provides a Budgetary Control System modeled after those commonly used by governments and other not-for-profit entities which satisfies the fiscal guidelines, policies and procedures of the Board of Trustees and the State University of New York. All student governments and clients for whom Sub-Board I acts as Fiscal Agent must use the Budgetary Control System.

UNDERSTANDING THE BUDGET

A budget is your management's plan or blueprint, in structured form, which projects or anticipates the desired outcome of financial activity for a specific set of resources, for a fixed period, usually one year. For our purposes, the Annual Operating Budget is divided into two separate components: Estimated Revenues - What are the anticipated sources of revenue and how much can management realistically expect to receive? Estimated Expenditures - How much does management expect to spend, and for what purposes are resources to be spent?

IMPORTANCE OF BUDGET

A budget acts as the formal process that establishes the authority on how funds are to be collected and spent. Management's objective is to provide a logical, detailed and realistic spending plan. Once a plan has been decided upon and is formally adopted by the student government/client governing body, the budget acts as an effective management tool by providing a means of identifying and allocating limited resources and monitoring their use.

The budget also is used to help prevent the student government/client from overspending. Budget reports provide management with information on operations, allowing the organization to monitor and control spending and revenue collection while they are in progress.

Hence, budgets alone are meaningless unless they are used to motivate responsible action and to direct operations towards accomplishing objectives that have been established by management as desirable. The budget is the single most important source of financial information. Almost all financial transactions are recorded in the budget.

The budget is used to track all cash receipts, encumbrances and cash disbursements, and provides a means of tracking these transactions back to original source documents.

STRUCTURE OF BUDGET

In determining the basic elements of Estimated Revenues and Estimated Expenditures, a logical structure must be developed to codify and arrange the elements into units or sections that reflect the nature and structure of the operations themselves. The basic structural tool is the budgetary account. A budgetary account identifies a specific source of revenue or a particular type of expenditure by using a budgetary account number.

Sub-Board's Budgetary Control System uses the following budgetary account number format:

- *Fund:* The first three digits of the account number identify the student government/client and the overall purpose of the funds accounted for in a particular budget, *e.g.* operating funds, capital funds, etc.

- *Department:* The next four digits of the account number identify the department, division, activity center, etc. within the internal operations of the student government/client.
- *Line Item:* The next four digits of the account number identify the specific source of revenue or the type of expenditure for a particular department, *e.g.* Advertising Revenue, or Telephone Expense.
- *Project:* In certain situations, the account number may be extended by an additional four digits to further identify a particular project.

HOW DOES THE BUDGETARY PROCESS BEGIN?

The first step in the budgetary process is for the student government/ client to review its operations. What is working well and what needs to be changed? What are the goals and objectives for the coming budget year? What projects does the student government/client wish to support? Which recognized clubs and organizations has management agreed to fund? What are the primary sources of revenue? Clubs, organizations, project managers and department heads may be required to submit budget requests to whoever is responsible for preparing the initial or "proposed" budget.

These requests can then be reviewed and modified before being incorporated into the proposed budget. It may also be helpful for whoever is preparing the proposed budget to review past budgets – historical information can be very helpful in determining how the student government/client has operated in the past and can help identify areas that management would like to continue, eliminate or change. All student governments/clients must prepare their budgets just as to the fiscal year.

The fiscal year begins on August 1 and ends on July 31 of the following year. Once the proposed budget has been prepared, it must be formally approved or adopted in accordance with the student government/client constitution, by-laws or governing rules. During this process, the budget may be discussed, modified, or challenged before being formally adopted. For student governments/clients that maintain more that one fund in addition to the operating budget, a separate budget for each Fund must be adopted.

AFTER THE BUDGET IS ADOPTED, WHAT IS THE NEXT STEP?

For all student governments/clients subject to administrative review and certification, approved budgets must be submitted using the Required Budget Format to the Administrative Designee no later than June 1 prior to the start of the fiscal year. A copy of the approved budget must also be submitted to the SBI Accounting Office by the same date, June 1. For independent clients whose budgets are not subject to administrative review and certification, approved budgets must be submitted to the SBI Accounting Office no later than June 1 prior to the start of the Fiscal Year.

Budgets must be accompanied by a completed Certification of Budget Form signed by at least two officers or authorized representatives of the student government/client, attesting that adoption and approval procedures were correctly followed. For student governments/clients that maintain more than one budget, a separate Certification of Budget Form must be submitted with each budget. In order to continue operating without an interruption in accounting services, budgets must be submitted by the due date of June 1.

WHAT HAPPENS AFTER THE BUDGET IS SUBMITTED AND CERTIFIED

Upon receiving the adopted budget, Sub-Board I will review the budget for accuracy and conformity to fiscal guidelines. Budgets must be balanced; *i.e.* Total Estimated Revenue must equal or exceed Total Estimated Expenditures. Unbalanced budgets will be returned to the student government/client unprocessed.

Estimated Revenues and Estimated Expenditures must be based on realistic projections. Assuming that budgets have been submitted by the required deadline, in the required format, and with the proper officer certification, and the administrative designee, where applicable, has approved the budgets, Sub- Board I will enter the adopted budgets into the accounting system. On August 1, the adopted budgets will go into effect. All student governments/clients will receive initial budget reports as of August 1, before any activity begins, as verification that Sub-Board I has accurately entered the budgets. The student government/client should closely review these initial budget reports and report any problems or errors immediately to the SBI Accounting Office for correction.

WILL ANY ACTIVITY FROM THE PRIOR YEAR BUDGET HAVE AN EFFECT ON THE CURRENT BUDGET

Since there may be financial activity in process between the end of one fiscal year and the beginning of the next, the budget will be affected in several ways.

- On the revenue side, the Fund's cash balance as of July 31 will be added to Estimated Revenues and Annual Revenue Receipts in the new budget on the first day of the new fiscal year, August 1. This cash balance, if sufficient, can be used as a reserve to accommodate outstanding encumbrances and accrued payroll expenses. Any remaining cash balance not reserved for other purposes may be re-appropriated in the new budget. This adjustment will take place as soon as all cash activity has been recorded and reconciled for July, usually sometime in early August.
- On the expenditure side, any encumbrances outstanding at the end of the fiscal year will be added to budgeted expenditures in the next fiscal year's budget. The date that this adjustment actually takes place

depends on the final accounting of year-end activity, preparation of year-end financial statements, the progress of the annual independent audit, etc., and usually takes place sometime after October 15. Until this final accounting for outstanding encumbrances is completed and the prior year budget is "closed", the accounting system will automatically account for encumbrances from the prior fiscal year that are paid in the new fiscal year. This is done so that budgetary expenditures for the new fiscal year are not depleted by payments for which encumbrances existed in the prior fiscal year's budget.

- Accrued payroll expenses, if any, as of July 31 will be added to Estimated Expenditures in the next fiscal year when the new budget goes into effect on August 1. You must provide a sufficient reserve in your budget to accommodate this additional appropriation and to maintain a balanced budget. This adjustment to the budget will take place after all payroll activity has been received and recorded, usually sometime in September.

WHAT IF THE BUDGET NEEDS TO BE MODIFIED OR ADJUSTED DURING THE COURSE OF THE FISCAL YEAR

It is not realistic to prepare a budget at the beginning of the fiscal year and then leave it as a rigid plan of action. Important unforeseen changes in internal or external conditions may require budget revisions during the fiscal year. It is essential that management receive timely information on its actual results in comparison with the plan. A comparison of actual operating results with the original budget plan would show management what the organization did in comparison with what it initially planned to do.

It may not reveal, however, how well the organization did with regard to how it should have performed under the conditions which actually existed. Therefore, Sub-Board I will provide periodic budget reports to assess performance of actual results with the original plan and the adjusted budget plan. Whenever an adjustment or revision to the original budget is necessary, the student government/client must notify Sub-Board I of the adjustment(s) to be made by entering a Budget Adjustment into the on-line KVS Accounting System. Budget Adjustments require the approval of two officers.

In addition, student governments and independent clients who are subject to administrative review must have all budget adjustments or changes to the budget reviewed and certified by the administrative designee. All approvals can be done on-line. Sub-Board I will update the budget adjustments only after all approvals have been obtained.

9

Operating and Service Costing

OPERATING COST

Operating costs are the recurring expenses which are related to the operation of a business, or to the operation of a device, component, piece of equipment or facility.

BUSINESS OPERATING COSTS

For a commercial enterprise, operating costs fall into two broad categories:

1. Fixed costs, which are the same whether the operation is closed or running at 100 per cent capacity
2. Variable costs, which may increase depending on whether more production is done, and how it is done (producing 100 items of product might require 10 days of normal time or take 7 days if overtime is used. It may be more or less expensive to use overtime production depending on whether faster production means the product can be more profitable).

Business Overhead Costs

Overhead costs for a business are the cost of resources used by an organization just to maintain its existence. Overhead costs are usually measured in monetary terms, but non-monetary overhead is possible in the form of time required to accomplish tasks.

Examples of overhead costs include:

- Cost of electricity for the office lights
- Payment of rent on the office space a business occupies
- Some office personnel wages

Non-overhead costs are incremental costs, such as the cost of raw materials used in the goods a business sells. Operating Cost is calculated by Cost of goods sold + Operating Expenses. Operating Expenses consist of:. Administrative and office expenses like rent, salaries, to staff, insurance, directors fees etc.. Selling and distribution expenses like advertisement, salaries of salesmen.

EQUIPMENT OPERATING COSTS

In the case of a device, component, piece of equipment or facility, it is the regular, usual and customary recurring coststing or purchasing the equipment. Operating costs are incurred by all equipment—unless the equipment has no cost to operate, requires no personnel or space and never wears out. In some cases, equipment may appear to have low or no operating cost because either the cost is not recognized or is being absorbed in whole or part by the cost of something else.

Equipment operating costs may include:

- Salaries or Wages of personnel
- Advertising
- Raw materials
- License or equivalent fees imposed by a government
- Real estate expenses, including
  - Rent or Lease payments
  - Office space
  - Furniture and equipment
  - Investment value of the funds used to purchase The land, if it is owned instead of rented or leased
  - Property taxes and equivalent assessments
  - Operations taxes, such as fees assessed on transportation carriers for use of highways
- Fuel costs such as power for operations, fuel for production
- Public Utilities such as telephone service, Internet connectivity, etc.
- Maintenance of equipment
- Office supplies and consumables
- Insurance
- Depreciation of equipment and eventual replacement costs
- Damage due to uninsured losses, accident, sabotage, negligence, terrorism and routine wear and tear.
- Taxes on production or operation
- Income taxes

Some of these are not applicable in all instances.

For example:

- A solar panel placed on one's home for use in generating electric power generally has only capital costs; once it's running there are no personnel costs, utility costs or depreciation and it uses no extra land so it has no real operating costs; however there may need to be taken into account costs of replacement if damaged.
- An automobile or any other item purchased for personal use has no salary cost because the owner does not charge themselves for operating the device.

- An item which is leased may have some or all of these costs included as part of the purchase price.

It might be questionable to assert that the cost of ten extra people on the sales force are an incremental cost or an overhead cost, since the wages for these people are both overhead and incremental. The staff needed to keep the shop operational are mostly considered as overhead.

COST ACCOUNTING AND OPERATIONS

Now it is time to give due attention to support of operations as the primary responsibility of a cost accounting system. Consider the following questions, this time in light of cost accounting responsibilities to operations, compared to its obligations to financial reporting requirements.

How might the accounting system:

- Support understanding of the nature and behaviour of cost?
- Promote, track, and give feedback on value creation?
- Assist management in wise use of resources?

The answers lie in the design of the cost management system. Deliberate and careful design of a cost management system promotes organizational control, as well as workforce focus. The managerial cost accounting system mandates specific control processes by means of the design of its cost management system. More and more organizations look to their CFOs, controllers, and accountants for vital decision-making information and participation in strategic and long-term planning. In contrast, operations-oriented firms often see accounting systems as a necessary evil, required by government and creditor agencies, but for the most part simply a nuisance to internal managers. The difference in viewpoint largely depends on the accounting system design. CMS designs that remain in Stage I and II may quickly become irrelevant to management's decision-making responsibilities. The importance of CMS design extends throughout the entire organization. Dr. CJ McNair summarizes the situation eloquently. "What cost management chooses to make visible—the focus of its work—will inform and constrain the organizations of the future.

In choosing a future for cost management, the future of business will be shaped." Cost management system design is a conscientious and deliberate process that avoids irrelevant detail and integrates seamlessly with the financial system. CMS design requires rigorous, periodic review to ascertain its continuing relevance.

To reiterate:

- *Cost accounting exists for a conceptually simple purpose*: Provide accurate cost information.
- The purpose of cost management is equally clear: Promote improvement in cost structure.

This part will address the essential steps that executives and managers can take to achieve these elusive goals and thereby develop a CMS that is easy to use, aimed at the most important targets of analysis, and supportive of management decision making. In Cost and Effect, Kaplan and Cooper conclude their introductory chapter by describing the vision for such cost systems where,"cost and performance measurement systems are explicitly designed to produce the right information at the right time for essential managerial learning, decisions, and control."

HISTORICAL OBSTACLES

Any executive with even a few years of experience knows the sharp difference between an accounting function that is pro-operations and one that is pro-finance. Likewise, any experienced accountant can tell when other functions (*e.g.*, operations, marketing) see the finance function as a necessary burden and when the function is appreciated for the value it adds to the organization. As in most complex situations, the ideal practice is a blend of both perspectives. Until this becomes true in their own organizations, managers must come to understand and acknowledge the historical animosity and inherent conflicts between operations and accounting. Passions would not run so high if the relationship between operations and accounting were not essential to business health. At the root of this friction is that, financial staff and operations people see their work from culturally different perspectives and business worldviews. These unspoken viewpoints generate misunderstandings and outright conflict. The different perspectives must be discovered, exposed, and reconciled before they can be blended. All too often, nothing happens. Both sides fear the loss of control, and each is reluctant to take on new roles.

Not long ago, a financial accounting professional might spend an entire career never setting foot on the factory floor or talking with a customer face-to-face. Huddled in back rooms with whirring pencils scratching numbers on green ledgers (and erasing them, too), accountants literally had no time for any activities other than tallying, ticking, and tying the numbers. Today, although computerized accounting systems have replaced the demanding drudgery of manual ledgers, some accountants still seldom set foot in the land of operations. Cost accountants who match this profile—then or now—cannot serve their organizations to the best of their abilities.

The connections and the conflicts within the accounting/operations dynamic are easiest to conceptualize in the manufacturing sector where the tangible nature of production makes conflict stand out.

Making the Numbers Count, Brian Maskell cites five key shortcomings with management accounting:

- Lack of relevance,
- Cost distortion,

- Inflexibility,
- Incompatibility with world-class approaches, and
- Inappropriate links to financial accounts.

By inversely examining each of these shortcomings as attributes, the inherent connections between cost accounting and operations, whereby a CMS brings value to management, can be explored in terms of:

- Relevance,
- Cost visibility,
- Flexibility,
- Support for advanced approaches, and
- Appropriate links to financial accounts.

APPROPRIATE LINKS TO FINANCIAL ACCOUNTS

Financial statements address the information needs of a range of constituents and government regulators. Since financial statements target external users and are governed by external standards and formats, at best they provide internal managers with a highly aggregated and shallow "report card" of business performance. Consequently, while the CMS should provide external managers the necessary and sufficient information to meet financial reporting requirements, the system should do so with all due dispatch in terms of the needs of internal managers for information focus and efficiency. Inventory valuation, COGS, expense classification, and absorption are among the few important connection points at issue between the financial accounting system and the CMS.

SUPPORT FOR ADVANCED APPROACHES

Because traditional accounting systems position cost accounting in the status of servant to the general ledger/financial statement system, the poorly designed CMS may consequently attempt to make vassals out of the other business functions. Practice the reverse. The most mature cost accountants have been given permission to support their executives to design a budgeting and cost reporting system that rapidly supports decision making, encourages efficiency throughout the organization, and requires value-added information from functional managers. In this context, all standard financial accounting-related routines should be automated and transparent to non-financial staff.

Capital spending is another connection point between accounting and operations functions for CMS value creation.

Typically, North American companies use discounted cash flow (DCF) or return-oninvestment (ROI) measurements to choose between capital spending alternatives. These financially focused frameworks are based on tenuous estimates and forecasts that frequently prove grossly inaccurate. Additionally, these traditional, exclusively financial analysis tools look for rapid returns on invested capital. This is not always congruent with operations management or long-term strategic plans.

FLEXIBILITY

Protocols often become highly standardized when financial accounting perspectives control the cost accounting system. In contrast, when the CMS serves operations first and financial accounting second, its system and report designs adapt to changing operational environments.

COST VISIBILITY

As service organizations become a larger business sector and the business landscape loses its stability in terms of organizational structure (due to mergers, acquisitions, and virtual offices), traditional cost types become increasingly irrelevant. Cost types do not facilitate cost visibility—a transparency of the nature and behaviour of costs and resource spending that sustains informed decision making. More advanced cost management systems such as activity-based costing and resource consumption accounting, clarify cost dynamics and enable wise choices grounded on business interrelationships that more closely reflect business performance.

RELEVANCE

Closing the circle, a CMS that serves operations, supports advanced cost management approaches, adapts flexibly, and clearly displays the nature and behaviour of cost, de facto, becomes relevant. In a relevant CMS, cost work investments are generally viewed as valueadded activities, and organizational management relies on them for essential decision-making information.

When a CMS exhibits these five attributes it becomes a valuable organizational asset. Inversely, for organizations missing some of these attributes, the executives and managers see one more reason for non-financial functions to pay less attention to CMS information.

OUTPUT COSTING AND OTHER COSTING METHODS

JOB COSTING

Job costing is the basic costing method applicable to those industries where the work consist of separate contracts, jobs, or batches, each of which is authorized by a specific order or contract.

- Contract costing is the form of specific order costing, generally applicable where work is undertaken to customer's special requirements and each order is of long duration, such as building construction, ship building, structural for bridge, civil construction, etc. The work is usually done outside the factory.

- Batch costing is that form of specific order costing which applies where similar articles are manufactured in batches either for sale or for use within the undertaking. Costs are collected according to batch order number and total costs are divided by total numbers in a batch to arrive at unit cost of each job. The method is applicable in aircraft, toy making, printing industries, etc.

Operation Costing – Process and Services

Process costing method is applicable where goods or services result from a sequence of continuous or repetitive operations or processes and products are identical and cannot be segregated. Costs are charged to processes and averaged over the units produced during the period.

- Single or output costing is used when the production is uniform and identical and a single article is produced. The total production cost is divided by the number of units produced to get unit or output cost. Examples are mining, breweries, brick making, etc.
- Operation costing refers to the methods where each operation in each stage of production or process is separately costed. Thereafter, the cost of finished unit is determined. This is suitable to industries dealing with mass production of repetitive nature for example, motor cars, cycles, toys, etc.
- Departmental costing refers to the method of ascertaining the cost of operating a department or cost centre. Total cost of each department is ascertained and divided by total units produced in that department to arrive at unit cost. If one product passes through a number of departments for completion, cost of each department will be picked up and the total unit cost will be the aggregate of unit cost of the departments through which the product passes.

Process Costing

Process costing is a form of operations costing which is used where standardized homogeneous goods are produced. This costing method is used in industries like chemicals, textiles, steel, rubber, sugar, shoes, petrol etc. Process costing is also used in the assembly type of industries also. It is assumed in process costing that the average cost presents the cost per unit. Cost of production during a particular period is divided by the number of units produced during that period to arrive at the cost per unit.

MEANING OF PROCESS COSTING

Process costing is a method of costing under which all costs are accumulated for each stage of production or process, and the cost per unit of product is ascertained at each stage of production by dividing the cost of each process by the normal output of that process. Features of Process Costing:

- The production is continuous
- The product is homogeneous
- The process is standardized
- Output of one process become raw material of another process
- The output of the last process is transferred to finished stock
- Costs are collected process-wise
- Both direct and indirect costs are accumulated in each process
- If there is a stock of semi-finished goods, it is expressed in terms of equalent units
- The total cost of each process is divided by the normal output of that process to find out cost per unit of that process.

ADVANTAGES OF PROCESS COSTING

- Costs are be computed periodically at the end of a particular period
- It is simple and involves less clerical work that job costing
- It is easy to allocate the expenses to processes in order to have accurate costs.
- Use of standard costing systems in very effective in process costing situations.
- Process costing helps in preparation of tender, quotations
- Since cost data is available for each process, operation and department, good managerial control is possible.

LIMITATIONS

- Cost obtained at each process is only historical cost and are not very useful for effective control.
- Process costing is based on average cost method, which is not that suitable for performance analysis, evaluation and managerial control.
- Work-in-progress is generally done on estimated basis which leads to inaccuracy in total cost calculations.
- The computation of average cost is more difficult in those cases where more than one type of products is manufactured and a division of the cost element is necessary.
- Where different products arise in the same process and common costs are prorated to various costs units. Such individual products costs may be taken as only approximation and hence not reliable.

10

Cost and Inventory Accounting

THE IMPORTANCE OF INVENTORY CONTROL

Managing inventory is like going to the dentist. It's dreaded, postponed and causes anxiety attacks. But in the end both must be done.

Here are three simple facts about inventory:

- You need it to create sales.
- You need to know what you have so you know what to order.
- You need to maintain it throughout the year because of shrinkage

Here are three simple results if you don't manage your inventory:

- Your employees are less productive because they are asked to count stock to determine ordering or fulfillment needs, constantly being interrupted.
- There is no knowledge of what money is being spent on inventory.
- Your balance sheet is incorrect.

Here are three simple ways to manage inventory:

- Conduct a physical inventory. Either close your business for a day or two or come in over weekend and count everything you have. Involve the staff because you'll need counters and data entry support.
- Do not process an order until the information is entered into the system. Depending on the size of your inventory this could be done in two days. The hours are long and the work is tedious, but it's imperative that it's done and done correctly.
- Maintain the inventory. Have a part that gets counted every week and rotated throughout the warehouse. This allows adjustments to be made more often so your inventory reports are correct.

Unmanaged inventory is like having a tooth that needs a root canal. For a long time you can get by without getting it fixed. But one day you wake up with a pounding tooth ache that needs immediate attention. You put your life on hold, get to the dentist and leave feeling much better. Inventory is no different. You can function without controls in place. However, you realise one day that you have no idea how much money you have sunk into inventory. It's usually a day when cash flow is tight. You decide to get it under control, conduct an inventory count, put processes in place and become more efficient. And you and your company begin feeling much better.

INVENTORY TURNOVER

THE CONCEPT OF INVENTORY TURNOVER

Say you sell $10,000 worth of a product each year. Total revenue received from sales of the product is $12,500. If we bought the entire $10,000 worth of the product on January 1st, at the end of the year we would have made a $2,500 gross profit on an investment of $10,000. But do we have to buy the entire $10,000 worth of the product at one time? What if we bought $5,000 worth of the product on January 1st. Then, just before running out of stock, we bought an additional $5,000 worth of the product with part of the revenues received from selling the first shipment. At the end of the year we've still sold $10,000 worth of the product, still made $2,500 gross profit, but on an investment of about $5,000.

Could we make the same gross profit on an even smaller investment? What if we were to buy $2,500 dollars worth of material. Sell most of it. Buy another $2,500 dollars worth of the product. Sell most of that shipment and then repeat the process two more times before the end of the year.

The annual gross profit of $2,500 is now generated with an investment of about $2,500. Which investment option is better? Selling $10,000 worth of a product with an investment of $10,000, $5,000 or $2,500? The best option is $2,500. Investing $2,500 frees up $7,500 that can be used for other purposes... such as stocking other products that have the potential of generating additional profits. Every time we sell an amount of a product, product line, or other group of items equal to the average amount of money we have invested in those items, we have "turned" our inventory.

THE INVENTORY TURNOVER FORMULA

Inventory turnover is calculated with the following formula: Cost of Goods Sold from Stock Sales during the Past 12 Months Average Inventory Investment during the Past 12 Months. There are several things to keep in mind when calculating turnover rates:

- Only consider cost of goods sold from stock sales which are filled from warehouse inventory. Non-stock items and direct shipments are not included. Sure, these sales are important, but don't involve your warehouse stock.
- The cost of goods sold figure in the formula includes transfers of stocked products to other branches and quantities of these products used for internal purposes such as repairs and assemblies.

- Inventory turnover is based on the cost of items. Inventory turnover depends on the average value of stocked inventory.

To determine your average inventory investment:

- Calculate the total value of every product in inventory every month, on the same day of the month. Be sure to be consistent in using the same cost basis in calculating both the cost of goods sold and average inventory investment.
- If your inventory levels tends to fluctuate throughout the month, calculate your total inventory value on the first and fifteenth of every month.
- Determine the average inventory value by averaging of all of inventory valuations recorded during the past 12 months.

TURNOVER GOALS

As you determine your inventory turnover goals, consider the average gross margin you receive on the sale of products. Most distributors who have 20 per cent - 30 per cent gross margins should strive to achieve an overall turnover rate of five to six turns per year. Distributors with lower margins require higher stock turnover. If your company enjoys high gross margins, you can afford to turn your inventory less often.

A turnover rate of six turns per year doesn't mean that the stock of every item will turn six times. The stock of popular, fast moving items should turn more often. Slow moving items may turn only once, or not at all. Finally, calculate inventory turnover separately for every product line in every warehouse. This will allow you to identify situations in which your inventory is not providing an adequate return on your investment.

To improve inventory turnover, consider reducing the quantity you normally buy from the supplier. Inventory turns improve when you buy less of product, more often. You have limited funds available to invest in inventory. You cannot stock a lifetime supply of every item.

In order to generate the cash necessary to pay your bills and return a profit, you must sell the material you've bought. The inventory turnover rate measures how quickly you are moving inventory through your warehouse. Combined with other measurements such as customer service level and return on investment, inventory turnover can provide an accurate barometer of your success.

BILLS OF EXCHANGE

According to the Negotiable Instruments Act 1881, a bill of exchange is defined as an instrument in writing containing an unconditional order, signed by the maker, directing a certain person to pay a certain sum of money only to, or to the order of a certain person or to the bearer of the instrument. The following features of a bill of exchange emerge out on the basis of this definition.

- A bill of exchange must be in writing and not oral.
- It is an order to make payment.
- The order to make payment is unconditional.
- The maker of the bill of exchange must sign it.
- The payment to be made must be certain.
- The date on which payment is made must also be certain.
- The bill of exchange must be payable to a certain person.
- The amount mentioned in the bill of exchange is payable either on demand or on the expiry of a fixed period of time.
- It must be stamped as per the requirement of law.

According to the Negotiable Instruments Act, a bill of exchange is generally drawn by the creditor on his debtor. It has to be accepted by the debtor or someone else on his behalf. It is called a draft before its acceptance. Therefore, one of the underlying features of a bill of exchange is that it has to be accepted either by the person upon whom it is drawn or by someone else on his/her behalf. For example, Amit sold goods to Rohit on credit for ₹.10,000 for three months. If agreed so, Amit can draw a bill of exchange upon Rohit for ₹ 10,000 payable after three months. Before it is accepted by Rohit it will be called a draft. It will become a bill of exchange only when Rohit writes the word "accepted" on it and puts his signature to communicate the acceptance.

PARTIES

There are three parties to a bill of exchange:

- Drawer is the maker of the bill of exchange. A seller/creditor who is entitled to receive money from the debtor can draw a bill of exchange upon the buyer/ debtor. The drawer after writing the bill of exchange has to sign it as maker of the bill.
- Drawee is the person upon whom the bill of exchange is drawn. Drawee is purchaser of the goods upon whom the bill of exchange is drawn. The dawee has to write the word "accepted" if he accepts to make the payment given in the bill on the due date and has to put his signatures on it. After the drawee of a bill has signed his assent on the face of the bill, he is called the acceptor and this process is called acceptance. A bill of exchange becomes a legal document after acceptance and binds the drawee to honour the bill on the due date. Acceptance however may be general or qualified. The general acceptance requires signatures of the acceptor only without stating any conditions, thereto. However, mention of a bank or a specified place of payment or part payment thereof, makes the acceptance qualified. A qualified acceptance varies the express terms of the bill as originally drawn and thereby the drawer can refuse to consider the bill as accepted. Sometimes the bill of exchange may be accepted

by another person on behalf of the drawee. For example a bill of exchange drawn by Ram upon Shyam may be accepted by Ghanshyam.

- Payee is the person to whom the payment is made. The drawer of the bill himself will be the payee if he keeps the bill with him till the date of its payment. The payee may change in the following situations.
  - In case the drawer has got the bill discounted, the person who has discounted the bill will become the payee;
  - In case the bill is transferred in favour of a creditor of the drawer then the creditor will become the payee.

Normally, the drawer and the payee is the same person. Similarly, the drawee and the acceptor is normally the same person. For example, Mamta sold goods worth ₹.10, 000 to Jyoti and drew a bill of exchange upon her for the same amount payable after three months. Here Mamta is the drawer of the bill and Jyoti is the drawee. If the bill is retained by Mamta for three months and the amount of ₹.10,000 is received by her on the due date than Mamta will be the payee.

If Mamta gives away this bill to her creditor, Ruchi then Ruchi will be the payee.If Mamta gets this bill discounted then the banker will become the payee. In the above mentioned bill of exchange, Mamta is the drawer and the bearer".

However, according to the Reserve Bank of India Act, a promissory note payable to bearer is illegal. Therefore, a promissory note cannot be made Jyoti is the drawee. Since Jyoti has accepted the bill she is the acceptor. Suppose in place of Jyoti the bill is accepted by Ashok then Ashok will become the acceptor.

INVENTORY CONTROL TECHNIQUES

There are several techniques a person can use to increase profitability and streamline workflow via proper inventory control. Through research, competitive analysis and experience, an effective business leader can balance costs versus benefits to storing and ordering the necessary supplies to ensure business vitality.

The supply chain is made of all materials that help you to produce, market and supply your product. Inventory control means that you have identified every facet of your supply chain and its logistics.

FIFO

If you deal in perishable items, FIFO is an important concept to understand and maintain throughout the supply chain. If a grocery store did not rotate their stock, new stock coming in would get taken immediately and older stock would expire, causing great loss. Stock must be arranged by date received.

CUTTING EDGE CONTROL

For a great deal of stock that needs constant management, consider bar codes or RFID where hand-held readers can immediately tell you where valuable merchandise is. Many IT inventory programmes on the market provide a wealth of features including tie-ins to USPS, Fed-Ex and/or UPS to track merchandise and provide real-time logistics.

COSTS VERSUS CONVENIENCE

A business owner must balance space available for extra stock versus speed of product turnover, fees for storage, cost in bulk versus regular ordering, and whether clients/end users would be willing to wait.

STOCK LEVELS

Defining your minimum stock level will allow you to set up regular inspections and re-ordering of supplies. Take into account emergencies and vendors taking longer than average to replenish stock. This will aid you in arriving at JIT ordering, where stock is held for a minimum amount of time before moving on to the next stage in the supply chain.

YOUR SECURITY

Stock security is a necessary cost. Many experts recommend separating staff that is responsible for stock management from staff that has financial responsibility. Many times, shoplifting and thievery is committed by employees rather than a stranger. Security guards, cameras, bar codes and security devices are used by most businesses since the cost of security is minimal compared to the millions of dollars that U.S. businesses lose each year to stolen goods.

Training staff in identifying potential security issues and having a clear method of reporting violations is important in reducing crime. Often, shoplifters and thieves use standard techniques to distract employees and take stock.

STOCK ON HAND

Having a great deal of stock on hand has both positive and negative consequences. Having an immediate supply means that end users get their product that much sooner. Speed and immediate gratification for a client can make the difference not only in a sale, but recommendations, repeat business and client loyalty. In the modern business environment where every business is a global business, an emergency or unforeseen circumstance anywhere in the world can render competition without resources you have on hand. Of course, one must take into account using capital in bulk buys, management and insurance costs as well as goods perishing or becoming obsolete.

ABC ANALYSIS

ABC analysis is a business term used to define an inventory categorization technique often used in materials management. It is also known as Selective Inventory Control. ABC analysis provides a mechanism for identifying items that will have a significant impact on overall inventory cost, while also providing a mechanism for identifying different categories of stock that will require different management and controls. When carrying out an ABC analysis, inventory items are valued with the results then ranked. The results are then grouped typically into three bands. These bands are called ABC codes.

CODES

- "A class" inventory will typically contain items that account for 80 per cent of total value, or 20 per cent of total items.
- "B class" inventory will have around 15 per cent of total value, or 30 per cent of total items.
- "C class" inventory will account for the remaining 5 per cent, or 50 per cent of total items..

ABC Analysis is similar to the Pareto principle in that the "A class" group will typically account for a large proportion of the overall value but a small percentage of the overall volume of inventory.

Another recommended breakdown of ABC classes:

- "A" approximately 10 per cent of items or 66.6 per cent of value
- "B" approximately 20 per cent of items or 23.3 per cent of value
- "C" approximately 70 per cent of items or 10.1 per cent of value

JUST-IN-TIME

Just-in-time is an inventory strategy that strives to improve a business's return on investment by reducing in-process inventory and associated carrying costs. Just In Time production method is also called the Toyota Production System. To meet JIT objectives, the process relies on signals or Kanban between different points in the process, which tell production when to make the next part.

Kanban are usually 'tickets' but can be simple visual signals, such as the presence or absence of a part on a shelf. Implemented correctly, JIT can improve a manufacturing organization's return on investment, quality, and efficiency. Quick notice that stock depletion requires personnel to order new stock is critical to the inventory reduction at the center of JIT.

This saves warehouse space and costs. However, the complete mechanism for making this work is often misunderstood. For instance, its effective application cannot be independent of other key components of a lean manufacturing system or it can "...end up with the opposite of the desired result."

In recent years manufacturers have continued to try to hone forecasting methods such as applying a trailing 13 week average as a better predictor for JIT planning, however some research demonstrates that basing JIT on the presumption of stability is inherently flawed.

- *Demand stability*: Karmarker highlights the importance of relatively stable demand, which helps ensure efficient capital utilization rates. Karmarker argues that without significantly stable demand, JIT becomes untenable in high capital cost production.
- *Price volatility*: JIT implicitly assumes a level of input price stability that obviates the need to buy parts in advance of price rises. Where input prices are expected to rise, storing inventory may be desirable.
- *Quality volatility*: JIT implicitly assumes that input parts quality remains constant over time. If not, firms may hoard high quality inputs. As with price volatility, a solution is to work with selected suppliers to help them improve their processes to reduce variation and costs. Longer term price agreements can then be negotiated and agreed-upon quality standards made the responsibility of the supplier. Fixing up of standards for volatility of quality according to the quality circle
- *Supply Stability*: In the U.S., the 1992 railway strikes caused General Motors to idle a 75,000-worker plant because they had no supply.
- *Transaction cost approach*: JIT reduces inventory in a firm. However, a firm may simply be outsourcing their input inventory to suppliers, even if those suppliers don't use Just in time. Newman investigated this effect and found that suppliers in Japan charged JIT customers, on average, a 5 per cent price premium.

JIT IMPLEMENTATION DESIGN

Based on a diagram modeled after the one used by Hewlett-Packard's Boise plant to accomplish its JIT programme:

- F Design Flow Process:
  - `F Redesign/relayout for flow
  - L Reduce lot sizes
  - O Link operations
  - W Balance workstation capacity
  - M Preventive maintenance
  - S Reduce Setup Times
- Q Total quality control:
  - C worker compliance
  - I Automatic inspection
  - M quality measures
  - M fail-safe methods
  - W Worker participation
- S Stabilize Schedule:
  - S Level Schedule
  - W establish freeze windows
  - UC Underutilize Capacity

- K Kanban Pull System:
  - B Backflush
  - L Reduce lot sizes
- V Work with vendors:
  - L Reduce lead time
  - D Frequent deliveries
  - U Project usage requirements
  - Q Quality Expectations
- I Further reduce inventory in other areas:
  - S Stores
  - T Transit
  - C Implement Carroussel to reduce motion waste
  - C Implement Conveyor belts to reduce motion waste
- P Improve Product Design:
  - P Standard Production Configuration
  - P Standardize and reduce the number of parts
  - P Process design with product design
  - Q Quality Expectations

Effects

A surprising effect was that factory response time fell to about a day. This improved customer satisfaction by providing vehicles within a day or two of the minimum economic shipping delay. Also, the factory began building many vehicles to order, eliminating the risk they would not be sold.

This improved the company's return on equity. Since assemblers no longer had a choice of which part to use, every part had to fit perfectly.

This caused a quality assurance crisis, which led to a dramatic improvement in product quality. Eventually, Toyota redesigned every part of its vehicles to widen tolerances, while simultaneously implementing careful statistical controls for quality control.

Toyota had to test and train parts suppliers to assure quality and delivery. In some cases, the company eliminated multiple suppliers. When a process or parts quality problem surfaced on the production line, the entire production line had to be slowed or even stopped.

No inventory meant a line could not operate from in-process inventory while a production problem was fixed. Many people in Toyota predicted that the initiative would be abandoned for this reason. In the first week, line stops occurred almost hourly.

But by the end of the first month, the rate had fallen to a few line stops per day. After six months, line stops had so little economic effect that Toyota installed an overhead pull-line, similar to a bus bell-pull, that let any worker on the line order a line stop for a process or quality problem. Even with this, line stops fell to a few per week. The result was a factory that has been studied worldwide. It has been widely emulated, but not always with the expected results, as many firms fail to adopt the full system. The just-in-time philosophy was also applied to other segments of the supply chain in several types of industries.

In the commercial sector, it meant eliminating one or all of the warehouses in the link between a factory and a retail establishment. Examples in sales, marketing, and customer service involve applying information systems and mobile hardware to deliver customer information as needed, and reducing waste by video conferencing to cut travel time.

Benefits

- *Reduced setup time*: Cutting setup time allows the company to reduce or eliminate inventory for "changeover" time. The tool used here is SMED.
- The flow of goods from warehouse to shelves improves. Small or individual piece lot sizes reduce lot delay inventories, which simplifies inventory flow and its management.
- Employees with multiple skills are used more efficiently. Having employees trained to work on different parts of the process allows companies to move workers where they are needed.
- Production scheduling and work hour consistency synchronized with demand. If there is no demand for a product at the time, it is not made. This saves the company money, either by not having to pay workers overtime or by having them focus on other work or participate in training.
- Increased emphasis on supplier relationships. A company without inventory does not want a supply system problem that creates a part shortage. This makes supplier relationships extremely important.
- Supplies come in at regular intervals throughout the production day. Supply is synchronized with production demand and the optimal amount of inventory is on hand at any time. When parts move directly from the truck to the point of assembly, the need for storage facilities is reduced.

Problems

Within a JIT System

Just-in-time operation leaves suppliers and downstream consumers open to supply shocks and large supply or demand changes. For internal reasons, Ohno saw this as a feature rather than a bug. He used an analogy of lowering the water level in a river to expose the rocks to explain how removing inventory showed where production flow was interrupted. Once barriers were exposed, they could be removed.

Since one of the main barriers was rework, lowering inventory forced each shop to improve its own quality or cause a holdup downstream. A key tool to manage this weakness is production levelling to remove these variations. Just-in-time is a means to improving performance of the system, not an end. Very low stock levels means shipments of the same part can come in several times per day. This means Toyota is especially susceptible to flow interruption. For that reason, Toyota uses two suppliers for most assemblies.

As noted in Liker, there was an exception to this rule that put the entire company at risk because of the 1997 Aisin fire. However, since Toyota also makes a point of maintaining high quality relations with its entire supplier network, several other suppliers immediately took up production of the Aisin-built parts by using existing capability and documentation. Thus, a strong, long-term relationship with a few suppliers is better than short-term, price-based relationships with many competing suppliers. Toyota uses this long-term relationship to send Toyota staff to help suppliers improve their processes. These interventions have been going on for twenty years and have created a more reliable supply chain, improved margins for Toyota and suppliers, and lowered prices for customers. Toyota encourages their suppliers to use JIT with their own suppliers.

Within a Raw Material Stream

As noted by Liker and Womack and Jones, it ultimately would be desirable to introduce synchronised flow and link JIT through the entire supply stream. However, none followed this in detail all the way back through the processes to the raw materials. With present technology, for example, an ear of corn cannot be grown and delivered to order.

The same is true of most raw materials, which must be discovered and/or grown through natural processes that require time and must account for natural variability in weather and discovery. The part of this currently viewed as impossible is the synchronised part of flow and the linked part of JIT.

It is for the reasons stated raw materials companies decouple their supply chain from their clients' demand by carrying large 'finished goods' stocks. Both flow and JIT can be implemented in isolated process islands within the raw materials stream. The challenge becomes to achieve that isolation by some means other than carrying huge stocks, as most do today.

Because of this, almost all value chains are split into a part made-to-forecast and a part that could, by using JIT, become make-to-order. Historically, the make-to-order part has often been within the retailer portion of the value chain. Toyota took Piggly Wiggly's supermarket replenishment system and drove it at least half way through their automobile factories.

Their challenge today is to drive it all the way back to their goods-inwards dock. Of course, the mining of iron and making of steel is still not connected to an order for a particular car. Recognising JIT could be driven back up the supply chain has reaped Toyota huge benefits and a dominant position in the auto industry.

Oil

It has been frequently charged that the oil industry has been influenced by JIT.

The argument is presented as follows:

- The number of refineries in the United States has fallen from 279 in 1975 to 205 in 1990 and further to 149 in 2004. As a result, the industry is susceptible to supply shocks, which cause spikes in prices and subsequently reduction in domestic manufacturing output. The effects of hurricanes Katrina and Rita are given as an example: in 2005, Katrina caused the shutdown of 9 refineries in Louisiana and 6 more in Mississippi, and a large number of oil production and transfer facilities, resulting in the loss of 20 per cent of the US domestic refinery output. Rita subsequently shut down refineries in Texas, further reducing output. The GDP figures for the third and fourth quarters showed a slowdown from 3.5 per cent to 1.2 per cent growth. Similar arguments were made in earlier crises.

Beside the obvious point that prices went up because of the reduction in supply and not for anything to do with the practice of JIT, JIT students and even oil and gas industry analysts question whether JIT as it has been developed by Ohno, Goldratt, and others is used by the petroleum industry. Companies routinely shut down facilities for reasons other than the application of JIT.

One of those reasons may be economic rationalization: when the benefits of operating no longer outweigh the costs, including opportunity costs, the plant may be economically inefficient. JIT has never subscribed to such considerations directly; following Waddel and Bodek, this ROI-based thinking conforms more to Brown-style accounting and Sloan management.

Further, and more significantly, JIT calls for a reduction in inventory capacity, not production capacity. From 1975 to 1990 to 2005, the annual average stocks of gasoline have fallen by only 8.5 per cent from 228,331 to 222,903 bbls to 208,986. Stocks fluctuate seasonally by as much as 20,000 bbls. During the 2005 hurricane season, stocks never fell below 194,000 thousand bbls, while the low for the period 1990 to 2006 was 187,017 thousand bbls in 1997.

This shows that while industry storage capacity has decreased in the last 30 years, it hasn't been drastically reduced as JIT practitioners would prefer. Finally, as shown in a pair of articles in the Oil and Gas Journal, JIT does not seem to have been a goal of the industry. In Waguespack and Cantor, the authors point out that JIT would require a significant change in the supplier/refiner relationship, but the changes in inventories in the oil industry exhibit none of those tendencies. Specifically, the relationships remain cost-driven among many competing suppliers rather than quality-based among a select few long-term relationships. They find that a large part of the shift came about because of the availability of short-haul crudes from Latin America. In the follow-up editorial, the Oil and Gas Journal claimed that "casually adopting popular business terminology that doesn't apply" had provided a "rhetorical bogey" to industry critics.

Confessing that they had been as guilty as other media sources, they confirmed that "It also happens not to be accurate."

BUSINESS MODELS FOLLOWING SIMILAR APPROACH

Vendor–Managed Inventory

Vendor-managed inventory employs the same principles as those of JIT inventory, however, the responsibilities of managing inventory is placed with the vendor in a vendor/customer relationship. Whether it's a manufacturer managing inventory for a distributor, or a distributor managing inventory for their customers, the management role goes to the vendor.

An advantage of this business model is that the vendor may have industry experience and expertise that lets them better anticipate demand and inventory needs. The inventory planning and controlling is facilitated by applications that allow vendors access to their customer's inventory data. Another advantage to the customer is that inventory cost usually remains on the vendor's books until used by the customer, even if parts or materials are on the customer's site.

Customer–Managed Inventory

With customer-managed inventory, the customer, as opposed to the vendor in a VMI model, has responsibility for all inventory decisions. This is similar to JIT inventory concepts. With a clear picture of their inventory and that of their supplier's, the customer can anticipate fluctuations in demand and make inventory replenishment decisions accordingly.

INVENTORY COST FLOW ASSUMPTIONS

Consider the following transactions for the Ramona Rice Company for the year 2012:

- Mar. 23—Purchased 10 kilos of rice, \$4 per kilo.
- Nov. 17—Purchased 10 kilos of rice, \$9 per kilo.
- Dec. 31—Sold 10 kilos of rice, \$10 per kilo.

The surprisingly difficult question to answer with this simple example is "How much income did Ramona make in 2012?" As you can see, it depends on which rice was sold on December 31. There are three possibilities.

	Case #1 Sold Old Rice	Case #2 Sold New Rice	Case #3 Sold Mixed Rice
Sales ($10 × 10 kilos)	$100	$100	$100
Cost of goods sold (10 kilos)	65	40	90
Gross margin	$60	$10	$35

In Case #1, it is assumed that the 10 kilos of rice sold on December 31 were the old ones, purchased on March 23 for $4 per kilo. Accountants call this a FIFO (first in, first out) assumption. In Case #2, it is assumed that the company sold the new rice, purchased on November 17 for $9 per kilo. Accountants call this a LIFO (last in, first out) assumption. In Case #3, it is assumed that all the rice is mixed together, so the cost per kilo is the average cost of all the rice available for sale, or $6.50 per kilo [($40 + $90) ÷ 20 kilos]. Accountants call this an average cost assumption. In most cases, as with Ramona, there is no feasible way to track exactly which units were sold. Accordingly, in order to compute cost of goods sold, the accountant must make an assumption. This is not a case of tricky accountants trying to manipulate the reported numbers; instead, this is a case in which income simply cannot be computed unless the accountant uses his or her judgement and makes an assumption. As suggested, examine in more detail the different cost flow assumptions used by companies to determine inventories and cost of goods sold.

SPECIFIC IDENTIFICATION INVENTORY COST FLOW

An alternative to the assumptions just described is to specifically identify the cost of each particular unit that is sold. This approach, called specific identification, is often used by automobile dealers and other businesses that sell a limited number of units at a high price. To illustrate the specific identification inventory costing method, consider the September 2012 records of Nephi Company, which sells one type of bicycle.

Sept. 1	Beginning inventory consisted of 10 bicycles costing $200 each.
3	Purchased 8 bicycles costing $250 each.
18	Purchased 16 bicycles costing $300 each.
20	Purchased 10 bicycles costing $320 each.
25	Sold 28 bicycles, $400 each.

These inventory records show that during September, Nephi had 44 bicycles (10 from beginning inventory and 34 that were purchased during the month) that it could have sold. However, only 28 bicycles were sold, leaving 16 on hand at the end of September.

Using the specific identification method of inventory costing requires that the individual costs of the actual units sold be charged against revenue as cost of goods sold. To compute cost of goods sold and ending inventory amounts with this alternative, a company must know which units were actually sold and what the unit cost of each was. Suppose that of the 28 bicycles sold by Nephi on September 25, 8 came from the beginning inventory, 4 came from the September 3 purchase, and 16 came from the September 18 purchase. With this information, cost of goods sold and ending inventory are computed as follows:

	Bicycles	Costs
Beginning inventory	10	$ 2,000
Net purchases	34	10,000
Goods available for sale	44	$12,000
Ending inventory	16	4,600
Cost of goods sold	28	$ 7,400

The cost of ending inventory is the total of the individual costs of the bicycles still on hand at the end of the month, or:

2 bicycles from beginning inventory, $200 each	$ 400
4 bicycles purchased on September 3, $250 each	1,000
0 bicycles purchased on September 18, $300 each	0
10 bicycles purchased on September 20, $320 each	3,200
Total ending inventory (16 units)	**$4,600**

Similarly, the cost of goods sold is the total of the costs of the specific bicycles sold, or:

8 bicycles from beginning inventory, $200 each	$1,600
4 bicycles purchased on September 3, $250 each	1,000
16 bicycles purchased on September 18, $300 each	4,800
0 bicycles purchased on September 20, $320 each	0
Total cost of goods sold (28 units)	**$7,400**

For many companies, it is impractical, if not impossible, to keep track of specific units. In that case, an assumption must be made as to which units were sold during the period and which are still in inventory.

It is very important to remember that the accounting rules do not require that the assumed flow of goods for costing purposes match the actual physical movement of goods purchased and sold—though in some cases, the assumed cost flow may be similar to the physical flow. A grocery store, for example, usually tries to sell the oldest units first to minimize spoilage.

Thus, the physical flow of goods would reflect a FIFO pattern, but the grocery store could use a FIFO, LIFO, or average cost assumption in determining the ending inventory and cost of goods sold numbers to be reported in the financial statements. On the other hand, a company that stockpiles coal must first sell the coal purchased last since it is on top of the pile. That company might use the LIFO cost assumption, which reflects physical flow, or it might use one of the other alternatives.

FIFO Cost Flow Assumption

With FIFO, it is assumed that the oldest units are sold and the newest units remain in inventory. Using the FIFO inventory cost flow assumption, the ending inventory and cost of goods sold for Nephi are:

	Bicycles	Costs
Beginning inventory	10	$ 2,000
Net purchases	34	10,000
Goods available for sale	44	$12,000
Ending inventory	16	5,000
Cost of goods sold	28	$ 7,000

The $7,000 cost of goods sold and $5,000 cost of ending inventory are determined as follows:

FIFO cost of goods sold (oldest 28 units):	
10 bicycles from beginning inventory, $200 each	$2,000
8 bicycles purchased on September 3, $250 each	2,000
10 bicycles purchased on September 18, $300 each	3,000
Total FIFO cost of goods sold	$7,000
FIFO ending inventory (newest 16 units):	
6 bicycles purchased on September 18, $300 each	$1,800
10 bicycles purchased on September 20, $320 each	3,200
Total FIFO ending inventory	$5,000

LIFO Cost Flow Assumption

LIFO is the opposite of FIFO. With LIFO, the cost of the most recent units purchased is transferred to cost of goods sold. When prices are rising, as they are for Nephi, LIFO provides higher cost of goods sold, and hence lower net income, than FIFO. This is because the newest (highpriced) goods are assumed to have been sold. Using the LIFO inventory cost flow assumption, the ending inventory and cost of goods sold for Nephi are:

	Bicycles	Costs
Beginning inventory	10	$ 2,000
Net purchases	34	10,000
Goods available for sale	44	$12,000
Ending inventory	16	3,500
Cost of goods sold	28	$ 8,500

The $8,500 cost of goods sold and $3,500 cost of ending inventory are determined as follows:

LIFO cost of goods sold (newest 28 units):	
10 bicycles purchased on September 20, $320 each	$3,200
16 bicycles purchased on September 18, $300 each	4,800
2 bicycles purchased on September 3, $250 each	500
Total LIFO cost of goods sold.	$8,500
LIFO ending inventory (oldest 16 units)	
10 bicycles from beginning inventory, $200 each	$2,000
6 bicycles purchased on September 3, $250 each	1,500
Total LIFO ending inventory	**$3,500**

Average Cost Flow Assumption

With average costing, an average cost must be computed for all the inventory available for sale during the period. The average unit cost for Nephi during September is computed as follows:

	Bicycles	**Costs**
Beginning inventory	10	$ 2,000
Net purchases	34	10,000
Goods available for sale	44	$12,000
$12,000 ÷ 44 units = $272.73 per unit		

With the average cost assumption, cost of goods sold is computed by multiplying the number of units sold by the average cost per unit. Similarly, the cost of ending inventory is computed by multiplying the number of units in ending inventory by the average cost per unit. These calculations are as follows:

Average Cost of Goods Sold: 28 units × $272.73 per unit = $7,636 (rounded)

Average Ending Inventory: 16 units × $272.73 per unit = $4,364 (rounded)

This information can be shown as follows:

	Bicycles	**Costs**
Beginning inventory	10	$ 2,000
Net purchases	34	10,000
Goods available for sale	44	$12,000
Ending inventory	16	4,364
Cost of goods sold	28	$ 7,636

A Comparison of All Inventory Costing Methods

The cost of goods sold and ending inventory amounts we have calculated using the three cost flow assumptions are summarized along with the resultant gross margins as follows. Note that the net result of each of the inventory cost flow assumptions is to allocate the total cost of goods available for sale of $12,000 between cost of goods sold and ending inventory.

	FIFO	LIFO	Average
Sales revenue (28 × $400)	$11,200	$11,200	$11,200
Cost of goods sold	7,000	8,500	7,636
Gross margin	$ 4,200	$ 2,700	$ 3,564
Ending inventory	$ 5,000	$ 3,500	$ 4,364

Conceptual Comparison

From a conceptual standpoint, LIFO gives a better reflection of cost of goods sold in the income statement than does FIFO because the most recent goods ("last in"), with the most recent costs, are assumed to have been sold. Thus, LIFO cost of goods sold matches current revenues with current costs. Average cost is somewhere between LIFO and FIFO.

On the balance sheet, however, FIFO gives a better measure of inventory value because, with the FIFO assumption, the "first in" units are sold and the remaining units are the newest ones with the most recent costs. In summary, LIFO gives a conceptually better measure of income, but FIFO gives a conceptually better measure of inventory value on the balance sheet.

Financial Statement Impact Comparison

As with Nephi, in times of rising inventory prices (the most common situation in the majority of industries today), cost of goods sold is highest with LIFO and lowest with FIFO. As a result, gross margin, net income, and ending inventory are lowest with LIFO and highest with FIFO.

With the impact on the reported financial statement numbers being so uniformly bad, you may be wondering why any company would ever voluntarily choose to use LIFO (during times of inflation). Yet over half of the large companies in the United States currently use LIFO in accounting for at least some of their inventories.

The attractiveness of LIFO can be explained with one word—TAXES. If a company uses LIFO in a time of rising prices, reported cost of goods sold is higher, reported taxable income is lower, and cash paid for income taxes is lower. In fact, LIFO was invented in the 1930s in the United States for the sole purpose of allowing companies to lower their income tax payments.

In most instances where accounting alternatives exist, firms are allowed to use one accounting method for tax purposes and another for financial reporting.

In 1939, however, when the Internal Revenue Service (1RS) approved the use of LIFO, it ruled that firms may use LIFO for tax purposes only if they also use LIFO for financial reporting purposes. Therefore, companies must choose between reporting higher profits and paying higher taxes with FIFO or reporting lower profits and paying lower taxes with LIFO.

INVENTORY SYSTEM

Inventory is basically the total amount of goods and materials held in stock by a factory, store and other business. This can be the food held in stock by a restaurant or the produce held for sale by a store. For a business to be run efficiently it is important that they keep a record of their inventory as this keeps them informed of when they are running short of something and need to restock to ensure they can serve their customers. An inventory system is used for this purpose.

An inventory system is basically a process whereby a business keeps track of the goods and material it has available. In its simplest sense it can be done manually by a count at the end of each day. In this way it is possible to keep a record of the goods coming in to the business and goods being sold. However this is only really appropriate for small businesses that do not have a lot of stock. For larger business it is more likely that a computerized system will be required.

There are many types of business that can benefit from using an inventory system. Retail outlets which stock and sell goods, warehouses that have goods and materials passing in and out on a daily basis and manufacturers that produce and sell products are just a few of this. It can be essential for companies that have a high turnover of stock and need a simple way of keeping track of this to ensure their business runs smoothly and efficiently.

These days a computerized inventory system is the most likely to be used by medium and large businesses although some small businesses may also use this. These typically use barcodes or radio frequency identification tags to keep a record of inventory objects. This can be used to keep a track of customer orders, monitor the stock a business has available for fulfilling orders and also provide details of when inventory needs to be restocked.

Buying inventory costs money. Therefore more efficient control of the amount of inventory required to be held in stock to fulfill orders can be better for a company in terms of its cash flow. Having a more efficient system in place to control inventory can also help to make a company more productive and this is also cost effective.

There are a number of companies that produce inventory computer software and systems for use by a business. Some of these include Computerized Inventory Systems Specialists (CISS), Skuflow and Executivpro. These companies produce inventory system software for a range of different businesses including warehouses, retailers, stores and restaurants. In many cases the companies allow free downloading of evaluation software that you can try out to find a system that is appropriate for your business. Most of the companies providing the systems can be contacted for a quote for a system.

Having an inventory system in place for your business can be a common sense idea. The initial cost outlay should be recouped by having a more efficient and productive working environment and this should help to ensure that the business is successful.

INVENTORY CONTROL

Inventory control means keeping the overall costs associated with having inventory as low as possible without creating problems. This is also sometimes called stock control. It is an important part of any business that must have a stock of products or items on hand. Correctly managing inventory control is a delicate balance at all times between having too much and too little in order to maximize profits. The costs associated with holding stock, running out of stock, and placing orders must all be looked at and compared in order to find the right formula for a particular business.

It is impossible to have an unlimited supply on hand, for a number of different reasons. Many businesses simply don't have enough money to keep excessively large inventories. There are costs associated with purchasing the items as well as storing them, and having too many products leads to further losses when they don't move off of the shelves.

At the same time, there are issues with inventory control when there isn't enough stock on hand. One common problem is running out of inventory, which is caused by trying to reduce inventory costs too much. This is something that no business wants to have happen, but it happens to virtually all of them at some point. Even the largest stores run out of certain products from time to time when they sell or use more than they expected. This can cause financial losses when inventory is not available for customers to purchase. Part of inventory control is trying to minimize shortages so these are rare occurrences. Most businesses expect they will have shortages on occasion and they have calculated that the small loss is worth the money saved by not having an overstock.

Another important element of inventory control is called reorder point. Businesses need to think ahead and calculate the best time for reordering products. Doing so too soon may cause financial difficulties or running out of space. On the other hand, waiting to long to reorder will result in a shortage and running out of inventory before the next shipment arrives. When figuring out a reorder point, it's necessary to calculate how long it will take the shipment to arrive and the amount of demand for a particular item. The overhead costs, fees, and shipping expenses of ordering large versus small quantities should also be looked at.

Inventory control is an ongoing process that is rarely, if ever, executed perfectly. Experience, expertise, and practice help people to make the best decisions regarding stock, but there are always unknown circumstances and variables. Stores can make good estimates about how many of a specific product they will sell, but they get things wrong from time to time. This is unavoidable.

Inventory control can break a business if it is executed poorly, because either expenses will be too high or customers will get tired of dealing with shortages and find another place to spend their money.

NATURE OF INVENTORY

Inventory means goods and materials, or those goods and materials themselves, held available in stock by a business. This word is also used for a list of the contents of a household and for a list for testamentary purposes of the possessions of someone who has died. In accounting, inventory is considered an asset.

In business management, inventory consists of a list of goods and materials held available in stock.

Labels: Inventory Management, Procurement, Supply Chain, Supply Chain Management.

INVENTORY MANAGEMENT

Inventory refers to the stock of resources, that possess economic value, held by an organization at any point of time. These resource stocks can be manpower, machines, capital goods or materials at various stages.

Inventory management is primarily about specifying the size and placement of stocked goods. Inventory management is required at different locations within a facility or within multiple locations of a supply network to protect the regular and planned course of production against the random disturbance of running out of materials or goods. The scope of inventory management also concerns the fine lines between replenishment lead time, carrying costs of inventory, asset management, inventory forecasting, inventory valuation, inventory visibility, future inventory price forecasting, physical inventory, available physical space for inventory, quality management, replenishment, returns and defective goods and demand forecasting. Balancing these competing requirements leads to optimal inventory levels, which is an on-going process as the business needs shift and react to the wider environment.

Inventory management involves a retailer seeking to acquire and maintain a proper merchandise assortment while ordering, shipping, handling, and related costs are kept in check.

Systems and processes that identify inventory requirements, set targets, provide replenishment techniques and report actual and projected inventory status.

Handles all functions related to the tracking and management of material. This would include the monitoring of material moved into and out of stockroom locations and the reconciling of the inventory balances. Also may include ABC analysis, lot tracking, cycle counting support etc. 7Management of the inventories, with the primary objective of determining/controlling stock levels within the physical distribution function to balance the need for product availability against the need for minimizing stock holding and handling costs.

BUSINESS INVENTORY

The Reasons for Keeping Stock

There are three basic reasons for keeping an inventory:

1. Time - The time lags present in the supply chain, from supplier to user at every stage, requires that you maintain certain amounts of inventory to use in this "lead time."
2. Uncertainty - Inventories are maintained as buffers to meet uncertainties in demand, supply and movements of goods.
3. Economies of scale - Ideal condition of "one unit at a time at a place where a user needs it, when he needs it" principle tends to incur lots of costs in terms of logistics. So bulk buying, movement and storing brings in economies of scale, thus inventory.

All these stock reasons can apply to any owner or product stage:

- Buffer stock is held in individual workstations against the possibility that the upstream workstation may be a little delayed in long setup or change over time. This stock is then used while that changeover is happening. This stock can be eliminated by tools like SMED.

These classifications apply along the whole Supply chain, not just within a facility or plant.

Where these stocks contain the same or similar items, it is often the work practice to hold all these stocks mixed together before or after the sub-process to which they relate. This 'reduces' costs. Because they are mixed up together there is no visual reminder to operators of the adjacent sub-processes or line management of the stock, which is due to a particular cause and should be a particular individual's responsibility with inevitable consequences. Some plants have centralized stock holding across sub-processes, which makes the situation even more acute.

Special Terms Used in Dealing with Inventory

- Stock Keeping Unit (SKU) is a unique combination of all the components that are assembled into the purchasable item. Therefore, any change in the packaging or product is a new SKU. This level of detailed specification assists in managing inventory.
- Stockout means running out of the inventory of an SKU.
- "New old stock" (sometimes abbreviated NOS) is a term used in business to refer to merchandise being offered for sale that was manufactured long ago but that has never been used. Such merchandise may not be produced anymore, and the new old stock

may represent the only market source of a particular item at the present time.

Typology

- Buffer/safety stock
- Cycle stock (Used in batch processes, it is the available inventory, excluding buffer stock)
- De-coupling (Buffer stock that is held by both the supplier and the user)
- Anticipation stock (Building up extra stock for periods of increased demand - *e.g.* ice cream for summer)
- Pipeline stock (Goods still in transit or in the process of distribution - have left the factory but not arrived at the customer yet)

Inventory Examples

While accountants often discuss inventory in terms of goods for sale, organizations - manufacturers, service-providers and not-for-profits - also have inventories (fixtures, furniture, supplies...) that they do not intend to sell. Manufacturers', distributors', and wholesalers' inventory tends to cluster in warehouses.

Retailers' inventory may exist in a warehouse or in a shop or store accessible to customers. Inventories not intended for sale to customers or to clients may be held in any premises an organization uses. Stock ties up cash and, if uncontrolled, it will be impossible to know the actual level of stocks and therefore impossible to control them.

While the reasons for holding stock were covered earlier, most manufacturing organizations usually divide their "goods for sale" inventory into:

- *Raw materials*: Materials and components scheduled for use in making a product.
- *Work in process, WIP*: Materials and components that have begun their transformation to finished goods.
- *Finished goods*: Goods ready for sale to customers.
- *Goods for resale*: Returned goods that are salable.

Manufacturing

A canned food manufacturer's materials inventory includes the ingredients to form the foods to be canned, empty cans and their lids (or coils of steel or aluminum for constructing those components), labels, and anything else (solder, glue...) that will form part of a finished can. The firm's work in process includes those materials from the time of release to the work floor until they become complete and ready for sale to wholesale or retail customers. This may be vats of prepared food, filled cans not yet labeled or sub-assemblies of food components. It may also include finished cans that are not yet packaged into cartons or pallets. Its finished good inventory consists of all the filled and labeled cans of food in its warehouse that it has manufactured and wishes to sell to food distributors (wholesalers), to grocery stores (retailers), and even perhaps to consumers through arrangements like factory stores and outlet centres.

Examples of case studies are very revealing, and consistently show that the improvement of inventory management has two parts: the capability of the organisation to manage inventory, and the way in which it chooses to do so. For example, a company may wish to install a complex inventory system, but unless there is a good understanding of the role of inventory and its perametres, and an effective business process to support that, the system cannot bring the necessary benefits to the organisation in isolation.

Typical Inventory Management techniques include Pareto Curve ABC Classification and Economic Order Quantity Management. A more sophisticated method takes these two techniques further, combining certain aspects of each to create The K Curve Methodology. A case study of k-curve benefits to one company shows a successful implementation.

Unnecessary inventory adds enormously to the working capital tied up in the business, as well as the complexity of the supply chain. Reduction and elimination of these inventory 'wait' states is a key concept in Lean. Too big an inventory reduction too quickly can cause a business to be anorexic. There are well-proven processes and techniques to assist in inventory planning and strategy, both at the business overview and part number level. Many of the big MRP/and ERP systems do not offer the necessary inventory planning tools within their integrated planning applications.

PRINCIPLE OF INVENTORY PROPORTIONALITY

Purpose

Inventory proportionality is the goal of demand-driven inventory management. The primary optimal outcome is to have the same number of days' (or hours', etc.) worth of inventory on hand across all products so that the time of runout of all products would be simultaneous. In such a case, there is no "excess inventory," that is, inventory that would be left over of another product when the first product runs out. Excess inventory is sub-optimal because the money spent to obtain it could have been utilized better elsewhere, *i.e.* to the product that just ran out.

The secondary goal of inventory proportionality is inventory minimization. By integrating accurate demand forecasting with inventory management, replenishment inventories can be scheduled to arrive just in time to replenish the product destined to run out first, while at the same time balancing out the inventory supply of all products to make their inventories more proportional, and thereby closer to achieving the primary goal.

Accurate demand forecasting also allows the desired inventory proportions to be dynamic by determining expected sales out into the future; this allows for inventory to be in proportion to expected short-term sales or consumption rather than to past averages, a much more accurate and optimal outcome.

Integrating demand forecasting into inventory management in this way also allows for the prediction of the "can fit" point when inventory storage is limited on a per-product basis.

Applications

The technique of inventory proportionality is most appropriate for inventories that remain unseen by the consumer. As opposed to "keep full" systems where a retail consumer would like to see full shelves of the product they are buying so as not to think they are buying something old, unwanted or stale; and differentiated from the "trigger point" systems where product is reordered when it hits a certain level; inventory proportionality is used effectively by just-in-time manufacturing processes and retail applications where the product is hidden from view.

One early example of inventory proportionality used in a retail application in the United States is for motor fuel. Motor fuel (*e.g.* gasoline) is generally stored in underground storage tanks. The motorists do not know whether they are buying gasoline off the top or bottom of the tank, nor need they care. Additionally, these storage tanks have a maximum capacity and cannot be overfilled. Finally, the product is expensive. Inventory proportionality is used to balance the inventories of the different grades of motor fuel, each stored in dedicated tanks, in proportion to the sales of each grade. Excess inventory is not seen or valued by the consumer, so it is simply cash sunk (literally) into the ground. Inventory proportionality minimizes the amount of excess inventory carried in underground storage tanks. This application for motor fuel was first developed and implemented by Petrolsoft Corporation in 1990 for Chevron Products Company. Most major oil companies use such systems today.

Roots

The use of inventory proportionality in the United States is thought to have been inspired by Japanese just-in-time (business) parts inventory management made famous by Toyota Motors in the 1980s.

HIGH-LEVEL INVENTORY MANAGEMENT

It seems that around 1880 there was a change in manufacturing practice from companies with relatively homogeneous lines of products to vertically integrated companies with unprecedented diversity in processes and products. Those companies (especially in metalworking) attempted to achieve success through economies of scope - the gains of jointly producing two or more products in one facility. The managers now needed information on the effect of product-mix decisions on overall profits and therefore needed accurate product-cost information. A variety of attempts to achieve this were unsuccessful due to the huge overhead of the information processing of the time. However, the burgeoning need for financial reporting after 1900 created unavoidable pressure for financial accounting of stock and the management need to cost manage products became overshadowed. In particular, it was the need for audited accounts that sealed the fate of managerial cost accounting. The dominance of financial reporting accounting over management accounting remains to this day with few exceptions, and the financial reporting definitions of 'cost' have distorted effective management 'cost' accounting since that time. This is particularly true of inventory.

Hence, high-level financial inventory has these two basic formulas, which relate to the accounting period:

- Cost of Beginning Inventory at the start of the period + inventory purchases within the period + cost of production within the period = cost of goods available
- Cost of goods available " cost of ending inventory at the end of the period = cost of goods sold

The benefit of these formulae is that the first absorbs all overheads of production and raw material costs into a value of inventory for reporting. The second formula then creates the new start point for the next period and gives a figure to be subtracted from the sales price to determine some form of sales-margin figure.

Manufacturing management is more interested in inventory turnover ratio or average days to sell inventory since it tells them something about relative inventory levels.

- Inventory turnover ratio (also known as inventory turns) = cost of goods sold/Average Inventory = Cost of Goods Sold/((Beginning Inventory + Ending Inventory)/2) and its inverse
- Average Days to Sell Inventory = Number of Days a Year/Inventory Turnover Ratio = 365 days a year/Inventory Turnover Ratio

This ratio estimates how many times the inventory turns over a year. This number tells how much cash/goods are tied up waiting for the process and is a critical measure of process reliability and effectiveness. So a factory with two inventory turns has six months stock on hand, which is generally not a good figure (depending upon the industry), whereas a factory that moves from six turns to twelve turns has probably improved effectiveness by 100 per cent. This improvement will have some negative results in the financial reporting, since the 'value' now stored in the factory as inventory is reduced.

Whilst these accounting measures of inventory are very useful because of their simplicity, they are also fraught with the danger of their own assumptions.

There are, in fact, so many things that can vary hidden under this appearance of simplicity that a variety of 'adjusting' assumptions may be used.

These include:

- Specific Identification
- Weighted Average Cost
- Moving-Average Cost
- FIFO and LIFO.

Inventory Turn is a financial accounting tool for evaluating inventory and it is not necessarily a management tool. Inventory management should be forward looking. The methodology applied is based on historical cost of goods sold. The ratio may not be able to reflect the usability of future production demand, as well as customer demand.

Business models, including Just in Time (JIT) Inventory, Vendor Managed Inventory (VMI) and Customer Managed Inventory (CMI), attempt to minimize on-hand inventory and increase inventory turns. VMI and CMI have gained considerable attention due to the success of third-party vendors who offer added expertise and knowledge that organizations may not possess.

ACCOUNTING FOR INVENTORY

Each country has its own rules about accounting for inventory that fit with their financial-reporting rules.

For example, organizations in the U.S. define inventory to suit their needs within US Generally Accepted Accounting Practices (GAAP), the rules defined by the Financial Accounting Standards Board (FASB) (and others) and enforced by the U.S. Securities and Exchange Commission (SEC) and other federal and state agencies. Other countries often have similar arrangements but with their own GAAP and national agencies instead.

It is intentional that financial accounting uses standards that allow the public to compare firms' performance, cost accounting functions internally to an organization and potentially with much greater flexibility. A discussion of inventory from standard and Theory of Constraints-based (throughput) cost accounting perspective follows some examples and a discussion of inventory from a financial accounting perspective.

The internal costing/valuation of inventory can be complex. Whereas in the past most enterprises ran simple, one-process factories, such enterprises are quite probably in the minority in the 21st century. Where 'one process' factories exist, there is a market for the goods created, which establishes an independent market value for the good. Today, with multistage-process companies, there is much inventory that would once have been finished goods which is now held as 'work in process' (WIP).

This needs to be valued in the accounts, but the valuation is a management decision since there is no market for the partially finished product. This somewhat arbitrary 'valuation' of WIP combined with the allocation of overheads to it has led to some unintended and undesirable results.

Financial Accounting

An organization's inventory can appear a mixed blessing, since it counts as an asset on the balance sheet, but it also ties up money that could serve for other purposes and requires additional expense for its protection. Inventory may also cause significant tax expenses, depending on particular countries' laws regarding depreciation of inventory, as in Thor Power Tool Company v. Commissioner.

Inventory appears as a current asset on an organization's balance sheet because the organization can, in principle, turn it into cash by selling it. Some organizations hold larger inventories than their operations require in order to inflate their apparent asset value and their perceived profitability.

In addition to the money tied up by acquiring inventory, inventory also brings associated costs for warehouse space, for utilities, and for insurance to cover staff to handle and protect it from fire and other disasters, obsolescence, shrinkage (theft and errors), and others. Such holding costs can mount up: between a third and a half of its acquisition value per year.

Businesses that stock too little inventory cannot take advantage of large orders from customers if they cannot deliver. The conflicting objectives of cost control and customer service often pit an organization's financial and operating managers against its sales and marketing departments. Salespeople, in particular, often receive sales-commission payments, so unavailable goods may reduce their potential personal income. This conflict can be minimised by reducing production time to being near or less than customers' expected delivery time. This effort, known as "Lean production" will significantly reduce working capital tied up in inventory and reduce manufacturing costs.

Role of Inventory Accounting

By helping the organization to make better decisions, the accountants can help the public sector to change in a very positive way that delivers increased value for the taxpayer's investment. It can also help to incentivise progress and to ensure that reforms are sustainable and effective in the long term, by ensuring that success is appropriately recognized in both the formal and informal reward systems of the organization.

To say that they have a key role to play is an understatement. Finance is connected to most, if not all, of the key business processes within the organization. It should be steering the stewardship and accountability systems that ensure that the organization is conducting its business in an appropriate, ethical manner. It is critical that these foundations are firmly laid. So often they are the litmus test by which public confidence in the institution is either won or lost. Finance should also be providing the information, analysis and advice to enable the organizations' service managers to operate effectively. This goes beyond the traditional preoccupation with budgets – how much have we spent so far, how much do we have left to spend? It is about helping the organization to better understand its own performance. That means making the connections and understanding the relationships between given inputs – the resources brought to bear – and the outputs and outcomes that they achieve. It is also about understanding and actively managing risks within the organization and its activities.

FIFO vs. LIFO Accounting

When a merchant buys goods from inventory, the value of the inventory account is reduced by the cost of goods sold (COGS). This is simple where the CoG has not varied across those held in stock; but where it has, then an agreed method must be derived to evaluate it. For commodity items that one cannot track individually, accountants must choose a method that fits the nature of the sale. Two popular methods that normally exist are: FIFO and LIFO accounting (first in - first out, last in - first out). FIFO regards the first unit that arrived in inventory as the first one sold. LIFO considers the last unit arriving in inventory as the first one sold. Which method an accountant selects can have a significant effect on net income and book value and, in turn, on taxation. Using LIFO accounting for inventory, a company generally reports lower net income and lower book value, due to the effects of inflation. This generally results in lower taxation. Due to LIFO's potential to skew inventory value, UK GAAP and IAS have effectively banned LIFO inventory accounting.

Standard Cost Accounting

Standard cost accounting uses ratios called efficiencies that compare the labour and materials actually used to produce a good with those that the same goods would have required under "standard" conditions. As long as similar actual and standard conditions obtain, few problems arise. Unfortunately, standard cost accounting methods developed about 100 years ago, when labour comprised the most important cost in manufactured goods. Standard methods continue to emphasize labour efficiency even though that resource now constitutes a (very) small part of cost in most cases.

Standard cost accounting can hurt managers, workers, and firms in several ways. For example, a policy decision to increase inventory can harm a manufacturing manager's performance evaluation. Increasing inventory requires increased production, which means that processes must operate at higher rates. When (not if) something goes wrong, the process takes longer and uses more than the standard labour time. The manager appears responsible for the excess, even though s/he has no control over the production requirement or the problem. In adverse economic times, firms use the same efficiencies to downsize, rightsize, or otherwise reduce their labour force. Workers laid off under those circumstances have even less control over excess inventory and cost efficiencies than their managers.

Many financial and cost accountants have agreed for many years on the desirability of replacing standard cost accounting. They have not, however, found a successor.

Theory of Constraints cost Accounting

Eliyahu M. Goldratt developed the Theory of Constraints in part to address the cost-accounting problems in what he calls the "cost world." He offers a substitute, called throughput accounting, that uses throughput (money for goods sold to customers) in place of output (goods produced that may sell or may boost inventory) and considers labour as a fixed rather than as a variable cost. He defines inventory simply as everything the organization owns that it plans to sell, including buildings, machinery, and many other things in addition to the categories listed here. Throughput accounting recognizes only one class of variable costs: the truly variable costs, like materials and components, which vary directly with the quantity produced.

Finished goods inventories remain balance-sheet assets, but labour-efficiency ratios no longer evaluate managers and workers. Instead of an incentive to reduce labour cost, throughput accounting focuses attention on the relationships between throughput (revenue or income) on one hand and controllable operating expenses and changes in inventory on the other. Those relationships direct attention to the constraints or bottlenecks that prevent the system from producing more throughput, rather than to people - who have little or no control over their situations.

NATIONAL ACCOUNTS

Inventories also play an important role in national accounts and the analysis of the business cycle. Some short-term macroeconomic fluctuations are attributed to the inventory cycle.

DISTRESSED INVENTORY

Also known as distressed or expired stock, distressed inventory is inventory whose potential to be sold at a normal cost has passed or will soon pass. In certain industries it could also mean that the stock is or will soon be impossible to sell. Examples of distressed inventory include products that have reached their expiry date, or have reached a date in advance of expiry at which the planned market will no longer purchase them, clothing that is defective or out of fashion, and old newspapers or magazines. It also includes computer or consumer-electronic equipment that is obsolete or discontinued and whose manufacturer is unable to support it. One current example of distressed inventory is the VHS format.

In 2001, Cisco wrote off inventory worth US $2.25 billion due to duplicate orders. This is one of the biggest inventory write-offs in business history.

INVENTORY CREDIT

Inventory credit refers to the use of stock, or inventory, as collateral to raise finance. Where banks may be reluctant to accept traditional collateral, for example in developing countries where land title may be lacking, inventory credit is a potentially important way of overcoming financing constraints. This is not a new concept; archaeological evidence suggests that it was practiced in Ancient Rome. Obtaining finance against stocks of a wide range of products held in a bonded warehouse is common in much of the world. It is, for example, used with Parmesan cheese in Italy. Inventory credit on the basis of stored agricultural produce is widely used in Latin American countries and in some Asian countries. A precondition for such credit is that banks must be confident that the stored product will be available if they need to call on the collateral; this implies the existence of a reliable network of certified warehouses.

Banks also face problems in valuing the inventory. The possibility of sudden falls in commodity prices means that they are usually reluctant to lend more than about 60 per cent of the value of the inventory at the time of the loan.

COUNTING INVENTORY AND CALCULATING COST OF GOODS SOLD

Regular physical counts of the existing inventory are essential to maintaining reliable inventory accounting records. With a perpetual system, the physical count can be compared to the recorded inventory balance to see whether any inventory has been lost or stolen. With a periodic system, a physical count is the only way to get the information necessary to compute cost of goods sold.

TAKING A PHYSICAL COUNT OF INVENTORY

No matter which inventory system a company is using, periodic physical counts are a necessary and important part of accounting for inventory. With a perpetual inventory system, the physical count either confirms that the amount entered in the accounting records is accurate or highlights shortages and clerical errors. If, for example, employees have been stealing inventory, the theft will show up as a difference between the balance in the inventory account and the amount physically counted.

A physical count of inventory involves two steps:

- *Quantity count.* In most companies, physically counting all inventory is a time consuming activity. Because sales transactions and merchandise deliveries can complicate matters, inventory is usually counted on holidays or after the close of business on the inventory day. Special care must be taken to ensure that all inventory owned, wherever its location, is counted and that inventory on hand but not owned (consignment inventory) is not counted.

- *Inventory costing.* When the physical count has been completed, each type of merchandise is assigned a unit cost. The quantity of each type of merchandise is multiplied by its unit cost to determine the dollar value of the inventory. These amounts are then added to obtain the total ending inventory for the business. This is the amount reported as Inventory on the balance sheet. The ending balance in the inventory account may have to be adjusted for any shortages discovered.

To illustrate the impact of a physical inventory count on the accounting records for both a periodic and a perpetual system, assume that Grantsville's physical count, combined with inventory costing analysis, suggests that the correct amount for ending inventory is $5,950. This information can be combined with previous information from the accounting system as follows:

	Periodic System	**Perpetual System**
Beginning inventory	$ 0	$ 0
Plus: Net purchases	15,876	15,876
Cost of goods available for sale	$15,876	$15,876
Less: Ending inventory	(5,950)	6,776
Cost of goods sold	$ 9,926	$ 9,100
Goods lost or stolen	unknown	826
Total cost of goods sold, lost, or stolen	$ 9,926	$ 9,926

(from inventory system)($6,776 - $5,950)

Recall that, in this example, the beginning inventory is assumed to be zero. The amount of net purchases is a combination of the items affecting the amount paid for inventory purchases during the period: purchase price, freight in, purchase returns, and purchase discounts. The $15,876 amount for net purchases was computed earlier in connection with the closing entry for the periodic system. This cost of goods sold computation highlights the key difference between a periodic and a perpetual inventory system. With a periodic system, the company does not know what ending inventory *should be* when the inventory count is performed.

The best the company can do is count the inventory and assume that the difference between the cost of goods available for sale and the cost of goods still remaining (ending inventory) must represent the cost of goods that were sold. Actually, a business using a periodic system has no way of knowing whether these goods were sold, lost, stolen, or spoiled—all it knows for sure is that the goods are gone.

With a perpetual system, the accounting records themselves yield the cost of goods sold during the period, as well as the amount of inventory that should be found when the physical count is made. For Grantsville, the predicted ending inventory is $6,776 (from the T-account shown earlier); the actual ending inventory, according to the physical count, is only $5,950. The difference of $826 ($6,776–$5,950) represents inventory lost, stolen, or ruined during the period. This amount is called inventory shrinkage. The adjusting entry needed to record this inventory shrinkage when using a perpetual inventory system is as follows:

Inventory Shrinkage	826	
Inventory ($6,776–$5,950)		826
Adjustment of perpetual inventory balance to reflect inventory shrinkage.		

For internal management purposes, the amount of inventory shrinkage would be tracked from one period to the next to detect whether the amount of "shrinkage" for any given period is unusually high. For external reporting purposes, the shrinkage amount would probably be combined with normal cost of goods sold, and the title "Cost of Goods Sold" would be given to the total. If this practice is followed, reported cost of goods sold would be the same under both a perpetual and a periodic inventory system. The difference is that, with a perpetual system, company management knows how much of the cost of goods sold was actually sold and how much represents inventory shrinkage. With a periodic inventory system, no journal entry for inventory shrinkage is made because the amount of shrinkage is unknown. Instead, the ending inventory amount derived from the physical count is used to make the second periodic inventory closing entry. Using the $5,950 ending inventory amount, the appropriate periodic inventory closing entry is:

Cost of Goods Sold	9,926	
Inventory ($15,876–$5,950)		9,926
Adjustment of inventory account to appropriate ending balance.		

The Income Effect of an Error in Ending Inventory

The results of the physical inventory count directly affect the computation of cost of goods sold with a periodic system and inventory shrinkage with a perpetual system. Errors in the inventory count will cause the amount of cost of goods sold or inventory shrinkage to be misstated. To illustrate, assume that the correct inventory count for Grantsville is $5,950 but that the ending inventory value is mistakenly computed to be $6,450. The impact of this $500 ($6,450–$5,950) inventory overstatement is as follows:

	Periodic System	Perpetual System
Beginning inventory	$ 0	$ 0
Plus: Net purchases	15,876	15,876
Cost of goods available for sale	$15,876	$15,876
Less: Ending inventory	6,450	6,776
Cost of goods sold	$ 9,426	$ 9,100
Goods lost or stolen	unknown	326
Total cost of goods sold, lost, or stolen (from inventory system)	$ 9,426	$ 9,426
(from inventory system)($6,776 - $6,450)		

The $500 inventory overstatement reduces the reported cost of goods sold, lost, or stolen by $500, from $9,926 (computed earlier) to $9,426. This is because if we mistakenly think that we have more inventory remaining, then as suggested, also mistakenly think that we must have sold less. Conversely, if the physical count understates ending inventory, total cost of goods sold will be overstated. Since an inventory overstatement decreases reported cost of goods sold, it will also increase reported gross margin and net income. For this reason, the managers of a firm that is having difficulty meeting profit targets are sometimes tempted to "mistakenly" overstate ending inventory. Because of this temptation, auditors must take care to review a company's inventory counting process and also to physically observe a sample of the actual inventory. When cost of goods sold is subtracted from revenues, the result is the gross margin. Management watches gross margin and the gross margin percentage very closely because a slight increase or decrease can dramatically affect a company's profitability.

ACCOUNTING FOR INVENTORY PURCHASES AND SALES

To begin a more detailed study of inventory accounting, we must first establish a solid understanding of the journal entries used to record inventory transactions. The accounting procedures for recording purchases and sales of inventory using both a periodic and a perpetual inventory system are detailed in this part.

OVERVIEW OF PERPETUAL AND PERIODIC SYSTEMS

Some businesses track changes in inventory levels on a continuous basis, recording inventory increases and decreases wiThe ach individual purchase and sale to maintain a running total of the inventory balance. This is called a perpetual inventory system. Other businesses rely on quarterly or yearly inventory counts to reveal which inventory items have been sold. This is called a periodic inventory system.

Perpetual

You own a discount appliance superstore. Your biggest-selling items are washers, dryers, refrigerators, microwaves, and dishwashers. You advertise your weekly sale items on local TV stations, and your sales volume is quite heavy. You have 50 salespeople who work independently of one another. You have found that customers get very upset if they come to buy an advertised item and you have run out. In this business environment, would it make sense to keep a running total of the quantity remaining of each inventory item and update it each time a sale is made?

Yes, the benefit of having current information on each inventory item would make it worthwhile to spend a little extra time to update the inventory records when a sale is made. This appliance store would probably use a perpetual inventory system.

With a perpetual system, inventory records are updated whenever a purchase or a sale is made. In this way, the inventory records at any given time reflect how many of each inventory item should be in the warehouse or out on the store shelves. A perpetual system is most often used when each individual inventory item has a relatively high value or when there are large costs to running out of or overstocking specific items.

Periodic

You operate a newsstand in a busy metropolitan subway station. Almost all of your sales occur during the morning and the evening rush hours. You sell a diverse array of items newspapers, magazines, pens, snacks, and other odds and ends. During rush hour, your business is a fast-paced pressure cooker; the longer you take with one customer, the more chance that the busy commuters waiting in line for service will tire of waiting and you will lose sales.

In this business environment, would it make sense to have each customer wait while you meticulously check off on an inventory sheet exactly which items were sold? No, the delay caused by this detailed bookkeeping would cause you to lose customers.

It makes more sense to wait until the end of the day, count up what inventory you still have left, compare that to what you started with, and use those numbers to calculate how many of each inventory item you sold during the day. This newsstand scenario is an example of a situation where a periodic inventory system is appropriate. With a periodic system, inventory records are not updated when a sale is made; only the dollar amount of the sale is recorded. Periodic systems are most often used when inventory is comprised of a large number of diverse items, each with a relatively low value.

Impact of Information Technology

Over the past 25 years, advances in information technology have lowered the cost of maintaining a perpetual inventory system. As a result, more businesses have adopted perpetual systems so that they can more closely track inventory levels. A visible manifestation of this trend is in supermarkets. Twenty years ago, the checkout clerk rang up the price of each item on a cash register. After the customers walked out of the store with their groceries, the store knew the total amount of the sale but did not know which individual items had been sold. This was a periodic inventory system. Now, with laser scanning equipment tied into the supermarket's computer system, most supermarkets operate under a perpetual system. The store manager knows exactly what you bought and exactly how many of each item should still be left on the store shelves.

Perpetual and Periodic Journal Entries

The following transactions for Grantsville Clothing Store will be used to illustrate the differences in bookkeeping procedures between a business using a perpetual inventory system and one using a periodic inventory system:

- *Purchased on account*: 1,000 shirts at a cost of $10 each for a total of $10,000.
- *Purchased on account*: 300 pairs of pants at a cost of $18 each for a total of $5,400.
- Paid cash for separate shipping costs on the shirts purchased in (a), $970. The supplier of the pants purchased in (b) included the shipping costs in the $18 purchase price.
- Returned 30 of the shirts (costing $300) to the supplier because they were stained.
- Paid for the shirt purchase. A 2 per cent discount was given on the $9,700 bill [(1,000 purchased " 30 returned) × $10] because of payment within the 10-day discount period (payment terms were 2/10, n/30).
- Paid $5,400 for the pants purchase. No discount was allowed because payment was made after the discount period.
- *Sold on account*: 600 shirts at a price of $25 each for a total of $15,000.
- *Sold on account*: 200 pairs of pants at a price of $40 each for a total of $8,000.
- Accepted return of 50 shirts by dissatisfied customers.

The journal entries for the perpetual inventory system should seem familiar to you—a perpetual system has been assumed in all earlier stages of the text. A perpetual system was assumed because it is logical and is the system all companies would choose if there were no cost to updating the inventory records each time a sale or purchase is made. A periodic inventory system is sometimes a practical necessity.

Purchases

With a perpetual system, all purchases are added (debited) directly to Inventory. With a periodic system, the inventory balance is only updated using an inventory count at the end of the period; inventory purchases during the period are recorded in a temporary holding account called Purchases. At the end of the period, the balance in Purchases is closed to Inventory in connection with the computation of cost of goods sold. Entries (a) and (b) to record the shirt and pants purchases are given below.

Perpetual			Periodic		
a. Inventory	10,000		Purchases	10,000	
Accounts Payable		10,000	Accounts Payable		10,000
b. Inventory	5,400		Purchases	5,400	
Accounts Payable		5,400	Accounts Payable		5,400

Transportation Costs

The cost of transporting the inventory is an additional inventory cost. Sometimes, as with the pants for Grantsville Clothing, the shipping cost is already included in the purchase price, so a separate entry to record the transportation costs is not needed. When a separate payment is made for transportation costs, it is recorded as follows:

Perpetual			Periodic		
c. Inventory	970		Freight In	970	
Cash		970	Cash		970

With a perpetual inventory system, transportation costs are added directly to the inventory balance. With a periodic inventory system, another temporary holding account, Freight In, is created, and transportation costs are accumulated in this account during the period. Like the purchases account, Freight In is added to Inventory at the end of the period in connection with the computation of cost of goods sold.

Purchase Returns

With a perpetual system, the return of unsatisfactory merchandise to the supplier results in a decrease in Inventory. In addition, since no payment will have to be made for the returned merchandise, Accounts Payable is reduced by the same amount. With a periodic system, the amount of the returned merchandise is recorded in yet another temporary holding account called Purchase Returns. Purchase Returns is a contra account to Purchases and is also closed to Inventory as part of the computation of cost of goods sold. If the returned merchandise had already been paid for, the supplier would most likely return the purchase price. In this case, the debit would be to Cash instead of to Accounts Payable.

Perpetual			Periodic		
d. Accounts Payable	300		Accounts Payable	300	
Inventory		300	Purchase Returns		300

Purchase Discounts

Sellers sometimes offer inducements for credit customers to pay quickly. Here, Grantsville takes advantage of purchase discounts to save money on the payment for the shirts. The amount of the purchase discount is $194 ($9,700 × 0.02), so the total payment for the shirts is $9,506 ($9,700–$194). The amount recorded for inventory should reflect the actual amount paid to purchase the inventory. With a perpetual inventory system, this is shown by subtracting the purchase discount amount from the inventory account. With a periodic inventory system, another holding account is created to accumulate purchase discounts taken during the period.

Perpetual			Periodic		
e. Accounts Payable	9,700		Accounts Payable	9,700	
Inventory		194	Purchase Discounts		194
Cash		9,506	Cash		9,506
f. Accounts Payable	5,400		Accounts Payable	5,400	
Cash		5,400	Cash		5,400

Note that the payment for the pants is made after the discount period, so the full amount must be paid. Since this transaction had no impact on Inventory, the entry is the same for both the perpetual and the periodic system. In terms of journal entries, the difference between a perpetual and a periodic inventory system is that all adjustments to inventory under a perpetual system are entered directly in the inventory account; with a periodic system, all inventory adjustments are accumulated in an array of temporary holding accounts: Purchases, Freight In, Purchase Returns, and Purchase Discounts.

Sales

The sales of shirts and pants would be recorded as follows:

	Perpetual			Periodic		
g.	Accounts Receivable	15,000		Accounts Receivable	15,000	
	Sales (600 × $25)		15,000	Sales		15,000
	Cost of Goods Sold	6,000				
	Inventory (600 × $10)		6,000	Accounts Receivable	8,000	
h.	Accounts Receivable	8,000				
	Sales (200 × $40)		8,000	Sales		8,000
	Cost of Goods Sold	3,600				
	Inventory (200 × $18)		3,600			

These entries reflect the primary difference between a perpetual and a periodic inventory system— with a periodic system, no attempt is made to recognize cost of goods sold on a transactionby- transaction basis.

In fact, with a periodic system, Grantsville would not even know how many shirts and how many pairs of pants had been sold. Instead, only total sales of $23,000 ($15,000 + $8,000) would be known. The cost of goods sold for the shirts recorded here is $10 each. The actual cost per shirt, after adjusting for freight in and purchase discounts, is $10.80, computed as follows:

Total purchase price (1,000 shirts)	$10,000
Plus: Freight in	970
Less: Purchase returns (30 shirts)	(300)
Less: Purchase discounts	(194)
Total cost of shirts (970 shirts)	$10,476

Total cost $10,476 ÷ 970 shirts = $10.80 per shirt

In practice, it is unlikely that a firm using a perpetual inventory system would bother to adjust unit costs for the effects of freight cost and purchase discounts on an ongoing basis. The cost of doing these calculations could easily outweigh any resulting improvement in the quality of cost information.

Sales Returns

Dissatisfied customers sometimes return their purchases. The journal entries to record the return of 50 shirts are as follows:

	Perpetual			Periodic		
i.	Sales Returns (50 × $25)	1,250		Sales Returns	1,250	
	Accounts Receivable		1,250	Accounts Receivable		1,250
	Inventory (50 × $10)	500				
	Cost of Goods Sold		500			

Under the perpetual system, not only are the sales for the returned items canceled, but the cost of the returned inventory is also removed from Cost of Goods Sold and restored to the inventory account.

Closing Entries

Two entries are made:

- Transfer all the temporary holding account balances to the inventory account. At this point, the inventory account balance is equal to the cost of goods available for sale (beginning inventory plus the net cost of purchases for the period).
- Reduce Inventory by the amount of Cost of Goods Sold. At this point, the inventory account balance is equal to the ending inventory amount, and the appropriate cost of goods sold amount is also recognized.

To illustrate, the information for Grantsville will be used. The entry to transfer all the temporary holding accounts to the inventory account is as follows:

Account	Debit	Credit
Inventory	15,876	
Purchase Returns	300	
Purchase Discounts	194	
Freight In		970
Purchases		15,400
Closing of temporary inventory accounts for periodic system.		

The inventory debit of $15,876 is the amount of net purchases for the period. Notice that, after this entry has been posted, the balances in all the temporary holding accounts will have been reduced to zero. After the addition of net purchases, the inventory account balance represents cost of goods available for sale (the sum of beginning inventory and net purchases). Remember that, in this example, beginning inventory is assumed to be zero. The second closing entry involves the adjustment of Inventory to its appropriate ending balance and the creation of the cost of goods sold account. This cost of goods sold account would be closed when other nominal accounts (*e.g.*, Sales Salaries, Interest Expense, etc.) are closed. If the year-end physical count indicates that the ending inventory balance should be $6,776, the appropriate entry is as follows:

Account	Debit	Credit
Cost of Goods Sold	9,100	
Inventory ($15,876 - $6,776)		9,100
Adjustment of inventory account to appropriate ending balance.		

Here, the values for boThending inventory ($6,776) and cost of goods sold ($9,100) are the same with either a perpetual or a periodic inventory system. So, what is the practical difference between the two systems? One difference is that a perpetual system can tell you the inventory balance and the cumulative cost of goods sold at any time during the period. With a periodic system, on the other hand, you must wait until the inventory is counted at the end of the period to compute the amount of inventory or cost of goods sold. Another difference is that, with a perpetual system, you can compare the inventory records to the amount of inventory actually on hand and thus determine whether any inventory has been lost or stolen. As described in the next part, this comparison is not possible with a periodic system.

INVENTORY AND COST OF GOODS SOLD

Inventory is the name given to goods that are either manufactured or purchased for resale in the normal course of business. A car dealer's inventory is comprised of automobiles; a grocery store's inventory consists of vegetables, meats, dairy products, canned goods, and bakery items; Sears' inventory is comprised of shirts, Kenmore appliances, DieHard® batteries, and more. Like other items of value, such as cash or equipment, inventory is classified as an asset and reported on the balance sheet. When products are sold, they are no longer assets. The costs to purchase or manufacture the products must be removed from the asset classification (inventory) on the balance sheet and reported on the income statement as an expense—cost of goods sold. The timeline in Exhibit illustrates the business issues involved with inventory as well as the financial statement effects of those business issues.

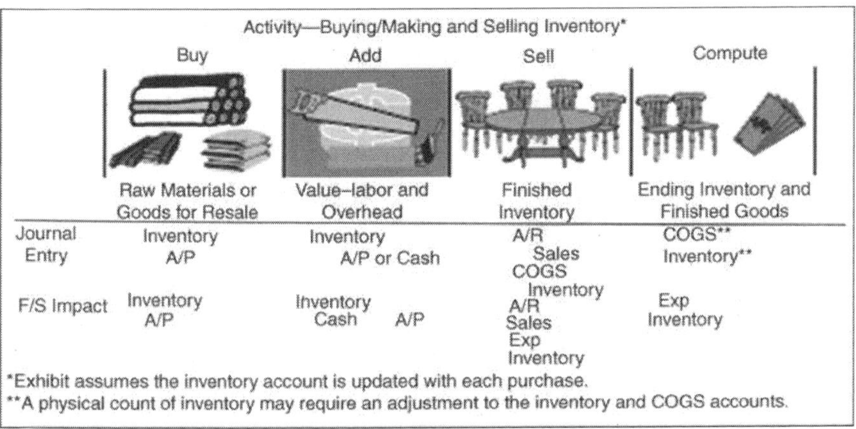

The accounting questions associated with the items in the timeline are as follows:

- When is inventory considered to have been purchased—when it is ordered, shipped, received, or paid for? Similarly, when is the inventory considered to have been sold?
- Which of the costs associated with the "value added" process are considered to be part of the cost of inventory, and which are simply business expenses for that period?
- How should total inventory cost be divided between the inventory that was sold (cost of goods sold) and the inventory that remains (ending inventory)?

What Is Inventory?

In a merchandising firm, either wholesale or retail, inventory is composed of the items that have been purchased in order to be resold to customers. In a supermarket, milk is inventory, a shopping cart is not. In a manufacturing company, there are three different types of inventory: raw materials, work in process, and finished goods.

Raw Materials

Raw materials are goods acquired in a relatively undeveloped state that will eventually compose a major part of the finished product. If you are making bicycles, one of the raw materials is tubular steel. For a computer assembler, raw materials inventory is composed of plastic, wires, and Intel Pentium® chips.

Work in Process

Work in process consists of partially finished products. When you take a tour of a manufacturing plant, you are seeing work-in-process inventory.

Finished Goods

Finished goods are the completed products waiting for sale. A completed car rolling off the automobile assembly line is part of finished goods inventory.

What Costs are included in Inventory Cost?

Inventory cost consists of all costs involved in buying the inventory and preparing it for sale. In the case of raw materials or goods acquired for resale by a merchandising firm, cost includes the purchase price, freight, and receiving and storage costs. The cost of work-in-process inventory is the sum of the costs of the raw materials, the production labour, and some share of the manufacturing overhead required to keep the factory running. The cost of an item in finished goods inventory is the total of the materials, labour, and overhead costs used in the production process for that item. As you can imagine, accumulating these costs and calculating a cost per unit is quite a difficult task.

The cost of a finished automobile includes the cost of the steel and rubber; the salaries and wages of assembly workers, inspectors, and testers; the factory insurance; the workers' pension benefits; and much more. This costing process is a key part of management accounting and in the management accounting part of *Accounting: Concepts and Applications.* The costs just described are all costs expended in order to get inventory produced and ready to sell. These costs are appropriately included in inventory costs. Those costs incurred in the sales effort itself are *not* inventory costs, but instead should be reported as operating expenses in the period in which they are incurred. For example, the costs of maintaining the finished goods warehouse or the retail showroom are period expenses. Salespersons' salaries are period expenses, as is the cost of advertising. In addition, general non-factory administrative costs are also period expenses. Examples are the costs of the corporate headquarters and the company president's salary.

Who Owns the Inventory

As a general rule, goods should be included in the inventory of the business holding legal title. So, a merchandising firm is considered to have purchased inventory once it has legal title to the inventory. Similarly, the inventory is considered to be sold when legal title passes to the customer. In most cases, this "legal title" rule is easy to apply—if you go into a business and look around, it is probably safe to assume that the inventory you see belongs to that business. In the case of goods in transit and goods on consignment, however, this "legal title" rule can be rather difficult to apply.

Goods Being Shipped

When goods are being shipped (in transit) from the seller to the buyer, who owns the inventory that is on a truck or railroad car—the seller or the buyer? If the seller pays for the shipping costs, the arrangement is known as FOB (free-on-board) destination, and the seller owns the merchandise from the time it is shipped until it is delivered to the buyer. If the buyer pays the shipping costs, the arrangement is known as FOB (free-on-board) shipping point, and the buyer owns the merchandise during transit. Thus, in determining which items should be counted and included in the inventory balance for a period, a company must note the amount of merchandise in transit and the terms under which it is being shipped. In all cases, merchandise should be included in the inventory of the party who owns it; for goods in transit, this is generally the party who is paying the shipping costs. The impact of shipping terms on the ownership of goods in transit is summarized in Exhibit.

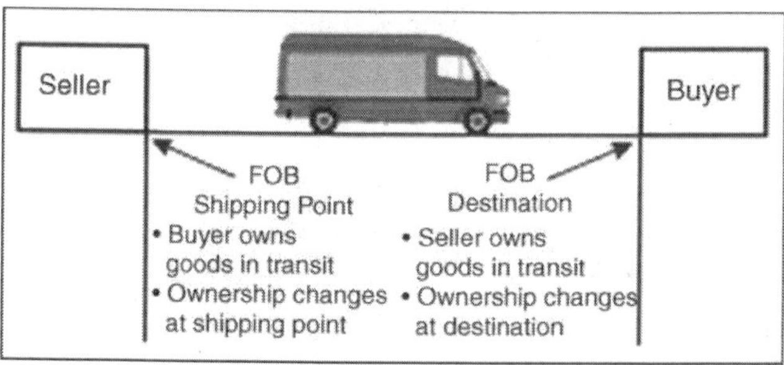

Exhibit. Ownership Transfer for Goods in Transit

Goods on Consignment

Sometimes the inventory a firm stocks in its warehouse has not actually been purchased from suppliers. With a consignment arrangement, suppliers (the consignors) provide inventory for resale while retaining ownership of the inventory until it is sold. (This is referred to in the business world as a "sale-through" arrangement as opposed to a "sell-in" arrangement where sales to distributors are recorded as revenue.)

The firm selling the merchandise (the consignee) merely stocks and sells the merchandise for the supplier/owner and receives a commission on any sales as payment for services rendered. Th rough a consignment arrangement, the manufacturer enables dealers to acquire a broad sample of inventory without incurring the purchase and finance charges required to actually buy the inventory. It is extremely important that goods being held on consignment not be included in the inventory of the firm holding the goods for sale even though they are physically on that firm's premises. It is equally important that the supplier/owner properly include all such goods in its records even though the inventory is not on its premises.

An example of a company that successfully uses consignment sales as part of its business strategy is International Airline Support Group, Inc. This company is a leading distributor of aircraft spare parts for large jet airplanes. The company uses consignments because, as stated in its annual report, this arrangement allows it "to obtain parts inventory on a favorable basis without committing its capital to purchasing inventory."

Ending Inventory and Cost of Goods Sold

Inventory purchased or manufactured during a period is added to beginning inventory, and the total cost of this inventory is called the cost of goods available for sale. At the end of an accounting period, total cost of goods available for sale must be allocated between inventory still remaining (to be reported in the balance sheet as an asset) and inventory sold during the period (to be reported in the income statement as an expense, Cost of Goods Sold). This cost allocation process is extremely important because the more cost that is said to remain in ending inventory, the less cost is reported as cost of goods sold on the income statement. This is why accurately determining who owns the inventory is such a big issue. Making a mistake with inventory ownership will result in misstating both the income statement and the balance sheet. For this reason, accountants must be careful of inventory errors because they directly affect reported net income. Inventory errors are discussed later in this stage. The cost allocation process also involves a significant amount of accounting judgement. Identical inventory items are usually purchased at varying prices throughout the year, so to calculate the amount of ending inventory and cost of goods sold, the accountant must determine which items (the low cost or high cost) remain and which were sold. Again, this decision can directly affect the amount of reported cost of goods sold and net income. Inventory cost flow assumptions are discussed later in the stage.

METHOD OF ESTIMATING INVENTORIES

We have assumed that the number of inventory units on hand is known by a physical count that takes place at the end of each accounting period. For the periodic inventory method, this physical count is the only way to determine how much inventory is on hand at the end of a period. For the perpetual inventory method, the physical count verifies the quantity on hand or indicates the amount of inventory shrinkage or theft. There are times, however, when a company needs to know the dollar amount of ending inventory, but a physical count is either impossible or impractical. For example, many firms prepare quarterly, or even monthly, financial statements, but it is too expensive and time consuming to count the inventory at the end of each period. In such cases, if the perpetual inventory method is being used, the balance in the inventory account is usually assumed to be correct. With the periodic inventory method, however, some estimate of the inventory balance must be made. A common method of estimating the dollar amount of ending inventory is the gross margin method.

The Gross Margin Method

With the gross margin method, a firm uses available information about the dollar amounts of beginning inventory and purchases, and the historical gross margin percentage to estimate the dollar amounts of cost of goods sold and ending inventory. To illustrate, assume the following data for Payson Brick Company:

Net sales revenue, January 1 to March 31	$100,000
Inventory balance, January 1	15,000
Net purchases, January 1 to March 31	65,000
Gross margin percentage (historically determined percentage of net sales)	40%

With this information, the dollar amount of inventory on hand on March 31 is estimated as follows:

	Dollars	**Percentage of Sales**
Net sales revenue	$100,000	100%
Cost of goods sold:		
Beginning inventory	$15,000	
Net purchases.	65,000	
Total cost of goods available for sale..	$80,000	
Ending inventory ($80,000 - $60,000)	20,000 (3)*	
Cost of goods sold ($100,000 - $40,000)	60,000 (2)*	60%
Gross margin ($100,000 × 0.40)	$ 40,000 (1)*	40%

*The numbers indicate the order of calculation.

Here, gross margin is first determined by calculating 40 per cent of sales (step 1). Next, cost of goods sold is found by subtracting gross margin from sales (step 2). Finally, the dollar amount of ending inventory is obtained by subtracting cost of goods sold from total cost of goods available for sale (step 3). Obviously, the gross margin method of estimating cost of goods sold and ending inventory assumes that the historical gross margin percentage is appropriate for the current period. This assumption is a realistic one in many fields of business. In cases where the gross margin percentage has changed, this method should be used with caution. The gross margin method of estimating ending inventories is also useful when a fire or other calamity destroys a company's inventory. In these cases, the dollar amount of inventory lost must be determined before insurance claims can be made. The dollar amounts of sales, purchases, and beginning inventory can be obtained from prior years' financial statements and from customers, suppliers, and other sources. Then the gross margin method can be used to estimate the dollar amount of inventory lost.

INVENTORY ERRORS

Incorrect amounts for inventory on the balance sheet and cost of goods sold on the income statement can result from errors in counting inventories, recording inventory transactions, or both. The effect of an error in the end-of-period inventory count was discussed earlier in the stage. To examine the effects of other types of inventory errors, assume that Richfield Company had the following inventory records for 2012:

Inventory balance, January 1, 2012	$ 8,000
Purchases through December 30, 2012	20,000
Inventory balance, December 30, 2012	12,000

Further assume that on December 31 the company purchased and received another $1,000 of inventory. The following comparison shows the kinds of inventory situations that might result:

	Incorrect*	**Incorrect**	**Incorrect**	**Correct**
The $1,000 of merchandise purchased on December 31 was	not recorded as a purchase and not counted as inventory	recorded as a purchase but not counted as inventory	not recorded as a purchase but counted as inventory	recorded as a purchase and counted as inventory
Beginning inventory	$ 8,000 (OK)**	$8,000 (OK)	$ 8,000 (OK)	$ 8,000 (OK)
Net purchases	20,000 (↓)	21,000 (OK)	20,000 (↑)	21,000 (OK)
Cost of goods available for sale	$28,000 (↓)	$29,000 OK)	$28,000 (↓)	$29,000 (OK)
Ending inventory	12,000 (↓)	12,000 (↓)	13,000 (OK)	13,000 (OK)
Cost of goods sold	$16,000 (OK)	$17,000 (↑)	$15,000 (↓)	$16,000 (OK)

Note:

*This calculation produces the correct cost of goods sold but by an incorrect route—the errors in purchases and ending inventory offset each other.

**For the amount, ˉ indicates it is too low, - means it is too high, and OK means it is correct.

In these calculations, the beginning inventory plus purchases equals the cost of goods that were "available for sale." In other words, everything that "could be sold" must have either been on hand at the beginning of the period (beginning inventory) or purchased during the period (net purchases). Then, ending inventory (what wasn't sold) was subtracted from the cost of goods available for sale. The result is the cost of goods that were sold. Everything on hand (available) had to be either sold or left in ending inventory. Clearly, inventory and cost of goods sold can be misstated by the improper recording of inventory purchases or counting of inventory. Similar errors can occur when inventory is sold. If a sale is recorded but the merchandise remains in the warehouse and is counted in the ending inventory, cost of goods sold will be understated, whereas gross margin and net income will be overstated.

If a sale is not recorded but inventory is shipped and not counted in the ending inventory, gross margin and net income will be understated, and cost of goods sold will be overstated. To illustrate these potential inventory errors, consider the following data for Richfield. Note that sales figures have been added and the ending inventory and the 2012 purchases now correctly include the $1,000 purchase of merchandise made on December 31, 2012.

Sales revenue through December 30, 2012 (200% of cost)	$32,000
Inventory balance, January 1, 2012	8,000
Net purchases during 2012	21,000
Inventory balance, December 31, 2012	13,000

In addition, assume that on December 31, inventory that cost $1,000 was sold for $2,000. The merchandise was delivered to the buyer on December 31. The following analysis shows the kinds of situations that might result:To reduce the possibility of these types of inventory cutoff errors, most businesses close their warehouses at year-end while they count inventory. If they are retailers, they typically count inventory after hours. During the inventory counting period, businesses do not accept or ship merchandise, nor do they enter purchase or sales transactions in their accounting records. As explained, an error in inventory results in cost of goods sold being overstated or understated.

	Incorrect*	**Incorrect**	**Incorrect**	**Correct**
The $2,000 sale on December 31 was	not recorded and the merchandise was counted as inventory	recorded and the merchandise was counted as inventory	not recorded and the merchandise was excluded from inventory	recorded and the merchandise was excluded from inventory
Sales revenue Cost of goods sold:	$32,000 (↓)*	$34,000 OK)	$32,000 (↓)	$34,000 (OK)
Beginning inventory	$ 8,000 (OK)**	$8,000 (OK)	$ 8,000 (OK)	$ 8,000 (OK)
Net purchases	21,000 (OK)	21,000 (OK)	21,000 (OK)	21,000 (OK)
Cost of goods available for sale	$29,000 (OK)	$29,000 (OK)	$28,000 (OK)	$29,000 (OK)
Ending inventory	13,000 (↑)	13,000 (↑)	12,000 (OK)	12,000 (OK)
Cost of goods sold	$16,000 (↓)	$16,000 (↓)	$17,000 (OK)	$17,000 (OK)
Gross margin	$16,000 (↓)	$18,000 (↑)	$15,000 (↓)	$ 17,000 (OK)

Note:

*For the amount, ˉ indicates it is too low, c means it is too high, and OK means it is correct.

This error has the opposite effect on gross margin and, hence, on net income. For example, if at the end of the accounting period $2,000 of inventory is not counted, cost of goods sold will be $2,000 higher than it should be, and gross margin and net income will be understated by $2,000. Such inventory errors affect gross margin and net income not only in the current year but in the following year as well. A recording delay resulting in an understatement of purchases in one year, for example, results in an overstatement in the next year. To illustrate how inventory errors affect gross margin and net income, assume the following correct data for Salina Corporation:

		2011		2012
Sales revenue		$50,000		$40,000
Cost of goods sold:				
Beginning inventory	$10,000		$ 5,000	
Net purchases	20,000		25,000	
Cost of goods available for sale	$30,000		$30,000	
Ending inventory	5,000		10,000	
Cost of goods sold		25,000		20,000
Gross margin		$25,000		$20,000
Operating expenses		10,000		10,000
Net income		$15,000		$10,000

Now suppose that ending inventory in 2011 was overstated; that is, instead of the correct amount of $5,000, the count erroneously showed $7,000 of inventory on hand. The following analysis shows the effect of the error on net income in both 2011 and 2012:

		2011		2012
Sales Revenue		$50,000		$40,000
Cost of Goods Sold:				
Beginning Inventory	$10,000		$ 7,000 (↑)	
Net Purchases	20,000		25,000	
Cost of Goods Available for Sale	$30,000		$32,000 (↑)	
Ending Inventory	7,000 (↑)*		10,000	
Cost of Goods Sold		23,000 (↓)		22,000(↑)
Gross Margin		$27,000 (↑)		$18,000 (↓)
Operating Expenses		10,000		10,000
Net Income		$17,000 (↑)		$ 8,000 (↓)

*For the amount, ↑ means it is too high ↓ means it is too low.

When the amount of ending inventory is overstated (as it was in 2011), both gross margin and net income are overstated by the same amount ($2,000 in 2011). If the ending inventory amount had been understated, net income and gross margin would also have been understated, again by the same amount. Since the ending inventory in 2011 becomes the beginning inventory in 2012, the net income and gross margin for 2012 are also misstated. In 2012, however, beginning inventory is overstated, so gross margin and net income are understated, again by $2,000. Thus, the errors in the two years off set or counterbalance each other, and if the count taken at the end of 2012 is correct, income in subsequent years will not be affected by this error.

Sears must pay its suppliers in 36 days but must wait for 106 days before receiving the cash from its customers. Sears must finance the remaining 70 days (106 days–36 days) of its operating cycle with bank loans or additional stockholder investment or by charging interest to those using its credit card debt. These calculations illustrate that proper management of the sales/collection cycle, coupled with prudent financing of inventory purchases on account, can reduce a company's reliance on external financing.

Bibliography

Archer, Stephen H.; Choate; G. Marc, Racette; George: *Financial Management: An Introduction*, New York: John Wiley and Sons, 1979.

Bailey; L. P.: *Management Accounting*, GASB's future role, 1989.

Berenyi; Eileen Brettler: "*Contracting Out Refuse Collection: The Nature and Impact of Change*.", The Urban Interest, Vol. 3, Nno. 1, spring, 1981.

Brackney; W. O.; H. R. Anderson: *Management Accounting*, Regulation of cost accounting, 1981.

Bryant; K. Jr.; C. U. Phillips: *Management Accounting,* Interest on equity capital and CASB standard, 1978.

Davis; S. W.; K. Menon: *Journal of Accounting and Public Policy,* The formation and termination of the Cost Accounting Standards Board: Legislative intervention in accounting standard-setting, 1987.

Dopuch; Nicholas; Birnberg; Jacob G.; Demski; Joel S: *Cost Accounting: Accounting Data for Management's Decisions, Third Edition*, Harcourt Brace Jovanovich, Inc, 1982.

Florestano; Patricia S.; Gordon; Stephen B: "*A Survey of City and County Use of Private Contracting*.", The Urban Interest, Vol. 3, No. 1, spring 1981.

Florestano; Patricia S; Gordon; Stephen B: "*Private Provision of Public Services: Contracting by Large Local Governments*", International Journal of Public Administration, Vol. 1, No. 3, 1979.

Gambino; Anthony J: *The Make or Buy Decision*, New York: National Association of Accountants and Society of Management Accountants of Canada, 1980.

Gecoma; Richard M.; Mohor; Arthur B.; Jackson; Michael G: *Energy Efficient Purchasing for Local Governments*, Athens: University of Georgia, 1979.

General Services Administration; Federal Supply Service: *Life Cycle Costing Workbook*, Washington, DC: General Printing Office, February 1977.

Gray; Jack; Johnston; Kenneth: "*Accounting and Management Action*.", New York: McGraw-Hill, 1977.

Griesemer; James R: *Budgeting for Results in Local Government*, Lake Park, FL: KJ David & Co., 1981.

Harbridge House: *Choosing and Using Professional Service Contractors*, Chicago: Municipal Finance Officers Association, 1980.

International City Management Association: "*Contracting with the Private Sector for Municipal Services: A Dialogue Between Practicioners*, "Management Information Service Report, Vol. 12, No. 4, April 1980.

Kehoe; Joseph; Dodson; William; Reeve; Robert; Plato; Gustav: *Activity-Based Management in Government,* Washington, DC: Coopers & Lybrand, L.L.P., 1995.

Lehan, Edward A: *Simplified Government Budgeting*, Chicago, IL: Municipal Finance Officers Association, 1981.

Lehan; Edward A: *Budget Making, A Workbook of Theory and Practice*, Cambridge, MA: Cantabrigia, Inc., 1981.

Logistics Management Institute: *Life Cycle Costing Guide*, Washington, DC: U.S. Department of Commerce, National Bureau of Standards, 1976.

Lynch, Thomas D: *Public Budgeting in America*, Englewood Cliffs, NJ: Prentice-Hall, Inc. 1979.

Lynn, Edward S; Freeman; Robert J": *Fund Accounting: Theory and Practice*, Engelwood Cliffs, NJ: Prentice-Hall, Inc, 1974.

McCarthy; Larry: *Citizens' Guide to Local Government Budgeting*, Sacramento: California Taxpayers' Association, 1977.

McRae, Robert D: *"The Cost-Burden Study: A Method for Recovering Costs from Nonresidents"*, Governmental Finance, March 1982.

Meyer; Michael E; Morgan; David R: *Contracting for Municipal Services: A Handbook for Local Officials*, Norman: University of Oklahoma, 1979.

Municipal Finance Officers Association: *Governmental Accounting, Auditing, and Financial Reporting*, Chicago: Government Finance Officers Association, 1994.

National Assocation of College and University Business Officers: *Contracting for Services*, Washington, DC: NACUBO, 1982.

Patitucci; Frank M: "*Governmental Accounting and Financial Reporting: Some Urgent Problems*", Public Affairs Report. Berkeley: University of California, June 1977.

Sheridan; Richard G.: *State Budgeting in Ohio*, Columbus: Legislative Budget Office, 1978.

White; Michael J; Budget Policy: "*Where Does It Begin and End?*" Government Finance, August 1978.

Index